WHAT EVERY MANAGER NEEDS TO KNOW ABOUT MARKETING AND THE LAW_____

WHAT EVERY MANAGER NEEDS TO KNOW ABOUT MARKETING AND THE LAW

ROBERT J. POSCH, JR.

McGRAW-HILL BOOK COMPANY

New York St. Louis San Francisco Auckland Bogotá
Hamburg Johannesburg London Madrid Mexico
Montreal New Delhi Panama Paris São Paulo
Singapore Sydney Tokyo Toronto

Library of Congress Cataloging in Publication Data

Posch, Robert J.
What every manager needs to know about marketing and the law.
Includes index.
1. Marketing—Law and legislation—United States.
I. Title.
KF2005.P67 1984   343.73′088   83-17572
ISBN 0-07-050567-5   347.30388

1234567890   BKP / BKP   89876543

ISBN 0-07-050567-5

The editors for this book were William A. Sabin and Susan B. West, the designer was Dennis Sharkey, and the production supervisor was Thomas G. Kowalczyk. It was set in Baskerville by Photo Data Inc.

Printed and bound by The Book Press.

This publication is designed to provide the author's opinion in regard to the subject matter covered. It is sold with the understanding that neither the publisher nor the author is engaged in rendering legal, tax, accounting, or similar professional services. While legal, tax, and accounting issues covered in this book have been checked with sources believed to be reliable, some material may be affected by changes in the laws or in the interpretations of such laws since the manuscript for this book was completed. For that reason the accuracy and completeness of such information and the opinions based thereon are not guaranteed. In addition, state or local tax laws or procedural rules may have a material impact on the general recommendations made by the author, and the strategies outlined in this book may not be suitable for every individual. If legal, accounting, tax, investment, or other expert advice is required, obtain the services of a competent practitioner. The publisher and author specifically disclaim any personal liability for loss or risk incurred as a consequence of the advice or information presented herein.

DEDICATION

To my wife, Mary Lou
For the past, the present, and the future

CONTENTS

PREFACE

A good manager "manages" to overcome obstacles—"muddling through" is not the way to manage. Having as much information as you can get avoids much needless risk. This book reduces your risk while telling you in conversational style both how to get things done within the framework of government regulations and how to keep government regulations from impinging on your management discretion.

As all managers in the 1980s are aware, government legislation and government agencies create and destroy marketing objectives or opportunities at a rate not even considered 10 to 15 years ago. For example, permitting comparative advertising creates opportunities, and banning cigarette advertising on television destroys them. As knowledge increases so will government intrusion in the form of laws, taxes, mandated copy, and the like. Today's manager who wants to be tomorrow's manager must know the current law and trends and how he or she can anticipate (and possibly influence) the government *before* it jeopardizes a market, a trademark, or a pricing or distribution policy. Failure to anticipate and interact with government and other political environments can lead your firm down the path of the nuclear power industry or the automakers in the 1960s.

This book will assist today's broad-visioned, multidimensional manager to include government in the "marketing concept." Traditionally, the marketing concept is the philosophy of focusing all the activities of the organization on satisfying customer needs through the use of integrated marketing to achieve maximum profits through customer satisfaction. However, all the positive publicity campaigns in the world won't overcome a government press release picked up by a wire service which alleges (but your buying public reads "states" or "confirms") that you've cheated customers or sold them television sets with excess radiation. You and your firm must be aware of the government at every stage of your management decision-making process—from obtaining a trademark for a new product idea through postsale warranty service.

The relatively low cost of this book may be deductible, yet it may help you interact with your counsel to avoid millions of dollars in fines which are *not* deductible. This book is written for *all* committed management professionals (because everyone in private enterprise is in marketing or assists marketing) who do not want to see the government feasting on their firms' profits or otherwise interfering in their business operations.

The writing has been kept simple, so you'll find no gratuitous legalese. Further, you'll find many checklists for easy review and overview—a feature that does not exist in current literature in the field.

A primary goal of this book is to help managers to spot issues or situations which may become legal issues. Any professional knows that in our complex world it is hard to fight all the fires. When you've seen a legal issue or anticipate that one may develop, review the matter with your counsel. Prompt consultation with your counsel in these circumstances could be the best career move you ever make.

ROBERT J. POSCH, JR.

Acknowledgments

This book bears the imprint of many persons. Although it goes without saying that it is impossible to list acknowledgments to all those who influenced this book, I'm going to try. I'd like to note special thanks to those individuals who, since I left Hofstra Law School, contributed decisively to my integration of law and marketing.

On April 23, 1975, I met Gerard H. Toner (now general counsel of Doubleday & Company, Inc.). Since then, he has been incontestably the single most important influence on my professional life. As a friend, he has always had time and as a professional, he has always set an example of disciplined excellence. He is the type of professional who excels in everything he does and imparts the leadership which motivates those around him to make their own commitment to professional excellence.

At Doubleday over the past eight years I've received much hands-on knowledge from a host of individuals who have assisted me in integrating law and business. If you, the manager, find this book lucid yet cogent, you can thank Peter Andresakis, Andy Danek, Bruce Degerdon, Doug Deptuch, Gary Edwards, Rick Engle, Walter Freese, Bob Galway, Tony Garramone, Joe Grabowski, Jim Guastavino, Craig Havemeyer, Alex Hoffman, L. C. Jacox, Heather Kilpatrick, Jeff Kunion, George Larie, Dick Malina, Barry Mark, Jon Mulford, Clarence O'Connor, John O'Neill, Ilene Skeen, Howard Weill, Bob Woods, and the late James T. McGrath.

Other professionals who've had a direct impact include John Beach, Anne Darr, Ron Docksai, Henry Hoke, Ted Krebsbach, Ed Markowitz, Terry McGoldrick, Ed Nash, Bill Newton, J. Gardiner Pieper (who operates New York State's best bar review course), Howard Phillips, Howard Weber, and three outstanding professors in the Hofstra MBA program: Dr. Dorothy Cohen, Dr. Joel Evans, and Dr. Saul Sands.

Specific editorial input came from many sources. Of particular note were the incisive legal comments by George Shively, Esq. Eileen De Milt was particularly helpful in offering insights into Section 2, one area of her current expertise.

My overriding debt is to my wife Mary Lou, who has been a star to steer by in helping to shape the contents of this book. The tone is hers as well as mine, and I hope that the reader will appreciate that the relative absence of legalese results from her efforts. Her patience and that of my children, Judith and Robert III, were greatly appreciated. To extol the merits of Mary Lou is to say the same about her parents, Vernon and Mary Collins. Finally, I thank my parents, Robert and Maryrose Posch, and my sister Eileen, who always encouraged me to write; now that I'm prolific, I trust that they feel vindicated.

SECTION
ONE
HOW TO READ
THIS BOOK

The sections and chapters in this book are not arranged in order of importance but rather are designed to follow one form of traditional decision analysis. Obviously, managers do not make their marketing decisions in "chapter-by-chapter" isolation, but some sequence was needed. Today's manager must interact with the organization's total marketing program, goals, and political environment. Because of the overall impact of the political environment, we begin with it.

Government legislation and government agencies create and destroy management opportunities in marketing a product or service. Both the creation and the destruction of these opportunities result from savvy input or lack of same by management into the public arena. The problem with prior books on this point is that they merely state this principle with not much more than a mention of the background of the various agencies and what they can do to you. There is a premium on passivity.

This book touches on the traditional approach and suggests tactics for staying abreast of current and future developments in your relationship with government bodies that can affect your business. Therefore, we begin with the need for the managers of your firm (no matter how small) to develop a profit preservation center. To prosper in this decade, management must constantly monitor changes in the business environment—not just as to action pending, but also as to which way the legislatures are going to act "down the road." Management at all levels of responsibility must plan for government change the same way it does for technological

1

change, tax change, or competitive changes. The failure to do so will hurt your firm's future as well as your career advancement.

Section 2 is written particularly for the small concern that cannot afford to retain ongoing in-house counsel, since the monitoring function can be done by any manager who wants to avoid adverse visibility to government. More importantly, this monitoring is fun—it's "newspaper law" or current events. Staying atop these areas will assist your professional career as well as make you a better citizen.

After you've reviewed this section, pick out the section you're most involved with professionally, that is, product development, channel design, pricing, or promotional policy. If you encounter "legalese," it will usually be explained in English, but the Glossary is a handy reference tool when you need a quick definition of a term. Also, give the references a chance; they have a lot of information useful to you without further follow-up.

Finally, no book can replace decent gut reaction to a questionable practice. Posch's rule of regulatory compliance is simple: If you would not like to be treated this way (unfair pricing, deceptive advertising, bait and switch, etc.), then someone else wouldn't either, and one of those "someone elses" probably has a law or regulation on point.[1]

If you encounter a questionable area of importance, never consult a book such as this as your sole source of information. You must consult your attorney. If you don't have an attorney who specializes in your field, contact the local bar association for a referral.

REFERENCES

[1] Throughout this book much reference will be made to Federal Trade Commission (FTC) decisions as well as to codified law and case law. Because of their precedent value, you should review these FTC decisions carefully.

Under Section 5(m) of the FTC act, you and your firm are bound by any cease and desist order, regardless of your firm's lack of involvement, if you or your firm had actual knowledge that such act or practice was unfair or deceptive and unlawful under Section 5(a) (1). Specifically, the FTC can commence a civil action in federal district court against any person, partner, and/or corporation which engages in an act or practice which the commission has determined in a cease and desist proceeding to be unfair or deceptive and prohibited by the FTC's decision. A violation of any such order may result in a civil penalty of up to $10,000 as well as in monitoring by the FTC, who will have access to internal records in matters pertaining to the order. The practical effect is that cease and desist orders are elevated to the level of trade regulation rules once you have actual knowledge. To establish such actual knowledge, the FTC will send copies of the order to industry members who may be engaging in the prohibited practice.

This may not afford you or your firm sufficient time to change policy. A more efficient way to do this is to routinely monitor all orders through an internal profit preservation center (see Section 2). This will keep you up to date as to compliance as well as assist you in planning for future trends.

At a minimum, get on the FTC's mailing list. Request that your name be added by writing to the Federal Trade Commission's Press Office, Washington, D.C. 20580.

SECTION
TWO
ESTABLISHING YOUR PROFIT PRESERVATION CENTER

Japanese management techniques and philosophies have recently attracted much attention, but managers can learn little from the Japanese until their companies establish profit preservation centers which interact effectively with all levels of government. The attitude that "this is not my job" is the reason so many jobs are being exported to Japan and elsewhere.

The Japanese manager is no creative genius. Japan did not prosper until business in the United States de facto ceased to compete in the midsixties. If you gave Japanese managers excessive affirmative action policies, regulations, and paperwork; "big is bad" antitrust enforcement; a president who believes profits are obscene; and counterproductive capital gains taxes and then made the Japanese defend themselves militarily, you would see how good they are. But, of course, the Japanese wouldn't tolerate this.

Nor should you. All managers must take an interest in government relations. Any manager can design a profit preservation center at a minimal cost. Depending on your resources, this center will anticipate, monitor, report, track, assess, and, where necessary, lobby for or against all state and federal legislation and regulation impacting your business.

If your business is large, you may be involved with as much as 5 to 10 percent of all state bills (and 150,000 to 200,000 are being introduced each biennium) in addition to those at the federal level. However, as a large industry you have the ability and the resources to develop an effective profit preservation center.

If your business is small, you may want to have input but may feel overwhelmed. Don't. You can stay abreast of and affect many issues without exorbitant cost. Our regulatory survival course can be self-taught.

WHO WILL RUN YOUR SYSTEM?

You should have a broad, up-to-date data base covering the social, political, technological, and economic trends affecting your business. The manager you select for this function must be able to learn how to learn, since government affairs are a lifetime education. This person must know your business to isolate the key laws and rules which may affect your business. The manager must understand the government process—who is a key sponsor, what committees really count in a given state and how receptive a sponsor's staff is to your input. Knowledge of computers also will help as more government bodies expand their electronic data transmission systems.

If you're running a small business and must do this yourself and the previous description doesn't sound like you, don't despair. Much of the law involved is newspaper law. It's easy to be familiar with the vernacular— you read about civil rights, age discrimination, and the like every day. Add this to your expertise in your own product line, and you're ready to go— on a limited basis. However, your exposure is probably more limited also.

HOW TO STAY ABREAST OF RULES AND LEGISLATION

You must monitor the government activity which affects your business. Monitoring requires an understanding of what signals precede an event (or have done so in the past). This is important not only because you wish to stay within the law but also because knowledge of future trends enables you to adjust your corporate planning in advance with a minimum of dislocation and inconvenience.

One good investment is the *Federal Register* (see reference for address and price).[1] You should also subscribe to the *Congressional Record*.[2] Most of the federal activity affecting your business will be found in these papers. If your business is small, these will probably be sufficient for your needs.

FEDERAL REGISTER

In 1935, Congress passed the Federal Register Act, setting up a basic centralized system to publicize government regulations. The *Federal Register* is published on a daily basis by the General Services Administration. It contains three types of documents: proposed rules, final rules, and notices, which are not rules but documents of general interest to the public. All agencies must give a 30-day notice in the *Federal Register* when a new rule is adopted. The language, although small in print, is straightforward and well indexed so that you may proceed to areas of interest to you and your business.

You may use the *Federal Register* merely to follow the rulemaking procedures of federal agencies impacting your business. Or, if you have the resources, you might consider using it as an alarm. When an agency intends to promulgate a new rule, a general notice of the proposed rule making must be published in the *Federal Register*. The agency *must* allow those with an interest in the area to be regulated an opportunity to submit written data, comments, or arguments, and it is within the agency's discretion to allow an oral presentation.

You can submit input as a citizen or, if possible, through your trade association, whose larger membership and possibly greater expertise might carry greater weight. You may not get the rule discarded, but your input may contribute to a more finely worded and narrowly drawn rule. This is important, since you cannot be held to any standards not expressed in the final rule. Further, legalese is not favored, and courts will construe the language of the rule literally and "according to the natural meaning of the words."[3]

CONGRESSIONAL RECORD

The *Congressional Record* is the full text of everything said in Congress each day, including all legislation introduced, subsequent votes, and certain articles, stories, and the like introduced and read into the record by various senators and representatives.

You'll want to read this in greater depth than you do the *Federal Register.* Not only are these debates and bills that directly affect your business, but there are daily debates on defense, taxes, water rights, highways, etc., that will often be of interest to you.

For a nominal price (see Ref. 2), you now have access to the public goings-on in Congress. If you support a bill, write your representative, the sponsor, and the head of the committee, in that order. If you don't think you count, try writing a personal letter. (Form letters, cards, and petitions are worth a lot less.) Your representative will respond to a personal letter from a constituent. Other representatives will respond to nonconstituents also.

I wrote to a number of senators concerning the Panama Canal treaties, including at least six out-of-state senators. I received in-depth responses from each in varying length. Senators Richard Schweiker, Paul Laxalt, Robert Dole, and Orin Hatch agreed with me and so their letters were barely a page. Senator Howard Baker disagreed and sent a three-page response apologizing for a 3-week delay, and candidly acknowledging that his Tennessee constituents come first. Remember, a lot of these people take their jobs as public servants seriously, as do their staffs. If you're cynical, remember that many representatives and senators consider running for president. Your state has a primary. You count.

In your letter of support or opposition, inform your representative why the bill is bad for the district or state. Talk about lost jobs, investment, tourism, and so on. You'll be surprised what *personal* letters from you, your friends, and trade associations can accomplish. Finally, don't forget the press—write to your local newspaper. Your local representatives don't want bad press, and an editorial may cause them to reconsider their votes.

How do you contact Washington people? There is no better book to answer this question than the *Almanac of American Politics.*[4] This book contains the state and Washington, D.C., addresses and phone numbers of all members of Congress as well as their voting records and ratings by various groups. This book, the *Federal Register,* and the *Congressional Record* provide a strong basis from which to monitor the federal scene as it affects your business.

FREE NEWSLETTERS

You may wish to take advantage of several free newsletters which are available.[5] Newsletters are available from the FTC (a must if you advertise and also need to keep abreast of consent agreements), the Consumer Product Safety Commission, and the Justice Department (especially for antitrust issues). However, you should write to all federal agencies that affect your business [for example, the Federal Communications Commission (FCC) or the Department of Agriculture] to ask if they have a newsletter. These are all "free," courtesy of your tax dollars.

Next write to all those in Congress who affect your business and get their newsletters and press releases. Since many senators and representatives distribute newsletters and/or press releases, you can have these indefinitely for the price of one stamp. You should follow anyone who heads a committee that impacts your business directly.

GETTING INFORMATION THROUGH THE FREEDOM OF INFORMATION ACT

Congress unanimously passed the Freedom of Information Act in 1966 to enable individual citizens to obtain information about the workings of their government.[6] You can use this act to find out general information about competitors. However, it is not the purpose of the act to obtain *private competitive* information. You will not get it, and your efforts may result in litigation filed against you if your competitor discovers what you tried to do.

The Freedom of Information Act provides that each agency shall make available to "any person" all records requested if they are reasonably identified unless the information falls into one of the nine enumerated exemptions. For purposes of this act, "records" include more than written records; for example, films[7] and tape recordings[8] are records.

As to exemptions, the one most clearly applicable to business information is Exemption 4, which exempts from mandatory disclosure "trade secrets" and commercial or financial information received which is privileged or confidential.[9] Another area of protection is Exemption 8, which protects the privacy of truth-in-lending compliance reports as well as reports concerning solvency.[10] However, the courts have generally construed such exemptions quite narrowly.[11]

Write to the agency from which you want records. If you have any problem getting an address, just call (202) 555-1212 to find the agency's phone number (often a toll-free one is available) and address. In your letter, include the following:

1. Cite that you are writing pursuant to 5 U.S.C. sec. 522 of the Freedom of Information Act.
2. Identify the records you are requesting as clearly and narrowly as possible.
3. State the limit of fees you are willing to pay.
4. Ask for all records not exempt (in case some are).

The agency must determine within 10 working days whether it will comply.[12] The time limit may be extended another 10 days if the agency notifies you of certain specific circumstances. If the request is denied, a specific reason must be given for the denial. You must be supplied with the name and title of the person responsible for the denial. You will be informed of your right to appeal to a higher official in the agency. If your appeal is subsequently denied, you can file suit in a district court, where you will often receive expedited preference under law.

However, you'll usually get the information quite painlessly. You'll pay a nominal fee to cover costs. The only possible drawback is that any requests under this act become a matter of public record. If discretion is important, you might consider using private stationery or having your attorney inquire for you.

Finally, be aware that information provided under this act does not have to be investigated for accuracy by an agency before it is released.[13]

EASING OF FEDERAL BURDENS?

The flood of papers and overly broad agency investigations of the past may be receding. The following are a few areas you should be alert to.

EXECUTIVE ORDER 12291 (1981). This executive order requires that regulatory action may not be undertaken unless the potential net benefits to society outweigh the potential costs to society. Furthermore, it directs the agencies to choose the least costly alternative among regulatory approaches and requires a regulatory impact analysis for every major rule that an agency intends to issue. This new emphasis on a cost-benefit approach amplifies the positive effects of conveying your firm's message when the agency first announces it is studying a rule.

PAPERWORK REDUCTION ACT. This act requires that each form sent to you by an agency have the name, address, and telephone number of a person who can help with any questions you might have. Also *all* federal forms must have an Office of Management and Budget clearance number on them. If they do not (usually in the top right-hand corner), you can legally ignore the form if your attorney so advises.[14] At a minimum you could consider contesting the form in a polite response letter.

EQUAL ACCESS TO JUSTICE ACT. This act became effective October 1, 1981, and provides that your business will be reimbursed for costs and fees if it prevails in litigation in certain suits involving the U.S. government, unless the court holds the agency's position to be "substantially justified" *or* certain special circumstances make the award unjust. The burden is on the government to justify its actions—you don't have to prove them unjustified.

Prior to this an agency with or without justification could conduct a fishing expedition into any business at the general taxpayers' expense. If the business "won," it had only the dubious satisfaction of winning an often Pyrrhic victory, since the business was out all costs and attorney fees incurred in defending itself and it lost goodwill through resulting bad publicity. This act will lessen the government burden on qualifying parties in both civil and administrative cases.

Are you a qualifying party? Eligible parties include individuals whose net worth does not exceed $1 million and who are sole owners of unincorporated businesses, partnerships, corporations, and associations of public and private organizations whose net worth does not exceed $5 million. No business employing more than 500 employees may recover under this act regardless of net worth (part-time employees are included on a proportional basis, and temporary or seasonal workers are excluded).

CONCLUDING COMMENTS ON FEDERAL IN-HOUSE COMPLIANCE

The cost of federal regulation compliance is now close to $130 billion per year (usually approximating the national debt, for obvious reasons).[15] This compliance does not include fines and other costs for violations (which are not tax-deductible).

You can reduce your costs and lower your adverse visibility to the federal government by creating a profit preservation center. The previous comments are useful particularly to managers of smaller businesses. Managers also need knowledge about state rulings and legislation, which the following section discusses.

GETTING A HANDLE ON STATE LEGISLATURES AND REGULATORY ACTIVITY

In certain areas the federal government preempts state authority. In other areas Congress will expressly permit "narrower" drafting of legislation in the interests of the public. Finally, there are areas in which the state alone chooses to act. This latter can be a problem for a nationwide business, since sales taxes, personnel policies, and advertising copy may vary from state to state.

There are many ways to approach the state legislative hurdle without drowning in a sea of paper. Many states will provide you with legislative and regulatory calendars for a nominal charge (the references contain state services costing less than $500 per year as of 1983).[16] Your trade association may be able to capsule a few specific topics as part of its dues. In some states the attorney general's office has a *free* newsletter which will update you on the state's activity as to consumer fraud, antitrust, and other issues.[17] The mailing list approach discussed in the federal area is useful here too. Get on newsletter mailing lists of key state representatives. They'll also send you bills free for the asking. Finally, there are services which specialize in state reporting and lobbying. These services will probably cost in excess of $10,000 per client, which may be prohibitive for small businesses.[18]

Another book you should seriously consider adding to your profit preservation center library is the *Consumer Protection Directory*.[19] This is a comprehensive guide to federal and state agencies as well as to consumer protection organizations in the United States and Canada. This book provides the address, phone number, and often the name of a direct contact for every agency you might need in the consumer field. In any state in which you're doing business, you'll be able to contact, for example, the attorney general's office, all state consumer services offices, and all state licensing boards. You'll also have direct contact with all local government agencies and private organizations such as the better business bureaus, credit unions, and consumer groups. This book is a necessary resource for any firm doing business in more than one state and a useful one for just intrastate business since it is better organized than a phone book.

Once you have access to the proposed laws and rules coming to your desk, start writing. Write to the key people concerned. If feasible, ask for an appointment to see them. This will almost always be possible if you are a constituent. Last but not least, contribute to candidates who support the free-enterprise goals you live by. If the incumbent doesn't, then work for the opponent. Finally, if you have the resources, discuss with your attorney the possibility of your firm's forming a political action committee (PAC).[20]

CONCLUSION

Section 2 is a primer for the businessperson in a small firm who doesn't believe interaction with government bodies can be so easy and so inexpensive. For less than $1000 (often tax-deductible) you can accomplish a lot.

Larger firms are already involved. Their interests may be yours generally but not specifically. It is important that you be heard. If you have any further questions or ideas, please write to me at the address given in Ref. 21.

REFERENCES

[1] The *Federal Register* can be ordered by calling the U.S. Government Printing Office at (202) 783-3238 and charging such subscription to a VISA or Mastercharge number (the present cost is $300, which is subject to change) or by ordering in writing with a prepayment to Superintendent of Documents, U.S. Government Printing Office, Washington, D.C., 20402. Another valuable tool to investigate is *The Business Action Network: Washington Watch*, a monthly newsletter published by the U.S. Chamber of Commerce. For more information and a price quote, call (202) 659-6000.

[2] The *Congressional Record* may also be ordered by calling or writing the U.S. Government Printing Office (see Ref. 1). The present cost is $218, which is subject to change.

[3] Diamond Roofing Co. v. OSHRC, 528 F.2d 645 (1976).

[4] Michael Barone and Grant Ujifusa, *The Almanac of American Politics 1982* (revised every 2 years), Barone, Washington, D.C. Should you need to contact any senator

or representative and this book is unavailable, the Capitol switchboard, at (202) 224-3121, will connect you with any senate or congressional office you specify.

5 To obtain press releases issued by the Department of Justice, write to Attorney General, Antitrust Division, Department of Justice, Washington, D.C., 20530.

The FTC issues a *News Summary,* which can be obtained by writing to the Public Reference Branch, Room 130, Federal Trade Commission, 6th and Pennsylvania Avenue N.W., Washington, D.C., 20580.

The Consumer Product Safety Commission newsletter can be obtained by writing to the U.S. Consumer Product Safety Commission, Room 342B, Washington, D.C., 20207.

The National Advertising Division of the Council of Better Business Bureaus, Inc. issues a newsletter, *NAD Case Report,* which can be obtained by writing to National Advertising Division, Council of Better Business Bureaus, Inc., 845 Third Avenue, New York, New York, 10022.

Copies of federal legislation may be obtained at no charge by contacting the sponsor's office or by writing to the following. For Senate bills, write to Senate Document Room, U.S. Capitol, Washington, D.C., 20510 and for House bills, write to H. 226, U.S. House Document Room, Washington, D.C., 20515. When writing to the House or Senate document rooms, provide a self-addressed label with your request.

For free information on the status of federal legislation, send the bill number or numbers along with a self-addressed stamped envelope to Legis Office, House Office Building Annex 2, 2d and D Street, S.W., Washington, D.C., 20515, and they will provide you with a printout of any activity on the bill or bills requested along with the current status.

6 5 U.S.C. sec. 552.

7 Save the Dolphins v. Dep't of Commerce, 404 F. Supp. 407 (1975).

8 Hrynko v. Crawford, 402 F. Supp. 1083 (1975).

9 5 U.S.C. sec. 552(b)(4). *See also* Chrysler Corp. v. Brown, 441 U.S. 281 (1979).

10 5 U.S.C. sec. 552(b)(8). *See also* Consumers Union of the United States, Inc. v. Heimann, No. 77-2115 (D.C. Cir. 1978).

11 Department of the Air Force v. Rose, 425 U.S. 352, 361 (1976). *See* McCarthy and Kornmeier, *Maintaining the Confidentiality of Confidential Business Information Submitted to the Federal Government,* 36 The Business Lawyer 57–78 (1980).

12 5 U.S.C. sec. 552(6)(A).

13 Price & Stevens Chem. Corp. v. United States Consumer Prod. Safety Comm'n 585 F.2d 1382 (1978).

14 For problems with federal department and agency forms, write or call the Office of Information and Regulatory Affairs, Office of Management and Budget, 726 Jackson Place N.W., Room 3208, Washington, D.C., 20503, (202) 395-6880. Also you might try the Business Advisory Council on Federal Reports, 1001 Connecticut Avenue N.W., Suite 925, Washington, D.C., 20036, (202) 331-1915. Finally, don't forget to call your local representative if you have an unresolved or burdensome problem with federal reports (obviously the same holds true for state reports which will be discussed further).

15 In addition to the *Almanac of American Politics,* you should also obtain a copy of *Conquering Government Regulations—A Business Guide* (McGraw-Hill, New York, 1982) edited by McNeill Stokes assisted by 10 contributing authors who are experts in their field. It contains a helpful jargon-free discussion of government regulations.

16 Free state services include the following free publications, listed by state.

Florida—*Daily Journal;* Mr. Allen Morris, Clerk of the House, Florida House of Representatives, 427 The Capitol, Tallahassee, Florida, 32301.

Kentucky—*Weekly Legislative Calendar;* Legislative Research Commission, State Capitol, Frankfort, Kentucky, 40601.

Maine—*Weekly Legislative Calendar;* Mr. Edwin H. Pert, Clerk of the House, House of Representatives, Augusta, Maine, 04333.

Minnesota—*Weekly Wrap Up;* House Information Office, Room 8 State Capitol, St. Paul, Minnesota, 55155.

Nebraska—*Unicameral Update;* Unicameral Information Office, State of Nebraska, State Capitol, Lincoln, Nebraska, 68509.

New Jersey—*Legislative Calendar;* Legislative Information Service, State House, CN-042, Trenton, New Jersey, 08625.

Washington—*Legislative Meeting Schedule;* Washington State Legislature, Legislative Building, Olympia, Washington, 98504.

In addition to these free publications, there are other inexpensive state services available. The following states provide legislative subscription services for nominal fees; the addresses and telephone numbers needed to discover what available services fulfill your requirements are included.

Delaware—Ms. Hedgecock, Legislative Council, P.O. Box 1401, Dover, Delaware, 19901.

Illinois—Legislative Reference Bureau, Room 112, State House, Springfield, Illinois, 62706.

Indiana—Legislative Services Agency, 302 State House, Indianapolis, Indiana, 46204.

Maine—Mr. Ed Pert, Clerk of the House, State House, Augusta, Maine, 04333.

Maryland—State Department of Legislative Reference, Attention: V. Tilghman, 90 State Circle, Room G-18, Annapolis, Maryland, 21401.

Missouri—Eric Luthi, Assistant Chief Clerk/House Administration, Missouri House of Representatives, State Capitol, Jefferson City, Missouri, 65101, or call the Missouri House of Representatives Legislative Information System at (314) 751-2357.

Montana—Legislative Bill Distribution, Capitol Station, Helena, Montana, 59601.

Nevada—Legislative Counsel Bureau, Legislative Building, Capitol Complex, Carson City, Nevada, 89710.

North Carolina—Publications Office, Institute of Government, Knapp Building 059A, The University of North Carolina at Chapel Hill, Chapel Hill, North Carolina, 27514, or call (919) 966-5381.

Oklahoma—Mr. LeRoy A. Ritter, Oklahoma Business News Co., P.O. Box 1177, 605 N.W. 13th, Suite C, Oklahoma City, Oklahoma, 73101, or call (405) 521-1405.

Oregon—Distribution Center, Room 49, State Capitol Building, Salem, Oregon, 97310.

Utah—House of Representatives, State of Utah, 318 State Capitol, Salt Lake City, Utah, 84114.

Vermont—Vermont Legislative Council, State House, Montpelier, Vermont, 05602.

Wisconsin—Legislative Document Room, State Capitol, Madison, Wisconsin, 53702, or call (608) 266-2400.

In addition to the specific state services mentioned, you might be interested in keeping abreast of national trends in the legislatures. Two magazines of interest in this area are *State Legislatures* published by the National Conference of State Legislatures, 1125 Seventeenth Street, Suite 1500, Denver, Colorado, 80202, (303) 623-6600 ($30 for a 1-year subscription) and *State Government News,* published by the Council of State Governments, P.O. Box 11910, Lexington, Kentucky, 40578 ($15 for a 1-year subscription).

One final source for state legislative information is *The State Slate,* which is prepared by Public Affairs Information. This contains the names, addresses, party affiliation, and committee membership of all legislators in the 50 states in addition to a listing of the information phone numbers in all the state capitols. The cost of a subscription is $165. To obtain more information or to order a copy, contact Lou O' Boyle, Public Affairs Information, 5203 Leesburg Pike, Suite 1201, Falls Church, Virginia, 22041, (703) 379-0222.

[17] State attorney general and consumer protection newsletters that are available include the following, listed by state:

Alaska—*Consumer Protection Newsletter;* Consumer Protection Section Department of Law, 1049 W. 5th, Suite 101, Anchorage, Alaska, 99501.

Arkansas—*Consumer Alert;* Consumer Protection Division, Justice Building, Little Rock, Arkansas, 72201.

Colorado—*A.G. Legal Newsbriefs;* Colorado Department of Law, 1525 Sherman Street, 3d Floor, Denver, Colorado, 80203.

Iowa—*Department of Justice Press Releases;* Consumer Protection Division, Hoover Building, 2d Floor, 1300 East Walnut, Des Moines, Iowa, 50319.

Kentucky—*News Release;* Office of the Attorney General, Capitol Building, Frankfort, Kentucky, 40601.

Maryland—*Attorney General's Digest;* Attorney General of Maryland, 1400 One South Calvert Building, Baltimore, Maryland, 21202.

Oregon—*Department of Justice Press Releases;* State of Oregon, Consumer Protection and Services Section, Justice Building, Salem, Oregon, 97310.

South Carolina—*Consumer Affairs Report;* South Carolina Department of Consumer Affairs, 2221 Devine Street, P.O. Box 5757, Columbia, South Carolina, 29250.

Texas—*The Consumer Alert;* Office of the Attorney General, Supreme Court Building, P.O. Box 12548, Austin, Texas, 78711-2548.

Wisconsin—*Consumer Protection Report;* Office of Consumer Protection, 114 East, State Capitol, Madison, Wisconsin, 53702.

For consumer news contact *Consumer News,* U.S. Office of Consumer Affairs, Washington, D.C., 20201. Should you be interested in a state not listed, address a letter to the attorney general of the state at the state capitol.

18 These services include Public Affairs Information, 5203 Leesburg Pike, Suite 1201, Falls Church, Virginia, 22041, (703) 379-0222; DeHart Associates, 1505 22d Street N.W., Washington, D.C., 20037, (202) 659-4000; and Legi-Slate, Suite 408, 444 North Capitol Street N.W., Washington, D.C., 20001, (202) 737-1888. Also, your trade association might have a targeted legislative service.

19 Write to Marquis Academic Media, Marquis Who's Who, Inc., 200 East Ohio Street, Chicago, Illinois, 60611.

20 For a very lucid description of PACs, see chapter 13 of Stoke's book, discussed in Ref. 15.

21 If you have any questions about starting your profit preservation center, write to me at 242 Elsie Avenue, Merrick, New York, 11566, or call me at (516) 868-9849. See also my article "To Survive You Must Follow Current Legislative Trends," *Direct Marketing,* July 1983, pp. 138–140.

SECTION

THREE

THE LAW YOU SHOULD KNOW AFFECTING PRODUCT DECISIONS

In the truly marketing-oriented firm, the "customer is king." A good manager therefore develops products which appeal to the general public or to a previously defined target market.

Before your product development program is put into effect, your company will decide its strategy and policy regarding product ideas. Traditionally, you approach various product-marketing questions such as the identification of the product's primary user and whether such primary user is the primary purchaser. You want to know where the product is purchased and whether this place of purchase is the optimum site. You'll consider whether you have the necessary distribution channels or the ability to develop them. These and many other routine questions impact the legal environment. If you approach your product-marketing decisions in a legal vacuum, you may find your firm encountering legal problems you hadn't anticipated.

This section will assist you in understanding the legal environmental issues so that you'll be more likely to spot a potential problem. *This* is the time to consult your counsel, *before* you make significant investments of your time and budget into market research and other initial preproduction investments. The section also includes a few pointers on potential issues involving both the production phase and the contractual phase.

Chapter 1 addresses your product liability exposure and how it can vary depending on the target market, communications mix, or distribution channel strategy you employ. The chapter briefs you on useful areas to document and provides some tips on how to build in and emphasize safety as a form of sales strategy. The chapter reviews the growing trend in case law to allow imposition of product liability costs on manufacturers *without* proof of the identity of the manufacturer whose product caused the injury or damage, and briefly explores some issues relevant to your potential criminal liability. Finally, we review the activities of the Consumer Product Safety Commission.

As a marketer you are a seller, and selling is the transfer of enthusiasm for your product downstream to your customer. This chapter encourages you to see the benefits of transferring enthusiasm for product safety upstream to your design and manufacturing people.

Chapter 2 reviews another essential in your sales strategy—your product's packaging. Does it look attractive on the shelf? Does it catch your eye? Can you mail it safely? A lot of marketing input goes into packaging, and your customers are increasingly relying on label information in their purchase decisions. The growth of self-service accelerates this trend. Visualize yourself as a consumer, and you'll find some useful information. To best provide this input, you should have an idea of the complexity of the regulations affecting packaging and labeling. Chapter 2 touches on these areas with a review of the Fair Packaging and Labeling Act.

Chapter 3 is an in-depth review of warranties, discussing both the Magnuson-Moss requirements (for consumers only) and those of the Uniform Commercial Code (UCC). You know from any recent automobile ad that a warranty is a valuable marketing vehicle. Your competitors are offering them, and your customer wants them—good ones. A knowledge of your obligations here is essential to the success of any warranty promotion. Just as important, don't forget that once you leave your office you are "one of them"—you're a consumer. *The law you learn here (as well as in other sections) will help you protect your own rights in the marketplace.*

Chapter 4 has a broad discussion of trademarks. In a more traditional book, you'd find this topic under advertising. However, the reality in the 1980s is "image," and your brand name and image can be as much a part of your strategy as any other factor. This chapter gives managers a thorough grasp of traditional trademark law and prepares them to compete in the world of product image built around such a mark.

So read on and enjoy, as often as possible consulting the references. Although many provide follow-up for the specialist, often you'll find general useful facts pertinent to your needs.

CHAPTER
ONE
YOUR PRODUCT
LIABILITY EXPOSURE

Why product liability? Isn't this an area of safety design for manufacturing? Although primary responsibility for a safe product rests in the product design and testing areas of your firm, your firm's communications mix, distribution system, labeling, and written instructions are all important factors in legal exposure. You can reduce your firm's risk of legal exposure to product liability as well as broaden your overall business knowledge by familiarizing yourself with the points raised in this chapter.

We'll review three traditional aspects of product liability and then discuss some evolving areas, including criminal exposure. We'll also briefly discuss the role of the Consumer Product Safety Commission, since this relates directly to the area of product liability. However, first it is important to stress that your firm must have a comprehensive in-house product liability program with your in-house counsel playing a leading role. This program should consist of a routine legal review of all warranties you offer, your purchase sales forms, your insurance coverage, new and revised labels and instructions books, document retention programs, and other relevant areas. Such a program needs the absolute and honest cooperation of all concerned parties. One way you can assist this program is to be aware of areas of exposure so that you can quickly contact your counsel if you see any potential problems.

When people are injured because of some defect in a product, they may have a claim for traditional negligence, strict product liability, or breach of warranty. Each of these three areas will be examined. There are three additional ways in which you may become exposed to a product liability charge: if your firm is a successor corporation, through market share liability, and through personal criminal liability. These latter areas have developed in recent years and may become increasingly "popular" in the years to come.

NEGLIGENCE

You may remember studying negligence law in your undergraduate or graduate business courses, and the definition you learned then holds you in good stead now. Negligence is your failure to use the amount of care you should reasonably have exercised under the circumstances, thereby resulting in an injury to a person. As with much of the law, there is an emphasis on reasonability, that is, the commonsense maturity the public has a right to expect from one in your position in a given set of circumstances.

The duty to exercise reasonable care extends to all phases of the production and distribution process. In general, this duty rests on the manufacturer, particularly if the wholesaler or retailer merely passes along sealed packages manufactured by reputable firms. If you don't manufacture the product, you cannot be held liable for injuries sustained from the contents of a sealed product, even though a test might have disclosed a potential danger not known to you at the time of sale. If you are required to inspect the goods sold, ordinarily you need not inspect them for *latent* defects. You are under a duty to discover any defects which a *reasonable* inspection would disclose. However, you are negligent if you fail to inspect or if a careless inspection results in your failure to discover a defect.

Further, a manufacturer which relies on its channels to inspect the product or perform other services can be held negligently liable if such channel members are lax in their duties or if the manufacturer fails to instruct them accordingly. For example, a firm designed a saw using all reasonable care at the time of design. However, after placing the saw into the marketplace, new safety improvements were introduced. A worker was injured and recovered $250,000. The court held that with little inconvenience or expense the firm could have instructed its dealers not to sell the saw without the latest safety attachments.[1]

Then there is the issue of whether you should repair a machine after an accident. Generally, the fact that you repaired a product after it injured someone is not relevant to show the product was defective at the time of the injury. The social policy is to encourage repair, and the defense is that it was repaired to make it even safer.

However, you're not off the hook. There are a number of ways you can expose yourself to liability in the postmanufacturing process. If you distribute the product of another as your own, the burden of liability shifts to you as well as the manufacturer. If you assume responsibility for assembling the product or otherwise preparing it for sale, you are charged with the responsibility for proper assemblage as well as for discovering and correcting obvious defects or other apparent problems.

A retailer may risk exposure by selling an otherwise safe product to the wrong consumer, for example, selling firearms, fireworks, or flammables such as kerosene or automotive flares to minors.[2] Here your test is the predictability of harm as well as the duty of care owed the particular buyer.

Products for children are especially important. It is estimated that there are as many as 750,000 injuries as a result of toy-related incidents each year.[3] You may be liable for an unintentional injury through faulty assembly, failure to warn, or selling to a child obviously not mature enough to handle such a toy.

Both a wholesaler and a retailer have a duty to warn when they have knowledge about a product's dangerous condition and the next recipient in the channel probably will not discover the danger. You should be aware that the negligent acts or omissions of one channel member may result in other channel members' being held liable if they should have anticipated the negligent act.

Obviously, if the distribution of a potentially dangerous product is strictly controlled and if there's no chance it will fall into the hands of outsiders unfamiliar with its specific hazards, your need to warn is greatly reduced. However, if there is even a remote chance that your product will find its way into the open market, you must post conspicuous warnings or give explicit explanations concerning safe and correct handling.

Labeling is important. Whenever you have a duty to warn (and you have such duty whenever you know or should anticipate that an inexperienced purchaser might use the item sold in a dangerous manner or might not comprehend the danger of such use) it is advisable to have a carefully worded, descriptive label on your product. The label must be worded in language the intended audience can grasp, which means basic English (or in the language of your particular target group). Where adequate warnings are given, the seller may reasonably assume that they will be read and followed. Here is where manufacturing, legal, and marketing sections must work together. Manufacturing must carefully explain the product's uses and dangers to counsel. You must work with your counsel to draft a well-worded label or instruction booklet. To make such a booklet and/or label readable to your audience, you must take into account who your audience is when reviewing the comprehensibility of the booklet or label. You might also suggest that a Flesch readability test be run.[4]

STRICT LIABILITY

Strict liability law is a rapidly emerging area; it represents the greatest potential hazard to you and your firm. The standards you are held to are much greater under strict liability law than under negligence law. For example, in negligence law the exercise of due care will exonerate you from liability. In strict liability law, this exercise of due care is little defense. The issue is the quality of the product. In strict product liability law, a defective product may involve:

1. A mistake in manufacturing, i.e., a flaw
2. A design defect (a product may be meticulously made but if it presents an unreasonable risk of harm it is defectively designed)[5]
3. An inadequate or nonexistent warning in connection with the use of the product

MISTAKE IN MANUFACTURING

A mistake in manufacturing is fairly straightforward: you have produced a "lemon." A traditional comment in this area is that "a manufacturer is strictly liable in tort when an article he places on the market, knowing that it presents a safety risk if defectively made or designed and that it is to be used without inspection for defects, proves to have a defect that causes injury to a human being."[6] In one case strict liability was imposed "to insure that the costs of injuries resulting from defective products are borne by the manufacturers that put such products on the market rather than by the injured persons who are powerless to protect themselves."[7]

The social policy involved is based both on consumer reliance on the manufacturer's expertise for protection when consumers are induced to purchase and on the manufacturer's superior ability to spread out the cost of injury through insurance. Also involved is the basic element of deterrence, whereby the ease of making out a strict product liability claim, along with the potential of losing large judgments, is thought to induce a manufacturer to impose greater control over product development and manufacture. However, such strict standards are not generally applied to commercial purchases that an expert buyer can inspect for defects.[8]

As you can see, this is an area of primary concern to manufacturers. However, those in the marketing distribution channels can involve themselves in product defect situations. One example occurred in a classic case on point, that of the "burning TV." As the court stated, "we can say that a television set properly manufactured and properly serviced by the seller does not, in normal operation, combust."[9] As a result a retailer was held strictly liable. The court noted that some accidents do not ordinarily occur in the absence of a defect and that in those situations a defect may be inferred from the circumstances as long as no alterations were made to the product. The court further commented that the retailer should have known about this danger because of the retailer's size, merchandising skills, and power to control the quality of its products.

Further, you can become liable for a product defect if you service the product. The doctrine of strict liability does not require a new product, but it does require that the product be in substantially the same condition after being serviced as when it was delivered to the purchaser.[10] Therefore, "the seller takes possession of the product when he undertakes to service it. *It becomes an extension of the manufacturing process.* Upon completion of servicing the product whether it is done on the seller's premises or on the premises of the purchaser, the effect is a re-delivery of the product with the same assurances and with the same obligations as the original sale."[11]

Although this discussion concerns your exposure to your customer, it does not mean that you have no right of recovery. Your attorney has included an indemnification clause in your contract with the manufacturer. The social policy for allowing a recovery by the consumer here is that you are distributing the goods and have an obligation of accountability. Even more important, you are the visible party a consumer will turn to for redress.

DESIGN DEFECT

When a design defect is involved, there is a balance between the likelihood of harm and the burden of taking precautions against the harm. The responsibility of a manufacturer is gauged as of the time the product left the manufacturer. This legal trade-off is important.

Once the injured party alleges that there is something about the design of your product which caused the injury, you must demonstrate that the design was safe, that a safer design would not have been practical, or that there was a substantial modification by the purchaser which subsequently altered the product. The latter involves testing the defective product to demonstrate that it was modified by the owner. Your duty is to produce items free of defects, not to produce products impossible to abuse (within reasonable predictability). The test here is whether the product has reached the user or consumer without substantial changes in the condition in which it is sold.[12]

When the issues of a safe product or safest practical product are involved, you must document, document, and then document. Here the "big three" (manufacturer, manager, and counsel) must work together carefully. Some topics your documents should show include:

1. Safety of the design of the product
2. All procedures, research, and testing that went into the design of the product
3. Documents detailing prior accidents or complaints (or lack of same) and how you responded
4. Records of parts and materials, quality control documents, and sales and marketing records to show what warranties were made
5. Proof that all government standards were met or preferably exceeded

Don't expect to rely on your buyer's compliance with Occupational Safety and Health Administration (OSHA) regulations. If you have the duty to install safety features (or your sales personnel must follow up on this during the installation of machinery), assume that the employer and/or buyer *won't*.[13]

One final note: Where possible, don't offer safety equipment as optional where it can be designed into the product. Although safety equipment offered as an option to reduce initial cost resistance or as a "sweetener" might seem preferable, in general, it greatly increases your potential liability.

No product can be absolutely safe. In design defects cases the injured party must show that a safer design would have been practical.[14] Your general test is whether a reasonable manufacturer who realizes the product's harmful propensities would sell the product in light of the risks involved, the utility of the product, its foreseeable use, and the availability and feasibility of safer, alternative designs. This trade-off is socially necessary to avoid discouraging the marketing of many products because their use involves some degree of risk.

Again, be able to document. The following precautions are advised:

1. Be able to document that any later design improvements were new to the state of the art and not a result of the inadequacy of your product's original design. In a small minority of states postaccident design changes can be used as evidence against a manufacturer in product

liability cases. Most states do not favor this view, because it penalizes the company for making safety improvements. Be alert to this issue and consult your counsel accordingly.

2. Prepare your documentation to show that you are committed to safety but that you must be able to price the product within the limits of your customer's ability to pay. Never phrase any cost-benefit analyses as a safety trade-off.

3. When in doubt phrase the documents in technical terms; don't draw conclusions. Never use words such as "defective."

4. Whenever possible you want to document that the design in question was in accordance with or mandated by the buyer's specifications and/ or that the buyer refused to purchase safety devices offered by you, the absence of which caused the design defect. Complying with the buyer's specifications is usually a good defense unless the designs supplied contain defects so extraordinarily dangerous that a prudent manufacturer would decline to produce them.[15]

5. Document all efforts to keep abreast of scientific, technological, and other developments in your ongoing product design and improvement efforts.

Stress to your people that they should keep all documentation in writing, assuming that it will someday be used as evidence in litigation.

Without adequate documentation, defending yourself in an action alleging design defect will be difficult. With adequate documentation you should be able to establish the inherent safety of your product and that your testing revealed that there was no safer state-of-the-art design technology at the time of production. The documents must show that you tested the product for use as intended as well as for all unintended yet reasonably foreseeable uses. Further, they must show that there was no available design modification that would reduce the risk of harm without *undue* cost to the consumer or interference with the performance of the product. This documentation enables you to establish the balancing test of the likelihood of your product's causing harm against the burdens of taking realistic precautions against that harm.[16]

DUTY TO WARN

Duty to warn is the area of greatest legal exposure for those in the distribution chain, although here, as elsewhere, the primary burdens fall on the manufacturer. The content and meaning of all labels, warnings, and instruction booklets are evaluated as to size of print, location, and effectiveness. Warnings, no matter how adequate, cannot absolve the manufacturer or designer of all responsibility for product safety. A warning alone is never a satisfactory replacement for a safety device.[17] Further, and this is all-important, the ultimate user must receive the warning if it is to have any value at all to you (or the user). To paraphrase a familiar statement, what is to be done? Your goal must be to warn any member of the consuming public who might use the product.

There is no duty to warn of a product-connected danger which is obvious or known to the person who claims to be entitled to the warning. "Awareness" is a defense when the consumer is aware of a possible defect and its potential danger but proceeds unreasonably to use the product.[18]

Place in your contracts a paragraph that your purchaser will read all instruction books and/or warning labels you provide and pass them along to the ultimate consumer. If the purchaser's employees will use the product, then the purchaser should agree to pass along all warnings to employees.

Write your instruction booklets as if you were preparing for a lawsuit. All warnings on the product should be included in the booklet. Work with your lawyer so that neither legalese nor too much complicated jargon is included in the book. If necessary, design and enclose a couple of instruction booklets addressed to varied individuals to whom your instructions are applicable.

On your product labels include a warning that the user must read the instruction booklet before proceeding to use the product. All product labels should be screened by your attorney as well as by experts who can determine the adequacy and audience "understandability" of your text. Understandability might include technical or complex wording analysis, convenience of the placement of the label to the reader, and the size of the print. Finally, remember that the label decal must last as long as the product.

Be alert as to the frequency and duration of your advertising campaign for a product, especially one directed at consumers. Advertisements may increase consumers' expectations regarding product performance.[19]

Your marketing communications can result in liability due to the *innocent omission* of facts. Retailers can be held liable for the goods they sell if they do not make the user aware of certain dangers. In one case the court held that the responsibility of a retailer was the same as that of a manufacturer, because the retailer held the product out as its own and because its size, volume, and merchandising practices brought it within the class of "professional vendors," who are presumed to know of defects in their wares. This relationship permits the retailer to exert pressure on the manufacturer to control its quality.[20] This case concerned a chipped hammer. It is well known in the tool industry that once a hammer is chipped it is dangerous and should be discarded. However, the court felt that the entire buying public should be made aware of this fact and went as far as to suggest a warning label stating "if this hammer chips, return to seller."[21]

The courts are interpreting defective labels, instruction books, and packaging as defective products. These are not product decisions strictly for the manufacturing and legal departments. Managers must get involved in these areas.

BREACH OF WARRANTY

A warranty is a representation by the seller about the product's qualities or characteristics. Warranties are discussed in more depth in the next chapter, but for now you should distinguish breach of warranty from the areas of negligence and strict products liability. The cause of action for breach of warranty is a contractual relationship, and only the parties to the contract may assert it. However, warranty protection is extended to a subpurchaser who bought the product under warranty and who justifiably relied on representations made by the seller to the public through advertisements or labels attached to the goods.

An initial question here is the degree of reliance the buyer placed on the salesperson's "pitch." A certain amount of puffery is permitted. However, any affirmation of fact which relates to the goods and becomes a part of the basis of the bargain will create an express warranty.[22] In general, catalog statements and other written advertisements are express warranties.

There is an implied warranty that a product is reasonably fit for the general purpose for which it is manufactured and sold. If a product doesn't satisfy this representation, an action for breach of warranty exists.[23]

SUCCESSOR CORPORATIONS

Under the product-line rule a firm which acquires a manufacturer's assets may be liable as a corporate successor if it holds itself out as an ongoing enterprise, if it maintains the same product name and personnel, or if it requires the predecessor corporation to dissolve.

The social policy articulated here is that "solvent corporations, going concerns, should not be permitted to discharge their liabilities to injured persons simply by shuffling paper and manipulating corporate entities."[24] Again, courts are seeking to impose liability based on the public policy of loss spreading across society rather than on an individual. This burden is imposed on the firm, even though the successor corporation has not put the defective article into commerce, as strict product liability mandates.[25]

For your planning and insurance purposes, it is important to review with counsel your state legal exposure when you seek to acquire the assets of another firm or to sell your firm. Further, awareness of your exposure here will enable you to include this potential liability when negotiating for your acquisition. You should then either purchase adequate product liability insurance or enter into an agreement under which your predecessor will indemnify you for any liability occasioned by the predecessor's product defects. You can assume that the courts will depart from the traditional rules and that liability will be imposed on a purchasing corporation if one of the following occurs:

1. The buyer expressly or implicitly agrees to assume the selling corporation's liabilities.
2. The transaction amounts to a consolidation or merger of the seller with or into the buyer.
3. The purchaser corporation is merely a continuation of the seller corporation.
4. The transaction is entered into fraudulently to escape liability for such obligations.
5. The court reviews the useless condition of the original manufacturer and the availability of resources to the successor corporation and the fairness of the successor in taking the benefit with the burden.

ENTERPRISE, MARKET SHARE, AND CONCERTED ACTION LIABILITY

If a person is injured and is unable to pinpoint a particular defendant, the injured party now may be able to recover on a theory of enterprise liability. In enterprise liability, the injured party does not have to prove that the injury was caused by a particular defendant but must show only that a member of a particular industry caused the injury or that the injury resulted from inadequate industrywide standards or practices.[26]

Market share liability is based on a similar social principle, that is, that these costs are foreseeable and should be borne by those financially able to spread the risk rather than by an individual.

Market share liability was announced in California in 1980.[27] A 22-year-old woman developed cervical cancer. Her mother had taken diethylstilbestrol (DES), a drug used in the early 1950s to prevent problems during pregnancy, when she was pregnant with her daughter. The court held that she could sue all the drug makers collectively because she could not prove which one produced the particular DES her mother had taken. The reasoning was that all the makers of this drug should be jointly and severally liable for the young woman's cancer and that, provided that she joined enough manufacturers in her suit to account for a broad market share (here about 85 percent of the entire market was joined), there would be enough likelihood that the defendant would be "caught." Each defendant was held liable for the percentage of its share of the market sales.

A major problem with this line of reasoning is the lack of a clear market. In this case national market shares were used, but equity would have seemed to dictate that the state where the injured party's mother resided or even the local market would have been a more realistic basis of market share.

Finally, there is the concert-of-action theory of recovery. This closely resembles the two theories just discussed.[28] The theory represents an expansion of product liability law, since it does not require that the defendant be guilty of any particular injurious conduct. The major case law on point arose from another DES litigation.[29] The injured party can proceed against any of the manufacturers, and they in turn may recover against manufacturers not brought into the action by the injured party.

CRIMINAL LIABILITY

The Ford Pinto case was a controversial criminal case in the product liability field. Although there is little precedential value in the case, do not disregard it. In general, reckless homicide (and similar charges) may result from a reckless failure to perform an act which one was under a duty to perform. Managers should assist the corporation in developing a product safety attitude. In light of the discussions throughout this chapter, such an attitude is clearly more than just good business.

For example, when involved in a product decision, be alert as to how much of the product's obvious (and occasionally fatal) defects you are aware of or someone could accuse you of being aware of. Failure to ask questions (if you have some) and to disassociate yourself from a potential injury-producing product could be as fatal to your career as it is to the product's user. Further, a criminal conviction not only can involve incarceration, it also allows victims or their families to press forward with civil liability suits.

THE CONSUMER PRODUCT SAFETY COMMISSION

President Ronald Reagan tried (halfheartedly) but could not kill the Consumer Product Safety Commission. This five-member board can set safety standards; require warning by producers and resellers; seize, ban, or recall merchandise; mandate consumer refunds; and *send violators to jail!* Clearly, the commission's powers are related to your product liability exposure. As part of your knowledge of this area you should know where this commission has been and where it is going.

In 1972 Congress promulgated the Consumer Product Safety Act, with the general aim of protecting the public against hazards posed by unsafe consumer products.[30] As stated in a declaration of purpose,[31] Congress enacted this act:

1. To protect the public against unreasonable risk of injury associated with consumer products
2. To assist consumers in evaluating the comparative safety of consumer products
3. To develop uniform safety standards for consumer products and to minimize conflicting state and local regulation
4. To promote research and investigation into the causes and prevention of product-related deaths, illness, and injuries

To carry out its aim, Congress created the Consumer Product Safety Commission, vesting it with broad investigative powers and with the authority to promulgate consumer product safety standards, ban hazardous products, and collect and disseminate product safety information.[32]

The commission may investigate a product within its jurisdiction; if it presents an "unreasonable risk of injury," it may develop rules to reduce the product's risk or, if no safety standard can protect the consumer, it may (although it rarely does) ban the product in question.[33]

Under the act, a proceeding to declare a product unsafe may also be initiated by any interested person (such as your disgruntled customer) or organization.[34] The commission may then elect to investigate further.

Naturally you'll bring in your counsel immediately. From a marketing point of view you must ensure that your counsel knows exactly what information provided by your firm is confidential and/or a trade secret. The commission has a duty not to disclose data that may injure a company. A recent decision[35] stated your rights well. The court noted that Congress specified that some information would be completely exempt from disclosure:

> All information reported to or otherwise obtained by the Commission or its representative under this Act which information contains or related to a trade secret or other matter . . . shall be considered confidential and shall not be disclosed. . . .
> It is wholly improper, and forbidden by this section, for the Commission to disclose information provided by a company if, taking a realistic view of the environment in which that company operates, such disclosure would result in any significant competitive harm to the company. While no conclusive formula can be devised, factors such as these are to be taken into account in determining whether a document comes within the prohibition: whether the information is considered confidential by the submittor and given appropriate protection; whether the information would reveal to competitors operational strengths and weaknesses or other valuable information to which the submittor does not have access about those competitors; whether the information is readily available from other sources.[36]

WHAT THE COMMISSION WILL LOOK AT

Congress expects the commission to weigh the cost of their standards against the cost of their absence. Each product reviewed is looked at as to its risk of injury. Then the commission evaluates whether the level of risk under the circumstances (which include maturity of users, social utility of the product, and so on) is an unreasonable one. For example, a court held on review that requirements to reduce the hazard of accidentally ignited matches were "reasonably necessary" under the act,[37] since there was substantial evidence that a sizable number of persons are injured annually by matchbooks which accidentally ignite and since the cost of reducing such a hazard to the industry was relatively small.[38]

This balancing test illustrates the need for the written documentation concerning the testing of your product as to safety that we discussed earlier in this chapter. Such documentation may be a critical element in establishing that the risk of any harm inherent in your product is balanced by other compelling factors. Can you demonstrate through your market research that a safety improvement will greatly increase the cost of your product beyond the reach of your customer's ability to purchase it? Consumers in lower-income brackets may willingly accept greater risks to save money. If you can document the utility of your product to them, you may be able to convince the commission (or a court) that denying the product to them is not worth a slight improvement in safety.

YOUR TARGET AUDIENCE

As a manager you know your market, and your target market may greatly increase your exposure to the commission's scrutiny. The commission has been criticized for relying on the National Electronic Injury Surveillance System (NEISS—the acronym is pronounced "nice") injury data to the exclusion of almost all else.[39] NEISS (at least initially) only reported product-related accidents which caused problems because certain products may relate to accidents without causing them. Also, the NEISS data counted only actual injuries, ignoring exposures.

If the old, the infirm, and children are your market, you may have increased exposure to the commission. For example, children under 10 years of age receive added weight: Accidents affecting this group are counted twice in the compilation of data as a result of the age-adjusted frequency severity index.

Products not remotely affecting children may come before the commission. Such an innocuous product as an extension cord warranted a specific safety standard to protect children, who had a high frequency of injuries resulting from such cord.

CONCLUSION

Your best protection against commission exposure is to follow these rules:

1. Test your products for safety as to their market and use by children where it is reasonable to anticipate that a child might come into contact with your product.
2. Carefully document the results of all testing.
3. Have your counsel review such tests and documents plus your labels, catalogs, and other promotional material as to wording and suitability to your target audience.
4. If you are investigated, identify for your counsel all documents which must be kept confidential.

5. Discuss with your counsel any unique characteristics of your product which might remove it from the statutory jurisdiction of the Consumer Products Safety Commission.[40]

This chapter has covered a lot of diverse areas. You must be alert to product design, safety features, the target audience variable, and many other areas of liability. This information will help you avoid risk—a goal dear to all business executives.

In view of the variety of court decisions and the varied state and federal legislative and regulatory activity on point, it is difficult to predict the future of industry liability (and your own). You must work closely with your counsel, particularly in drafting contracts with firms with whom you deal or for whom you distribute and in dealing with your advertising agency regarding their promotional proposals. You should also work with your counsel in establishing your own internal procedures for product selection and testing and control of product promotions which will reach the public (and come to the attention of federal and state government agencies). Your attorney's skilled input will see that you have proper indemnification and insurance protection.

REFERENCES

[1] Perkins v. Emerson Elec. Co., 482 F. Supp. 1347 (1980).

[2] Lake Washington School Dist. No. 414 v. Schuch's Auto Supply, Inc., 613 P.2d 561 (1980).

[3] Edward M. Swartz, "Toys-R-Dangerous," *Trial*, February 1982, p. 29.

[4] *See* Rudolph Flesch, *How to Test Readability*, Harper & Brothers, New York, 1951.

[5] Robinson v. Reed-Prentice, 49 N.Y.2d 471, 479, 403 N.E.2d 440, 446–7 (1980).

[6] Greenman v. Yuba Power Prods., Inc., 59 Cal. 2d 57, 377 P.2d 897, 900, 27 Cal. Rptr. 697, 700 (1963). Also of interest is the landmark case Mac Pherson v. Buick Motor Co., 217 N.Y. 382, 11 N.E. 1050 (1916).

[7] Greenman v. Yuba Power Prods., Inc., 59 Cal. 2d 57, 63, 377 P.2d 897, 901, 27 Cal. Rptr. 697, 701 (1963).

[8] Scandinavian Airlines Sys. v. United Aircraft Corp., 601 F.2d 425 (9th Cir. 1979). Most courts won't permit a recovery on strict liability if the parties (1) deal in a commercial setting, (2) negotiate concerning the risk of loss resulting from defects, (3) negotiate concerning product specifications, and (4) have relatively equal economic strength.

[9] Winters v. Sears, Roebuck & Co., 554 S.W.2d 565, 571 (1977).

10 *Id.* at 570.

11 *Id.* at 572.

12 *See* Ref. 4. *See also* Hatcher v. American Motors Corp. 241 So. 2d 147 (1970). After purchase, an independent auto mechanic improperly installed overload springs in a car. This subsequent modification and not a design defect resulted in the injury. For a more recent decision see Daberko v. Heil Co., 661 F.2d 445 (1982). Again, the fact that a manufacturer might have designed a safer product doesn't mean that the current one is unreasonably dangerous.

13 Jasper v. Skyhood Corp., 547 P.2d 1140 (1976).

14 Wilson v. Piper Aircraft Corp., 579 P.2d 1287 (1978).

15 McCabe Powers Body Co. v. Sharp, 594 S.W.2d 592, 595 (1980).

16 Micallef v. Miehle Co., 39 N.Y. 2d 376 (1976). Such documentation can also come back to haunt you; an injured party was permitted to show that about 4 years after the accident the manufacturer modified its design and cured the alleged defect by a modification known 8 years *before* the accident. *See* Capara v. Chrysler Corp., 52 N.Y.2d 114, 417 N.E.2d 545 (1981).

17 Uloth v. City Tank Corp., 384 N.E.2d 1188, 1192 (1978).

18 Hunt v. Harley-Davidson Motor Co., 248 S.E.2d 15 (1978).

19 McCann v. Atlas Supply Co., 325 F. Supp. 701 (1971).

20 Chappins v. Sears, Roebuck & Co., 358 So. 2d 926 (1978).

21 *Id.* at 930.

22 U.C.C. sec. 2–313 1(a).

23 U.C.C. sec. 2–314. For an excellent review of the traditional areas of liability, see Fred W. Morgan, "Marketing and Product Liability: A Review and Update," *Journal of Marketing*, vol. 46, no. 3, Summer 1982, pp. 69–78. Table 2 is particularly useful in highlighting reference cases according to your marketing function (e.g., selling, advertising, wholesaling).

24 Shannon v. Samuel Langston Co., 379 F. Supp. 797, 803 (W.D. Mich. 1979). For a similar articulation of social policy, *see* Dawejho v. Jorgensen Steel Co., 434 A.2d 106, 109 (1981).

25 Tucker v. Paxson Mach. Co., 645 F.2d 620 (8th Cir. 1981). *See also* Bernard v. Kee Mfg. Co., 394 So. 2d 552 (Fla. Dist. Ct. App. 1981). *But see* Armour Dial, Inc. v. Albar Eng'r Corp., 469 F. Supp. 1198 (1979). In 1982, Florida, Illinois, Michigan, and Nebraska rejected strict liability for successor corporations.

26 Hall v. E.I. DuPont De Nemours and Co., 345 F. Supp. 353 (E.D.N.Y. 1972).

27 Sindell v. Abbot Laboratories, 26 Cal. 3d. 588, 607 P.2d 924, 163 Cal. Rptr. 132, *cert. denied* 449 U.S. 912 (1980).

28 This theory is based on The American Law Institute's Restatement of Torts (second) Section 876 (1977) p. 315 which provides as follows:

> For harm resulting to a third person from the tortuous conduct of another, one is subject to liability if he (a) does a tortuous act in concert with the other

or pursuant to a common design with him, (b) knows that the other's conduct constitutes a breach of duty and gives substantial assistance or encouragement to the other so to conduct himself or (c) gives substantial assistance to the other in accomplishing a tortuous result in his own conduct, separately considered, constitutes a breach of duty to the third person.

29 Bickler v. Eli Lilly & Co., 436 N.Y.S.2d 625, 79 A.D.2d 317 (1981).

30 The term "consumer product" (15 U.S.C.S. sec. 2052):

... means any article, or component part thereof, produced or distributed (i) for sales to a consumer for use in or around a permanent or temporary household or residence, a school, in recreation, or otherwise, or (ii) for the personal use, consumption or enjoyment of a consumer in or around a permanent or temporary household or residence, a school, in recreation, or otherwise; but such term does not include:
(A) any article which is not customarily produced or distributed for sale to, or use or consumption by, or enjoyment of, a consumer.

This statutory definition requires that the product be "customarily" (not just occasionally) produced or distributed for the use of consumers.

31 15 U.S.C. sec. 2051.

32 15 U.S.C. secs. 2503–508. It is advisable to get on their mailing list. You might also wish to order a copy of the Commission's "Report of the Recall Effectiveness Task Force of the Consumer Products Safety Commission." To do so, write to the Office of the Secretary, Consumer Products Safety Commission, Washington, D.C., 20207.

33 15 U.S.C. sec. 2058(c)(2)(c).

34 15 U.S.C. sec. 2059(a).

35 Fountainhead Group v. Consumer Prod. Safety Comm'n, 527 F. Supp. 294 (1981).

36 *Id.* at 298–99.

37 Referred to in 18 U.S.C. sec. 1905 or subject to 15 U.S.C. sec. 552(b)(4). *See* 15 U.S.C. sec. 2055(a)(2).

38 15 U.S.C. sec. 2058(c)(2)(A).

39 D.D. Bean & Sons Co. v. Consumer Prod. Safety Comm'n, 574 F.2d 643 (1980).

40 *See What Is a Consumer Product for Purposes of Consumer Product Safety Act,"* 43 A.L.R. Fed. 827(1979).

CHAPTER
TWO
WHAT YOU NEED TO KNOW ABOUT THE FAIR PACKAGING AND LABELING ACT

Most marketing once was based on the personal advice and guidance of the local retailer in the general store, but the growth of the suburbs, resulting in large impersonal shopping centers, as well as the growth of direct mail has brought many innovations. One such innovation has been self-service, which puts a premium on packaging. The package can help sell itself: The color and shape of the packaging can call attention to the product as well as describe it. A label may discuss warranty information. The development of high-volume marketing has required both the marketing and legal professions to pay greater attention to the area of packaging and labeling early in the process of product development.

There is state regulation in this area, but the primary basis of compliance is the Fair Packaging and Labeling Act.[1] The basic purpose of the act is to enable consumers to obtain accurate information which will facilitate value comparison between products. The following is a brief review of both the general principles of the act and the FTC's very lucid interpretations on point.[2]

DEFINITIONS YOU SHOULD KNOW

There are three definitions in the act with which you should be familiar: package, label, and principal display panel.

A "package" is "any container or wrapping in which any consumer commodity is enclosed for use in the delivery or display of that commodity to retail purchasers."[3] There are specific containers and wrappings which are not included in this definition, but the distinctions are fairly technical, and your specific circumstances should be reviewed with your counsel.

A "label" is "any written, printed, or graphic matter affixed to or appearing upon any consumer commodity or affixed to or appearing upon a package containing any consumer commodity; *except* that (1) an inspector's tag or other nonpromotional matter affixed to or appearing upon a consumer commodity shall not be deemed to be a label requiring the repetition of the label information required by this part, and, (2) for the purposes of the regulations in this part the term 'label' does not include written, printed, or graphic matter affixed to or appearing upon containers or wrappers for commodities sold or distributed to industrial or institutional users."[4]

A "principal display panel" is "that part of a label that is most likely to be displayed, presented, shown, or examined under normal and customary conditions of display for retail sale. The principal display panel must be large enough to accommodate all the mandatory label information required to be placed thereon by this part without obscuring designs, vignettes, or crowding. This definition does not preclude utilization of alternate principal display panels on the label of a package, but alternate principal display panels must duplicate the information required to be placed on the principal display panel by this part."[5]

Given the complexity of these definitions, the need to review the wording of your labels and packaging with your counsel is clear.

LABELS

The principal display panel of a consumer commodity must identify the original marketer of the commodity in a type size and location which will be understandable to the consumer.[6] Thus the name (including corporate name) and address of the manufacturer, packer, or distributor must be on the label. Where the consumer commodity is not manufactured by the person whose name appears on the label, the name should be qualified by a phrase that reveals the connection such person has with the commodity, such as "Manufactured for _____," "Distributed by _____," or any other wording that clearly expresses the facts of the relationship.[7]

The net quantity must appear in the front in a fixed location as a distinct item on the principal display panel. It must be separated from other printed label information appearing above or below the declaration by at least a space equal to the height of the lettering used in the declaration. The net quantity statement must not include any term qualifying a unit of weight, measure, or count such as "jumbo quart," "full gallon," "when packed," "minimum," or words of similar import. This prevents consumer confusion in comparison shopping where the consumer could be confronted by one company's referring to its size as "jumbo" while its competitor referred to the same size as "large." The declaration of net quantity must be separated from the other printed label information appearing to the left or right of the declaration by at least a space equal to twice the width of the letter "N" of the style of type used in the net quantity statement.[8]

The quantity must be stated in standard measurements known to your purchasers, giving accurate information regarding the net quantity of the contents to facilitate comparison shopping. The act states specific measurements as to weight and measure,[9] units of fluid measure,[10] length and width,[11] area,[12] cubic measure and dry measure,[13] units of count,[14] and measurement of container type[15] as well as how to set forth fractional amounts[16] of any of the measurements.

As you can see, how to word and present label information is specified by law. All such required information must appear in conspicuous and easily readable boldface type or print in distinct contrast (by layout, color, etc.) to the other matter on the package.[17] The type size must be uniform for all labels and packages of substantially the same size. An official listing of definitions is also set forth.[18]

Variations from the stated weight or measure are permitted when caused by ordinary factors which are "conditions which normally occur in good distribution practices and which unavoidably result in a change of weight or measure."[19] In a California case, the state's labeling laws did not permit variations caused by moisture, and a firm was in trouble because the average net weight of its flour was less than the net weight stated on the packages. The Supreme Court, relying on the principle of national marketplace which this act affords through its preemption of state laws, held that varied state laws affecting weight measurements would defeat the act's purpose of facilitating value comparisons by consumers of similar products.[20] The federal act permits weight variations in flour packages caused by humidity. Unless allowance was made for moisture loss, consumers throughout the county would be misled by attempting to compare the value of identically labeled packages which did not contain identical amounts of flour solids. If you see a potential issue as to temperature, humidity, and the like affecting the weight of your product, consult your counsel as to your potential adverse legal exposure (or lack of same). Copies of published product standards are available.[21]

The act presents a variety of regulations as to multiunit packages,[22] variety of packages,[23] and combination packages.[24] There are exemptions affecting certain varied products such as camera film,[25] Christmas tree ornaments,[26] and pillowcases.[27] Again you must review your particular circumstances with your counsel, who can advise you as to your specific needs and compliance.

SPECIFIC REGULATIONS

Perhaps of most interest to managers is the section of the act that establishes requirements for the labeling and characterization of the following retail sale price representations.

"CENTS-OFF"

Any offer of a certain amount off the regular price is a powerful incentive to buy. (We'll discuss this in greater detail in Chapter 18.) You may not place a "cents-off" statement on your package or label unless:

1. "The commodity has been sold by the packager or labeler at an ordinary and customary price in the most recent and regular course of business in the trade area in which the 'cents-off' promotion is made."[28]
2. It is sold "at a reduction from the ordinary and customary price, which reduction is at least equal to the amount of the 'cents-off' representation imprinted on the commodity package or label."[29]
3. "Each 'cents-off' representation imprinted on the package or label is limited to a phrase which reflects that the price marked by the retailer represents the savings in the amount of the 'cents-off' the retailer's price, e.g., 'Price Marked is _____ ¢ Off the Regular Price.' 'Price Marked is _____ Cents-off the Regular Price of This Package.'"[30]

Further, you may not initiate more than three cents-off promotions of any single-size commodity in the same trade area within a 12-month period.[31] You must allow at least 30 days to lapse between cents-off promotions of any particular-size package or labeled commodity in a specific trade area.[32] And you must not sell any single-size commodity so labeled in your trade area for a duration in excess of 6 months within any 12-month period.[33]

Finally, there are commonsense requirements which state that you must not allow a cents-off promotion to be used in a deceptive manner and that you must retain invoices and/or other records for 1 year after the cents-off promotion occurs.

INTRODUCTORY OFFERS

The regulations on introductory offers are similar to those for cents-off offers. To place this term on your package or label, you must use the exact words "introductory offer." The product must be new (or new to your trade area) or changed in a functionally significant and substantial respect.[34] Your introductory offer may not be made for longer than 6 months.[35]

The requirements as to avoiding deception and the 1-year period for record keeping are the same as those for cents-off offers.

ECONOMY SIZE

Size characterization is important for comparison shopping because it affects the comparison of the same item produced by different manufacturers and/or distributors. To use the wording "economy size" on your package or label, the following are required.

1. You must have at least one other size of the same brand available when you have an economy size.
2. You must sell the commodity labeled with an economy-size representation at a price per unit of weight, volume, measure, or count which is substantially reduced (i.e., at least 5 percent) from the actual price of all other packaged or labeled units of the same brand of that commodity offered simultaneously.[36]
3. The economy-size package must never be made available for deceptive purposes.

CONCLUSION

Compliance with the Fair Packaging and Labeling Act is important. A federal standard avoids the chaos which state-by-state regulation would bring, and the consumer wants benchmark standards to facilitate comparison shopping. Without this act the consumer would lack a rational value comparison for products as to their size, weight, etc. If you have a good product which stands up to your competitors' in objective comparisons, then you'll appreciate the uniformity of standards imposed by this act.

Your best approach is to forward the format for your proposed market research as well as suggested packaging, wording, labeling, etc. to your counsel prior to formal research and testing. This early review will save both time and money, especially if the initial claims are not legally supportable as designed. When your package and label plans are approved, you should conduct a legal review of the finished materials.

Your counsel should then retain a complete set of supporting documents for all claims, statements, and similar items included in all your packaging and labeling material.

REFERENCES

[1] 15 U.S.C. secs. 1451–1461.

[2] 16 C.F.R. sec. 500, subchapter E—*Rules, Regulations, Statement of General Policy or Interpretation and Exemptions under the Fair Packaging and Labeling Act.* Note that the act is enforced primarily by two federal agencies, the Food and Drug Administration (FDA) and the Federal Trade Commission (FTC). The FDA's jurisdiction applies "to any consumer commodity that is a food, drug, device or cosmetic" as defined by the Food, Drug and Cosmetic Act. The FTC's jurisdiction applies to any other consumer commodity. *See also* Robert J. Posch, Jr., "What's On Your Package?," *Direct Marketing*, December 1983.

[3] 16 C.F.R. sec. 502.2(d).

[4] 16 C.F.R. sec. 502.2(e).

[5] 16 C.F.R. sec. 502.2(h).

[6] 16 C.F.R. sec. 500.4.

[7] 16 C.F.R. sec. 500.5(a).

[8] 16 C.F.R. sec. 500.6(b).

[9] 16 C.F.R. secs. 500.0, 500.9.

[10] 16 C.F.R. sec. 500.10.

[11] 16 C.F.R. secs. 500.11, 500.12

[12] 16 C.F.R. sec. 500.13.

[13] 16 C.F.R. sec. 500.14.

[14] 16 C.F.R. sec. 500.15.

[15] 16 C.F.R. sec. 500.15(a).

[16] 16 C.F.R. sec. 500.16.

[17] 16 C.F.R. sec. 500.17.

[18] 16 C.F.R. sec. 500.19.

[19] 16 C.F.R. sec. 500.22(b).

[20] Jones v. Rath Packing Co., 430 U.S. 519 (1977).

[21] Write to the National Bureau of Standards, Department of Commerce, Washington, D.C.

[22] 16 C.F.R. sec. 500.24.

[23] 16 C.F.R. sec. 500.25.

[24] 16 C.F.R. sec. 500.26.

[25] 16 C.F.R. sec. 501.1.

[26] 16 C.F.R. sec. 501.2.

[27] 16 C.F.R. sec. 501.5. *See* 16 C.F.R. secs. 500.1–501.8.

[28] 16 C.F.R. sec. 502.100(b)(1).

[29] 16 C.F.R. sec. 502.100(b)(2).

[30] 16 C.F.R. sec. 502.100(b)(3).

[31] 16 C.F.R. sec. 502.100(b)(5)(i).

[32] 16 C.F.R. sec. 502.100(b)(5)(ii).

[33] 16 C.F.R. sec. 502.100(b)(5)(iii).

[34] 16 C.F.R. sec. 502.101(b)(2). Obviously, new packaging is not enough. Qualification for a patent would be enough to comply with this section.

[35] 16 C.F.R. sec. 502.101(b)(3).

[36] 16 C.F.R. sec. 502.102(b)(3).

CHAPTER
THREE
WARRANTY
COMPLIANCE

As your products cost more, any failure to live up to advertised expecta·
tions becomes increasingly irksome to your customer. A relatively no-
growth economy also produces a customer who wants a long-life product.
A pleasurable or unsatisfactory purchase experience will determine
whether you retain your customer. A key determinant here is how well you
honor your warranty or that of your supplier. As we'll discuss later, as a
retailer or distributor you may not be liable for a manufacturer's warranty.
However, your customer will look to you for information and assistance,
and ignorance of the law on point may jeopardize a repeat purchase.
Thus, both legally and as a matter of good customer relations, read this
chapter thoroughly.

There is a lot of warranty activity in the news; the court calendars are
filling up with varied claims. Certain states have enacted laws to give new
car buyers the right to receive a new car or refund if their automobile
cannot be repaired within four tries for the same problem or if the car is
out of service for more than 30 days due to one or more defects. Increasingly, consumers want useful warranties, and they know how to
enforce them. Your competitive position may be significantly affected by
how well you satisfy the public demand for this benefit.

In developing your warranty policy, consider the following: performance data obtained from company research and development and product performance testing, consumer expectations and experience based on
market testing and complaint data, and the differences between full and
limited warranties. Weigh the costs to the company against the costs to

46

consumers of any limitations or conditions on warranty coverage. Finally, consider the federal and state laws and regulations governing warranties.[1]

The following discussion of federal and state laws first reviews the scope and coverage of the Magnuson-Moss law for marketing compliance, which requires that your customer receive a complete and understandable explanation of written product warranties *before* a purchase is made. Warranties under the Uniform Commercial Code, including traditional title, express, and implied warranties are also reviewed.

WARRANTIES UNDER THE MAGNUSON-MOSS WARRANTY ACT

A warranty is an expression of your firm's willingness to stand behind its product *after* the purchase is complete. The social policy behind the Magnuson-Moss Act is that your warranty is part of the product you sell and should be as readily available for examination prior to the sale as is the product itself.

The act applies only to *written* warranties[2] on *tangible* personal property which is normally used for personal, family, or household purposes (not products sold for resale).[3] However, any ambiguity as to whether an item is a personal or a consumer product will be resolved in favor of coverage under the act. This written warranty must be part of the "basis of the bargain." Thus it must be given at the time of sale, and the purchaser must not give any additional payment exceeding the purchase price of the product to benefit from the warranty. Again, the product must *not* be purchased by the consumer for resale purposes.

Generally the threshold figure for warranty compliance is where the actual cost to the consumer exceeds $10 (excluding taxes or shipping and handling charges). The warranty must cover a specified period of time to be considered a written warranty.[4] Taken alone, terms of sale such as "free examination period" or any other promotional wording allowing the consumer an unconditional right to revoke acceptance of your goods within a certain number of days after delivery are not sufficient for compliance under the act.

FULL OR LIMITED WARRANTY

You *are* free to offer no warranties at all on your product. The act does not require any product or service to carry a written warranty regardless of product category or price of the item. However, once you elect to offer a written warranty on a product costing the consumer more than $10 (again, excluding sales tax and other charges), it must be designated as either a "full" or a "limited" warranty. Such designations should appear conspicuously as a caption or prominent title, clearly separated from the text of your warranty. This creates a headline that your customers will be able to recognize easily.

A full warranty promises the customer the following:

1. A defective product will be fixed (or replaced) free, including removal and reinstallation, if necessary.
2. A defective product will be fixed within a reasonable time after the first complaint.
3. Your customer will not have to do anything unreasonable to get warranty service. Any duties imposed on your customer must be conspicuously disclosed.
4. The warranty is good for anyone who owns the product during the warranty period unless it is materially altered. However, you may limit this in clear and conspicuous language by stating that the duration of the warranty expires automatically if the consumer transfers the item.[5] For example, an automobile battery or muffler warranty may be designated as "full warranty for as long as you own your car."[6]
5. If the product cannot be fixed (or hasn't been after a reasonable number of tries), the customer is entitled to the choice of a new product or his or her money back.[7]
6. Warranty coverage is not contingent on returning a registration card (either expressly or even implicitly).[8] This does not prohibit the use of such cards as a proof of the date of purchase. You might encourage the return of these cards (useful for market research) by stating that you can use them to notify your customer of a defect or recall. However, any such suggestion to the consumer must include a notice that the failure to return the card will not affect rights or service under the warranty, so long as the customer can show in a reasonable manner the date the product was purchased.[9]
7. Implied warranties may not be disclaimed or limited during the duration of the full warranty. There is one important thing that the word "full" doesn't promise—a full warranty doesn't have to cover the whole product. It may cover only part of the product, like the picture tube of a television. Or it may leave out some parts, like tires on a car. If your warranty covers only the picture tube and the sound goes bad, the customer pays.[10]

A limited warranty gives anything less than what a full warranty offers. A product may have both limited and full warranties for different parts or aspects of performance. A limited warranty might cover parts only, and your customer would have to pay labor or vice versa. You may require the return of a registration card for a limited warranty only if you do not provide service on products for which the card has not been returned.

Both forms of warranty prohibit any tying arrangement that *conditions* warranty coverage on the consumer's use of an article or service identified by brand, trade, or corporate name unless that article or service is provided free of charge to the consumer.[11] Likewise, no warranty may condition its continued validity on the use of only authorized repair service and/or authorized replacement parts for nonwarranty service and maintenance. For example, a provision such as "this warranty is void if service is performed by anyone other than an authorized ABC dealer and all replacement parts must be genuine ABC parts" is prohibited when the service and parts are not covered by the warranty.[12]

DISCLOSURE OF WARRANTY TERMS

A warranty for a product costing the consumer more than $15 shall clearly and conspicuously disclose the following in a *single document* in simple and readily understood language:

1. The identity of the party or parties to whom the warranty is extended (i.e., whether offered to every consumer during the duration of the warranty or to the first purchaser only).
2. When the warranty begins and ends.
3. A clear description and identification of all products covered (including components) as well as excluded from the warranty.
4. A statement of what your consumer will receive once a defect is reported, including which repair services and replacement costs the warrantor will provide and will *not* provide.
5. A step-by-step procedure customers must follow to secure their rights, including the warrantor's name and mailing address and the title or department to contact. The warrantor might also elect to provide a toll-free number in lieu of these, which your customer may use to obtain information on securing warranty performance rights.
6. Any information as to informal dispute settlement procedures.
7. Certain notifications of possible broader rights available to your customer under state law.[13]

These disclosures must be written as clearly as possible in lay English, possibly in a promotion piece. However, you are not responsible for your customer's ability or lack of ability to digest information although you should consider printing instructions and other terms in languages other than English when justified by your market. The inability to understand the warranty remains a major impediment to the usefulness of warranty protection.

If you are the party extending the warranty, you should establish standardized forms for warranty repairs and all warranty procedures. These forms should be consistent with or identical to your warranty disclosure material and should spell out to your service agent what is included and excluded from warranty coverage.

PRESALE AVAILABILITY

When products cost the consumer more than $15, retail sellers must display the text of the warranty in close conjunction with each warranted product and/or retain a binder with copies of all written warranties, displaying the binder or placing signs in prominent locations in the store "in a manner calculated to elicit the prospective buyer's attention."[14] A major problem for the consumer is clutter and the lack of systematic organization. Written warranties are often organized differently for different brands, inhibiting comparison price shopping.

The Magnuson-Moss Act offers the retailer four methods of making warranties available to consumers. You may elect one or more of the following:

1. Clearly and conspicuously display the text of your written warranty in close conjunction to each warranted product.
2. Maintain a binder or series of binders which contains copies of your warranties for the products sold in each department in which any consumer product with a written warranty is offered for sale. Such binders should be maintained in each department or in a location which provides your prospective buyer with ready access to such binders; they should be clearly identified as the binders containing the warranties. You may display the binders in such a way as to catch the prospective buyer's attention, or you may make the binders available to your prospective buyers on request. If you choose the latter, you must place signs which will catch prospective buyers' attention in the store or department. These signs must advise them of the availabilty of the binders and must include instructions for obtaining access to them.

3. Display the package of any consumer product on which the text of the written warranty is disclosed in a manner such that the warranty is clearly visible to your prospective buyers at the point of sale.
4. Place a notice which discloses the text of the written warranty in close proximity to the warranted product in a manner which clearly identifies to your prospective buyers the product to which the notice applies.[15]

You should be aware of whatever warranties are offered by the manufacturers of merchandise you sell. The nature of such warranties (if available) should be spelled out in all contracts you sign with your vendors. You might discuss with your counsel inserting a clause in your merchandise contract requiring your vendor to explicitly state what, if any, warranties are expressed or implied.[16]

What if you are involved in direct marketing? Do you have to disclose the presale availability of any warranties, and, if so, how? The act specifically addresses two forms of direct-marketing categories—mail and door to-door sales.

DIRECT MAIL. First, what constitutes a catalog or mail-order sale? "Catalogue or Mail Order Sale means *any offer for sale or any solicitation* for an order for a consumer product with a written warranty, which includes instructions for ordering the product which do not require a personal visit to the seller's establishment."[17]

If you are a catalog and/or mail-order seller, you must include in your catalog or solicitation either the full text of the written warranty *or* the fact that the warranty can be obtained from you free on specific written request. The address to which such requests may be sent must be included, and, if this option is elected, you must *promptly* provide requested copies to the consumer. The text of your warranty or the statement that your warranty will be provided on request must appear in close conjunction to the description of your warranted product or must be clearly referenced to an information section of the catalog or solicitation, including a page number. "Close conjunction" here means on the same page as the description of the product or on the facing page.

However, here as elsewhere, even if you did not mention the warranty your vendor has provided for the product you're selling, your vendor alone and not you is liable for any defect in the warranty or in performance under it.[18] However, make sure that your vendor is required by contract to inform you of the existence of any warranties offered on a product—even if you are not actually promoting them.

When a retailer takes full responsibility for part of the warranty service, this constitutes a separate retailer's warranty. Furthermore, promotional representations in connection with making a sale may make the retailer a "cowarrantor" and, therefore, obligate him or her under the warranty. Advertising and verbal representation such as "We stand behind our products" may bind the retailer as well.

DOOR-TO-DOOR SALES. Anyone involved in door-to-door sales should be aware of the following warranty provision directly impacting their operations:

> Any seller who offers for sale to consumers consumer products with written warranties by means of door-to-door sales shall, prior to the consummation of the sale, disclose the fact that the sales representative has copies of the warranties for the warranted products being offered for sale which may be inspected by the prospective buyer at any time during the sales presentation. Such disclosure shall be made orally and shall be included in any written materials shown to the prospective buyers.[19]

BROADCAST MEDIA AND TELEPHONE SALES

In broadcast media your customers have a limited time to absorb information. Your customer cannot control the sequence and the rate of the information presentation, and the continuous pace does not permit careful study.

The broad definition of "mail order," that is, "*any* solicitation for an order which does not require a personal visit to the seller's establishment," appears to include radio, television, telephone, and cable sales. Interactive cable (and related technologies such as videotext) have the capabilities to provide instant access to a central data base and thereby obtain the warranty information through the media itself. This instantaneous retrieval could offer a significant competitive advantage over all other media both per product and in overall comparison shopping. Review your media communications mix disclosure strategy with your counsel.

INFORMAL DISPUTE SETTLEMENT PROCEDURES

Voluntary procedures to settle a dispute informally should be carefully reviewed with counsel.[20] The trade-off is often the burden of setting them up and disclosing them versus the possibility of saving a costly litigation fee.[21] This saving may result from your ability to require the consumer to resort to the informal procedures (specifically arbitration) before taking you to court.

An informal settlement procedure is called a "mechanism."[22] Your mechanism must comport with the standards of the FTC's dispute settlement rule, which governs the disclosure of the mechanism in written warranties as well as the mechanism's organization, operation, and record keeping. An example of a qualifying mechanism is a panel established by a trade association, a local better business bureau, an accounting firm, or other sponsor insulated from your influence and in no way a party to the dispute.

With one narrow exception you may require consumers to resort to a qualifying mechanism before commencing a civil action (including small-claims court).[23] However, your customers are free at any time to pursue alternate state or federal remedies. Warrantors with mechanisms may also encourage, but may not require, consumers to seek redress from the warrantor directly without raising a complaint to the level of a dispute.[24] The decisions are not binding on the parties but are admissible in evidence in any related civil action.[25] The nonbinding feature of the procedure may, of course, significantly diminish the procedure's utility to both warrantors and consumers.

Meetings are open to observers, and either party has access to all records of the hearings, including the right to copy the records. Records must be retained for 4 years after the final disposition of the dispute.

It is good customer relations to treat these informal hearings as customer service rather than as adversarial proceedings. You should use the consumer experience and complaints as a means for improving quality, discovering latent defects, and designing products for simplified serviceability.

CONCLUSIONS ON THE MAGNUSON-MOSS WARRANTY ACT

Magnuson-Moss is a truth-in-warranty law. It mandates that all warranties be written so as to be understandable to your average lay customer. If you can't understand it, your customer can't and may not buy. Therefore, review your warranty as to who is protected, what parts of the product are covered, whether it is full or limited, and what are the effective date and total life of the warranty. Also, does the warrantor attempt to disclaim any implied warranty? This is illegal. Finally, review the steps your buyer must take if the product is defective. Is notification of the seller (you) involved? If so, review with your counsel whether you should establish informal procedure mechanisms to deal with such contingencies. Consumer good-will and your company's reputation may depend on how well you exercise this option.[26]

PRODUCT WARRANTIES UNDER THE UCC

The UCC (Uniform Commercial Code) warranties are in many ways similar to the Magnuson-Moss warranties. The scope of the UCC (adopted in all states except Louisiana) covers many commercial transactions concerning "goods." You must take *both* the UCC and Magnuson-Moss consumer warranty provisions into account, depending on the parties to the contractual relationship into which you are entering.

In this section we'll review four UCC warranties: warranties of title, express warranties, implied warranties of merchantability, and implied warranties of fitness for a particular purpose. Warranties are important because of their impact on your firm's goodwill. Further, approximately 25 percent of all UCC litigation involves warranty disputes; clearly, we are discussing a very significant area of commercial law. You may best enjoy this section if you first refer to the chapter on sales law (Chapter 8) in Section 4. However, remember that UCC warranties are limited to the sale of goods only; they do not affect services.

Since the warranty field is rather technical, I strongly suggest that you have your counsel review all your warranties in light of your marketing objectives. Failure to use the UCC prescribed language does create some additional warranty exposure, and your counsel can describe the amount of that exposure so that you can evaluate your risks.

WARRANTY OF TITLE

The warranty of title is the most common warranty.[27] The seller need not be a merchant dealing in goods of the kind involved.[28] *Any* sales contract warrants as to the goods that there is clean title and that the goods are free from all incumbrances and liens.

The title warranty can be disclaimed or modified only by specific language in your contract or by circumstances which give your buyer notice that you do not claim title. The disclaimer should specifically mention the word "title." For example, later we'll discuss that the words "as is" exclude the implied warranty of merchantability and fitness for a particular purpose. However, "as is" standing alone does not exclude the warranty of title.

EXPRESS WARRANTIES

Any affirmation of fact or promise made by a seller to a buyer can result in an express warranty if such statement is part of the basis of the bargain.[29] A statement becomes part of the basis of a bargain when your buyer *could* (not did) have relied on it when she or he entered into the contract or agreement of sale.

Express affirmations of fact can be created by *objective* promises or descriptions such as those found on a label or in a brochure or catalog. *Subjective* statements relating merely to the value of the goods or a statement purporting to be only the seller's opinion or commendation of the goods does not create an express warranty. A statement that an article is "excellent," "well made," "unbeatable," or "the best machine made" is rarely a warranty. Rather, it is usually considered puffery.

Examples always seem to include used car dealers making rosy statements about their cars such as "Ford cars are better." However, this is an audience sophistication issue. If you are selling to sophisticated businesspersons in your field, there is greater latitude than for claims made to the "average" consumer. Even with sophisticated persons in your trade, if you move from subjective conjecture, opinions, guessing, or predictions into the realm of a commitment (such as "we'll meet your deadline"), you create an express warranty.[30] It is always safest to stick to the facts.

We've reviewed puffing and how *not* to create an express warranty. There are, however, various ways such a warranty may be created. Remember that an express warranty is any affirmation of fact which is made to induce the buyer to buy and which the buyer relies on; the affirmation of fact becomes part of the basis of the bargain in the actual purchase decision.

Any description of the goods on which your buyer relies creates an express warranty that your goods will conform to that description. The FTC and state regulatory agencies are increasingly active in protecting consumers in this area, and thus your catalog wording must be submitted to your counsel as well as to your promotional personnel or advertising agency.

When dealing in commercial transactions, remember that your catalog is provided to induce the purchase of your product, and thus such statements form the basis of the bargain. Technical specifications in a contract do not supercede catalog statements unless they expressly state that they do. For example, a court ordered a company to pay damages when the television transmitting tower it built for a customer collapsed in heavy winds. In the company's catalog (although not the contractual wording), performance specifications stated that the tower could withstand maximum wind velocities. The courts stated that the catalog's "broad affirmations were not superceded or corrected by the technical specifications in the contract."[31]

Illustrations as well as words in a catalog or brochure are descriptions of goods and as such are express warranties. In one instance the court noted that such promotional vehicles "are thrust upon the public as invitation to purchase" and are replacements for the traveling salesperson.[32] If you have any questions, consult your counsel as to the advisability of placing in your catalog any indication that the items are not as illustrated. This may relieve you of express warranty responsibility for your illustrations.

In addition to the express warranty of description, there is a warranty created by sample. When you offer the buyer the right to inspect samples and your buyer relies on the samples in the purchase decision, then such samples become part of the basis of the bargain. Thereafter your buyer has the right to assume that *all* goods covered by the order will take the form of the sample you showed.[33]

Managers must know when a distributor or dealer has *adopted* a manufacturer's express warranty. A seller is liable for the breach of an express warranty only when through conduct or communication the seller creates *or* adopts a warranty and the buyer relies on it as the basis of the bargain.[34] If a dealer only passes on a manufacturer's warranty and does not adopt it, the dealer is not bound by the warranty.[35] A dealer adopts the manufacturer's warranty when it attempts to carry out the repair obligations under the warranty.[36] Note that if you as a purchaser want the warranty period *tolled* during downtime for repairs, such provision *must* be stated in your express warranty.[37]

Finally, you should be aware of the disclaimer issues for express warranties. Between merchants there is little second-guessing if your documents follow UCC provisions correctly. You can disclaim warranties and limit your liability in a commercial setting without too much fear of a court's imposing liability on the grounds of public policy or fairness. The precise language of the UCC is that "words or conduct relevant to the creation of an express warranty and words or conduct tending to negate or limit such warranty shall be construed wherever reasonable as consistent with each other."[38] The negation of such warranties is inoperative to the extent that such construction is unreasonable. Any disclaimer must be conspicuous. As stated by a New Jersey court: "an exclusion or limitation of express warranties is strongly disfavored in the UCC." A court will not uphold a warranty disclaimer which is a linguistic maze.[39]

One idea is to have separate paragraphs where you state your warranty and then disclaim it! Never use the back of your documents to disclaim a warranty unless you call attention to your disclaimer language on the front page. Then the disclaimers, too, become part of the basis of the bargain.

Obviously only your counsel should create disclaimer wording and decide on its location. When dealing with two commercial enterprises on a relatively equal footing, your counsel can usually disclaim express warranties.[40] However, the situation is much more complicated when dealing with a consumer, because of the requirements of Magnuson-Moss as well as the general UCC provisions as to unconscionability.[41]

IMPLIED WARRANTY OF MERCHANTABILITY

The implied warranty of merchantability can be made *only* by a *merchant* who deals in goods of the kind sold (see the discussion relating to merchants in Section 4). In *every* sale by a merchant who deals in goods of the kind sold, there is an implied warranty that the goods are merchantable. The buyer need not rely on the seller for this warranty. One example is the serving of food or drink on the premises. This would be a sale of goods subject to the warranty of merchantability. The full text of the seven elements of this warranty is as follows:

> To be merchantable, goods must be at least such as (a) pass without objection in the trade under the contract description; (b) in the case of tangible goods, are of fair average quality within that description; (c) are fit for the ordinary purposes for which such goods are used; (d) run of even kind, quality and quantity within each unit; (e) are adequately packaged and labelled as the agreement may require;[42] (f) conform to promises and affirmations made in the contract or label, if any; (g) unless excused or modified, other implied warranties may arise from course of dealing or usage of trade.[43]

These elements are fairly straightforward. One area not readily apparent but included is the sale of used or second-hand goods. The UCC does not distinguish between new and used goods, and so the sale of used goods gives rise to implied warranties. If you sell used goods, you are warranting that they are fit for the purpose for which they are sold.[44]

To exclude or modify any part of the implied warranty of merchantability, you must use language which mentions merchantability. If the warranty is in writing, the disclaimer must be conspicuous.[45] A term or clause is conspicuous when it is so written that a reasonable person against whom it is to operate ought to have noticed it. A printed heading in capitals is conspicuous. Language in the body of a form is conspicuous if it is larger or in a contrasting color.[46] Indenting and underlining the language will also assist in distinguishing and setting apart your disclaimer language from the text of the other contractual provisions.[47] Other ways to exclude this warranty include:

1. The use of expressions such as "as is," "with all faults," or other expressions are generally understood to call to your buyer's attention the fact that you are offering no implied warranties.
2. When you have demanded that your buyer inspect the goods and the buyer refuses, then there is no warranty as to patent defects which a reasonable examination would have revealed. You remain liable under the warranty for any latent defects.[48]
3. Under certain circumstances implied warranties may be disclaimed by the course of dealing, course of performance, or usage of trade.[49]

Finally, review the suggestions made in the prior discussion of express warranties, concerning where to locate your disclaimers, setting them apart, etc.[50] You must have counsel draft your warranty provisions and/or any modifications and disclaimers in all your commercial dealing. In general, you won't be able to disclaim a written warranty given to a consumer.[51] In addition to the law, there is the issue of your goodwill, since the buyer may think that any small-print disclaimers are in bad faith, and you may lose a repeat purchase. However, you should consult with your counsel as to the as-is sale and other possible options available to you in consumer warranty limitations.

THE IMPLIED WARRANTY OF FITNESS FOR A PARTICULAR PURPOSE

The implied warranty of fitness for a particular purpose basically means that the buyer is relying on your specific skill and expertise *and* that you know the buyer is so relying.[52] For this warranty you need not be a merchant. You are held to a higher standard of care here than you are for the previous warranty of merchantability. As the comment to the UCC says: "A particular purpose differs from an ordinary purpose for which goods are used in that it envisages a specific use by the buyer which is peculiar to the nature of his business whereas the ordinary purposes for which goods are used are those envisaged in the concept of merchantability."[53]

The purpose of this warranty is to protect the buyer of goods from bearing the burden of loss when goods, although not violating express warranties, do not meet your buyer's particular purpose. Such expertise can vary from your expertise in electronic circuitry design[54] to your knowledge of the age and dependability of a punch press.[55]

Another area of increasing importance to managers is compliance with various flammability acts. If your buyer requests clothing fit for the particular purpose of compliance with these acts and you agree, you must provide clothing which complies with the flammability acts and is fit for your buyer's purposes.[56]

However, common sense tells you a buyer receives no warranty of fitness for a particular purpose if you manufacture or supply goods on the basis of specifications provided by the buyer. In one case a buyer ordered carts, supplying the exact specifications and then inspecting them. The buyer then claimed that the goods breached his warranty of fitness. The court actually moved the carts about in front of the courthouse and found them fit for the purpose intended! Since the buyer designed them and they were found fit, the buyer received no further warranty protection.[57]

To disclaim these warranties, refer back to the general disclaimers previously discussed (as is, inspection or refusal to inspect, course of dealing, conspicuous language, and so on). Wording such as "There are no warranties which extend beyond the description of the face hereof" is sufficient to exclude a warranty of fitness for a particular purpose.[58]

Disclaimer language properly drafted by your counsel will invariably accomplish its purposes with parties who have equal bargaining power and expertise. However, when dealing with consumers, a court may hold your disclaimer unconscionable even though it is in literal compliance with the formal requirements we've discussed. The court may find that such things as your customer's lack of bargaining position, lack of choice, lack of expertise concerning your goods, or failure to understand the language would be more important issues than the mere fact that your disclaimer wording was correct. Consult your counsel for advice as to your specific exposure with your specific market.

CUMULATION AND CONFLICT OF WARRANTIES EXPRESS OR IMPLIED

Finally, the "priority" of warranties when there is a problem of ambiguity is a UCC issue.

The UCC reads concisely here:

> All warranties, express or implied, are to be construed as consistent and cumulative, but if this is unreasonable, the [parties'] intention determines which warranty is dominant. To get that result, certain rules are followed:
>
> 1. Exact or technical specifications displace an inconsistent sample or model or general descriptive language.
> 2. A sample from an existing bulk displaces general inconsistent language of description.
> 3. Express warranties displace inconsistent implied warranties, other than an implied warranty of fitness for a particular purpose. Thus though the seller delivers an item as described in the contract, it would not bar an action for breach of warranty of fitness for the purpose intended, if it was not suited for the work intended as known by the seller and upon whose judgment the buyer relied.[59]

CONCLUSION

Your warranty is the expression of your willingness to stand behind your products. There is much goodwill at stake. Sears' simple "we service what we sell" has been an excellent warranty used in conjunction with its promotional campaigns. Anyone offering a warranty must be acquainted with the laws on point. This knowledge assists you to be a better manager and all-purpose business executive; this knowledge also informs you of your own rights and protections as a consumer.

REFERENCES

1 Note that law of a given state in which you do business may be narrower than construed by federal agencies or the courts. For example, sections 1793.1 and 1975.6 of the California Civil Code require that all orders or repair invoices must contain a statement, in 10-point boldface type, informing consumers of their rights. These sections also extend the warranty period by the number of days a product is out of a customer's hands because of repairs. Review the particular statutes and the various deceptive trade practices acts with your counsel. You might also contact your trade association to see if they compile and distribute information as to consumer rights and remedies applicable in the various states. *Product Warranties and Servicing*, Office of Consumer Affairs, U.S. Department of Commerce (October 1980), is an excellent booklet on point. Direct marketers should also see Robert J. Posch, Jr., *The Direct Marketer's Legal Adviser*, McGraw-Hill,

New York, 1983, pp. 27–30 and Robert J. Posch, Jr., "Warranty Disclosures for Direct Marketers," *Direct Marketing*, November 1982, pp. 110–112.

2 For the purposes of this act, there is no legal difference between the words "warranty" and "guarantee." For you they both mean your promise to stand behind your products.

3 16 C.F.R. sec. 700.1(a). If an *oral* express warranty is at issue, your customer may have protection under the U.C.C. sec. 2–213 or under the states' "little FTC acts." For this reason it is particularly important to familiarize your sales staff with the proper presentation of warranty information.

4 16 C.F.R. sec. 700.3.

5 The act does not define "conspicuous," but UCC language [sec. 1–201(10)] may be useful as a guide. It defines "conspicuous" as a term or clause that is "so written that a reasonable person against whom it is to operate ought to have noticed it . . . . Language in the body of a form is conspicuous if it is in larger or other contrasting type of color. But in a telegram any stated term is conspicuous."

6 *See* Federal Trade Commission, *Warranties: There Ought to Be a Law . . .* , FTC Informational Pamphlet.

7 16 C.F.R. sec. 700.6(b).

8 16 C.F.R. sec. 700.7(b).

9 16 C.F.R. sec. 700.7(c). The information you request should be limited to that necessary to fulfill your warranty program. Before you request additional information (such as retail prices), you should consult your counsel.

10 *See* Ref. 3.

11 16 C.F.R. sec. 700.10(a). See also Robert J. Posch, Jr., "How to Avoid Getting Tied Up with Tie-Ins," *Direct Marketing*, August 1982, pp. 104–106.

12 16 C.F.R. sec. 700.10(c).

13 16 C.F.R. sec. 701.3.

14 16 C.F.R. sec. 702.3.

15 "Reasonably calculated to elicit the prospective buyer's attention" must be read, in context with the three nonbinder options, to require that notice of the availability of warranty information in the form of binders or signs be in sufficient proximity to the point of sale so that buyers are likely to see such notice before making their purchases.

16 16 C.F.R. sec. 702.3(a).

17 16 C.F.R. sec. 702.3(c)(i) (emphasis my own).

18 16 C.F.R. sec. 700.4. Again, it is important to review your purchase agreements with counsel. If you are merely a supplier of a product, you should make sure you know if the manufacturer is offering a warranty with the product as delivered.

19 16 C.F.R. sec. 702.3(d)(2).

20 16 C.F.R. sec. 703.

21 16 C.F.R. sec. 703.2

22 16 C.F.R. sec. 703.2(a).

23 16 C.F.R. sec. 703.2(b)(3).

24 16 C.F.R. sec. 703.2(d).

25 16 C.F.R. sec. 703.5(j).

26 Related to the issue of warranties is the disclosure of unassembled merchandise (with the logical exception of toy hobby kits). Review this area with your counsel. Although there are no specific formal guidelines as to the exact language needed in the promotion piece, failure to include some form of clear, up-front (not buried in copy text) language indicating that the product requires assembly or special tools could result in a charge of deceptive advertising based on FTC case history and also certain state laws (e.g., New York).

Finally, you may wish to review a few FTC decisions discussing the extent of disclosure and manner of performance for the warranty under the act:

a   Redman Indus., Inc., 85 F.T.C. 309 (1975).
b   Fleetwood Enters. Inc., 85 F.T.C. 414 (1975).
c   Skyline Corp., 85 F.T.C. 444 (1975).
d   Soxomy Pools, 86 F.T.C. 349 (1975).
e   North American Pools, Inc., 86 F.T.C. 615 (1975).
f   Lifetime Filter Equip. Corp., 86 F.T.C. 608 (1975).
g   Mutual Const. Co., 87 F.T.C. 608 (1975).
h   Levitz Furniture Corp. 88 F.T.C. 263 (1976).
i   Korvette's, Inc., 94 F.T.C. 318 (1979).
j   Montgomery Ward & Co., 97 F.T.C. 363 (1979).
k   George's Radio and Television Co., 94 F.T.C. 1135 (1979).

27 U.C.C. sec. 2–312. Although we'll be citing federal statutes, all types of warranties are governed by state law. Further, different states have modified their own UCCs in different ways, and their courts have rendered varying interpretations. Complying with the federal law on point may not be enough, so review with your counsel the laws of the states in which you're doing business.

28 UCC sec. 2–104. A "merchant" is "a person who deals in goods of the kind or otherwise by his occupation holds himself out as having knowledge or skill peculiar to the practices or goods involved in the transaction or to whom such knowledge or skill may be attributed by his employment of an agent or broker or other intermediary who by his occupation holds himself out as having such knowledge or skill."

29 U.C.C. sec. 2–313.

30 Vance Pearson, Inc. v. Alexander, 408 N.E.2d 782 (1980). See also Investors Premium Corp. v. Burroughs Corp., 389 F. Supp. 39 (D.S.C. 1974).

31 Community Television Servs., Inc. v. Dresser Indus. Inc., 586 F.2d 637, 640 (1978). See also M-A-S-H, Inc. v. Fiat-Allis Constr. Mach. Inc., 461 F. Supp. 79 (1978).

[32] Arlis, Inc. v. Gojer Inc., 75 Misc. 2d 962, 349 N.Y.S.2d 948 (Civ. Ct. Queens Co. 1973).

[33] Indus-Ri-Chem. Par Laboratory, Inc. v. Pak Co., 602 S.W.2d 282 (1980).

[34] *Id.* at 296. However, consistent with the code's overall policy of commercial reasons you should be aware of comment 2–313 with regards to express warranties: "Of course, all descriptions by merchants must be read against the applicable trade usages with the general rules as to merchantability resolving any doubts." Thus, express warranties running to your buyer and the buyer's objections must be read in terms of their significance in the trade and relative to what would normally pass in the trade without objection under the catalog description.

[35] Courtesy Motor Sales, Inc. v. Farrior, 298 So. 2d 26 (1974).

[36] Matthews v. Ford Motor Co., 479 F.2d 399 (1973).

[37] Mountain Fuel Supply Co. v. Central En'g and Equip. Co., 611 P.2d 863 (1980).

[38] U.C.C. sec. 2–316(1). You should be alert to U.C.C. sec. 2–202 (see discussion in Section 4), since consistent additional oral express warranties may be proven unless the written contract is stated to complete or unless the writing negates any other warranties.

[39] Henningsen v. Bloomfield Motors, Inc., 32 N.J. 358, 373, 161 A.2d 69 (1960). *See also* Gladden v. Cadillac Motor Car Div. 416 A.2d 394, 399, 401 (1980).

[40] *See* Filures, Inc. v. Proctor & Schwartz, Inc. 509 F.2d 1043 (1979).

[41] See discussion in Section 4. Also, the U.C.C. sec. 2–207 material term issue is discussed in Section 4. A *disclaimer* is an additional *material term* for purpose of U.C.C. sec. 2–207 and can't be accepted by silence.

[42] U.C.C. sec. 2–301.

[43] See the discussion of the Fair Labeling and Packaging Act in Chapter 2.

[44] U.C.C. sec. 2–314(2).

[45] Perry v. Lawson Ford Tractor Co., 613 P.2d 458 (1980).

[46] U.C.C. sec. 2–316.

[47] U.C.C. sec. 2–201(10). *See also* Transcontinental Refrigeration Co. v. Figgins, 585 P.2d 1301 (1978).

[48] R.D. Lowrance, Inc. v. Peterson, 178 N.W.2d 277 (1970).

[49] Country Clubs, Inc. v. Allis-Chalmers Mfg. Co., 430 F.2d 1394 (1970).

[50] *See* Hunt v. Perkins Mach. Co., 226 N.E.2d 228 (1967). *See also* Dekalb Agresearch, Inc. v. Abbott, 391 F. Supp. 152 (1974).

[51] 15 U.S.C. sec. 2308. However, see 15 U.S.C. sec. 2308(b) and 15 U.S.C. sec. 2304(a)(3). Obviously, you and your counsel must discuss the applicable state laws governing your warranty.

[52] U.C.C. sec. 2–315.

[53] U.C.C. sec. 2–315 comment 2. *See also* Coisson Corp. v. Ingersoll-Rand Co., 622 F.2d 672 (1980).

[54] Controltek, Inc. v. Kwikee Enters. Inc., 585 P.2d 670 (1978).

[55] Miller v. Hubbard-Wrory Co., 630 P.2d 880 (1981).

[56] Trinkle v. Schumacher Co., 301 N.W.2d 255 (1980). *See* Flammable Fabrics Act, 15 U.S.C. secs. 1191–1204.

[57] Sam's Marine Park Enters. Inc. v. Admar Bar & Kitchen Equip. Corp. 103 Misc. 2d 276, 425 N.Y.S.2d 743 (1980).

[58] U.C.C. sec. 2–316(2).

[59] U.C.C. sec. 2–317.

CHAPTER
FOUR

YOUR TRADEMARK AS PART OF YOUR PACKAGE

Today managers are increasingly emphasizing a product or service name rather than price or quality. They are selling image as well as merchandise. They carefully select their market segments and then protect their well-differentiated audience by hooking them on an image. This appeal to image results from a number of social and economic forces:

1. Prohibitive labor costs have forced cutbacks on servicing in many firms.
2. Location is less of an advantage because of the proliferation of competitive outlets located nearby.
3. Product proliferation and wide distribution (compounded by the demise of fair trade laws) have robbed many firms of merchandise exclusivity.
4. In an increasingly socialistic and impersonal nation, consumers are showing a growing need for individuality in style and products.
5. The middle-class gospel of "work hard, save, and buy goods with a significant utility" is giving way to a social hedonism.
6. Finally, what worked in merchandising before doesn't work as well now. People's habits and tastes have changed and they've begun to make and spend more money. Shopping has become a fun thing to do, a weekend sport, a way to be entertained.

The image brand marketer attempts to satisfy these needs through less emphasis on traditional factors and more on ego-gratification.

Even if you are in the traditional and unglamorous areas of hard goods, work clothes, or such, strong brand identification can be the most important factor in a product's success. However, if you are going to spend a lot of money on name selection, packaging, generation of publicity, consumer testing, and promotion, you need a brand that you can obtain a monopoly on. A brand with a legal monopoly is a trademark.[1] As used in this book, the words "trademark," "mark," and "brand" are synonymous. You will want to work closely with your counsel in developing a mark. In fact your involvement here may be the most practical interaction you can have with your lawyer to ensure your product's success. Since this area can be very important, familiarize yourself with this entire section and reread it before beginning any significant product development plans. *This is not a time to make business decisions in isolation from legal realities.*

WHAT IS A TRADEMARK?

By law, a trademark "includes any word, name, symbol or device or any combination thereof adopted and used by a manufacturer or merchant to identify his/her goods and distinguish them from those manufactured or sold by others."[2] The law is very jealous of your rights here. The following is an observation by Justice Frankfurter on the importance of trademarks in our economic system:

> The protection of trademarks is the law's recognition of the psychological function of symbols. If it is true that we live by symbols, it is no less true that we purchase goods by them. A trademark is a merchandising short-cut which induces a purchaser to select what he wants, or what he has been led to believe he wants. The owner of a mark exploits this human propensity by making every effort to impregnate the atmosphere of the market with the drawing power of a congenial symbol. Whatever the means employed, the aim is the same—to convey through the mark, in the midst of potential customers, the desirability of the commodity upon which it appears. Once this is attained, the trademark owner has something of value. If another poaches upon the commercial magnetism of the symbol he has created, the owner can obtain legal redress.[3]

In a society with a high literacy rate, words are the most common and most favored form of trademark. However, any type of symbol or design can be a trademark, provided that it functions as a trademark. Essentially a trademark is used for three reasons:

1. To distinguish and identify your goods

2. To serve as a guarantee of consistent quality
3. To advertise and sell your products

A product packaged in an unmistakable color and stamped with a famous logo in a stylish script can serve all three functions.

In addition to trademarks there are service marks. A service mark is a "mark used in the sale or advertising of services to identify the services of one person and distinguish them from the services of others."[4] Where it might matter, we'll distinguish between the terms. However, the differences are more important to your counsel in light of the unique facts of your given product and/or service development.

CHOOSING YOUR TRADEMARK

You'll want brand name wording which will best communicate your product's novel and important benefits to your target audience. You might also wish to study a distinctive package shape to complement your product. This analysis should be done in isolation from legal input. You may wish to bring it in line with your other house marks or you may wish to adopt Procter and Gamble's theory of brand management, which is that any brand stands as an independent self-sustaining competitive unit. A drawback here is that customers satisfied with the house mark are unfamiliar with your new mark. A plus is that to the extent that any brand becomes the victim of adverse publicity, the damage will be limited to that brand and will not spill over to the company's other brands.[5] If you remember the Tylenol problems in 1982, you can see the merit of separate brands.

Once you've developed a good mark, see your counsel. It is not cost-effective to see your counsel after spending a lot of money to develop the product. Your counsel will review your wording and the thrust of your marketing plans and may be able to tell you immediately whether your wording is generic, descriptive, or distinctive. If it is the latter, your counsel will make sure you have a present intent to market the goods. Trademark protection comes from use, not mere adoption. Shipment of goods in interstate commerce to which your marks are attached will suffice for registration. If you intend to use your mark soon, your counsel will then undertake a search to see if the mark is already in use. If it is in use, your counsel may recommend certain strategies to save your mark.

WHAT IS A GENERIC MARK? _____

A generic term refers to or has come to be understood as referring to the genus of which the particular product specifies, such as soap or coffee.[6] These are common or universal terms whose words are the common property of all. No one can obtain an exclusive right to one.

A term may also *become* generic. This happens when the term has come to be understood as a name for a *kind* of product, rather than the name for the product itself. You're probably aware that DuPont lost the mark "cellophane" in 1937[7] and that Bayer lost "aspirin" in 1921.[8] "Escalator" and "Thermos Bottle" were once proprietary rights of one firm, and Sanka and Xerox spend millions each year to publicize their marks. Once a term becomes generic, it remains so; no company can later claim it as its own.[9]

Finally, don't expect to get away with a slight modification of a generic name. "Lite" was held not to be a valid trademark for a low-calorie beer because of its similarity to the generic term "light," and "Alo" is not a valid trademark for a skin cream due to its likeness to the generic "aloe."

Another example of the distinction between trademarks and generic terms was a firm's attempt to make "trillion" a trademark for triangular-shaped diamonds. The competition argued that "trillion" is nothing but a variation of "trilliant"—the industry's generic contraction for triangular diamonds. The court agreed; it was not impressed with the simple substitution of "o" for "a" and dropping the final "t." It held that the term was not distinct in spelling, pronunciation, or meaning from the generic term.[10]

The court also reviewed pronunciation in the trade. It held that the words, while somewhat dissimilar visually, are virtually indistinguishable in sound: "When dealing with goods which are frequently purchased or traded by the spoken word, similarity of sound has been given particular importance."[11]

Thus a review with your counsel of generic phrases before undertaking a major new product promotion effort is a worthwhile investment.

WHAT IS A DESCRIPTIVE MARK? _____

A descriptive mark describes the product as to its quality, function, or place of origination. In general, a descriptive term which characterizes your product—its uses, functions, or characteristics—is available to all in a descriptive sense. For example, one firm put out a mark "Trim" which the court felt was a weak mark at best because it was descriptive of the product's function.[12] However, unlike a generic term, a descriptive term can acquire trademark rights by taking on a "secondary meaning." This may occur where a mark has been so extensively advertised or promoted that your purchasers have come to associate the mark with your firm prior to the first sale or distribution of goods bearing the mark.[13]

Therefore, if there are compelling reasons for you to employ a descriptive mark, your counsel will conduct a search on the mark. If there is no danger of infringement, your counsel will help develop a descriptive mark into a distinctive mark. Your counsel may suggest alternate registration. Supplemental registration is the appropriate procedure for registering marks which are not inherently distinctive but which are capable of acquiring trademark significance in the *future* through exclusive use by the registrant. The *Supplemental Register* is also the *only* proper place for registering marks which are more like slogans (for example, "You deserve a break today").

Once you are actively using the mark, your counsel may argue that it has developed a secondary meaning because your purchasing public has come to associate your mark with the product through length of use, sales volume, and the extent of your steady advertising and publicity of your mark.[14]

WHAT IS A DISTINCTIVE MARK?

A distinctive mark uses words which are "meaningless" or suggestive without being descriptive. A so-called meaningless word mark is not meaningless to you, since this kind of mark is the most protectable. Any arbitrary wording which connotes nothing about a product or its use can be a strong trademark. Examples of these include coined words, such as "Exxon," which are not found in the dictionary, common words such as "Shell" for gasoline, or a character and picture mark such as the famous Green Giant. A suggestive word hints at but does not describe characteristics or properties of a product—a classic here is Ivory Soap. The word evokes an image of purity and luxury.

You might consider the shape of your product or its container. Will it be primarily functional? If so, it probably won't be entitled to registration. Since the appearance of your package on the shelf often helps to sell the product, you might consider designing it less for utility features and more for selling features, possibly entitling it to protection.

Finally, there are times when registering a joint mark of the design and name together will strengthen your mark. Explore this with your counsel.

If you have a distinctive mark, your counsel will then conduct a search in the U.S. Patent and Trademark Office to determine whether your mark might infringe on an existing mark. The test for infringement is whether the use of the word in question is likely to cause confusion, to cause a mistake as to origin, or to deceive the public.[15] There is no need to show actual deception or confusion—merely that such deception or confusion would be a natural and probable result.[16] The following are areas to consider when you read the search report (and also when you are evaluating whether someone is infringing on your mark):

1. The degree of resemblance between the designation and the other's trade name, trademark, or certification mark in the following:
   a. Appearance
   b. Pronunciation of the words involved
   c. Translation of the words involved
   d. Verbal translations of the pictures or designs involved
   e. Suggestiveness, connotation, or meaning of the actor's designation and the trade name, trademark, or certification mark involved
   f. Identity of retail outlets and other retail channels and purchasers
   g. Identity and similarity of advertising media used
2. The intent of the user in adopting and using the designation.
3. The similarity of circumstances and conditions surrounding the purchase of the goods or services involved.
4. The degree of care likely to be exercised by purchasers of the goods or services involved.[17]
5. Examination of prior litigation history of the user (the claimant):
   a. The public record may demonstrate whether the mark is weak or strong.
   b. An examination of prior litigation may also reveal the degree to which a competitor is willing to litigate to protect its marks. If a company has been aggressive in policing its rights against third parties, your counsel may advise you to refrain from using a potentially conflicting mark unless you are willing to expend substantial sums in litigation defending it.
6. Abandonment of the mark. Two years of nonuse constitutes abandonment.[18]

Your next step is to register your mark.

REGISTRATION

Your counsel will explain the advantages of formal registration. Priority of use is the basic criterion (your rights arise through the use of the mark, not the registration), but it's generally not preferable to registration.

Consider the case of another firm (not necessarily a competitor) that introduces a mark identical or similar to yours. This duplication or similarity would probably result in public confusion as to the source of goods or services. Prior registration of your descriptive mark with the U.S. Patent and Trademark Office will enable you to obtain the following advantages:

1. Other firms receive notice of your right to use the mark. With registration, notice to the world is presumed in your favor. It creates presumptions as to ownership of the mark and the exclusive right to use it. Although the infringer need not have had prior knowledge that you were using your mark, it is helpful if you can prove this for an infringement claim.
2. Registration gives you the right to sue in a federal rather than state court. Federal courts tend to be more sophisticated in these matters and may also be more inclined to stop the infringement, since a state court might favor a local interest.
3. The notice discourages a good-faith firm from "accidentally" infringing. Even where there is no intention to infringe, it still costs money and time to alert and stop the infringer. Further, you've lost exclusive use of your mark, even if only for a short time.
4. Registration may be used as the basis for obtaining registrations in foreign countries.
5. Finally, registration asserts and increases distinctiveness. A trademark, otherwise protectable, could conceivably lose its distinctiveness if the owner is not careful in asserting it (see the discussion concerning generic marks).

DISPLAYING YOUR MARK

What is formal identification? The usual procedure is to use ™ (or SM for a service mark) on all material where the mark is used (such as stationery, business forms, and advertising) while the registration procedure is pending. Once the product or service mark is registered, the mark is followed by the letter "R" enclosed within a circle; thus ® indicates a *registered* trademark.[19] This notice should appear with all uses or references to the trademark. Legibility is the only standard in regard to the mark's size.

Once you're registered, don't let your company's trademark cross the line from a unique product designation to a common descriptive term for all products of that type. You'll lose your exclusive protection. Protect such exclusivity and distinctiveness by taking the following precautions:

Where there is a risk of generic adaptation, use your mark in conjunction with the generic name for your product. One method is to insert the word "brand" between the trademark and the generic term, for example, "Scotch-brand tape." Some other preventive measures are:

1. Always spell your trademark in exactly the same manner (changes in form detract from its status) and in capital (never lower-case) letters.
2. Have the trademark appear in the style of printing in which it is registered whenever possible.
3. Use the symbol ® after registration is secured.

Fight infringement immediately. The test for infringement is whether the other mark would confuse or deceive the normal purchaser. (See discussion of policing your mark later in chapter.)

Be concerned with how your mark is used on products. In cases of unauthorized use, there may be no confusion or deception per se, but the use may reflect adversely on your image. Under state as well as federal laws, you may have an action for "dilution" of your mark.

Be careful if you cease use—even temporarily. Although a short period of nonuse may be permissible, nonuse for 2 years or more may result in the presumption of abandonment.

POLICING YOUR MARK

If you begin to receive misdelivered mail, experience mix-ups in equipment deliveries, and/or receive telephone calls or orders intended for a competitor, contact your counsel immediately.[20] Your competitor may be employing a mark confusingly similar to your own.

For instance, a competitor may be using your geographic area's name. You are not entitled to the exclusive use of geographic terms, but you can prevent others from misleading the public as to geographic origin. "Black Hills jewelry" must come from the Black Hills![21]

When a competitor employs a similar trade dress on its product, such similarities tend to obscure whatever differences exist between the marks and may contribute significantly to confusion in the minds of your purchasers. Ask yourself whether your customers are likely to purchase another product in the mistaken belief that it is yours. For example, a court felt that a firm was copying the unique trade dress of certain Johnson & Johnson products. Their clear plastic baby oil bottle was identical, and their baby powder was packaged in a straight, rectangular-shaped white plastic container that was also identical to Johnson & Johnson's. The firm's label had the same pink bar across the top and bottom and was written in the same typeface.

The court felt that the competitor's trade dress was a "fraternal twin." In some figurative language, the court stated: "Having been caught with a hand in the cookie jar, defendants cannot avoid the claims by taking fewer or smaller cookies. They should have never reached into the cookie jar in the first place, and having done so must keep far away from it."[22]

However, there may be no confusion that you can demonstrate. Your company can't have trademark protection for obvious configurations or where the marks are not so similar that the average viewer could not readily detect the differences.[23] As perceived by the adjudicate court, the sophistication of your customers is as relevant to the likelihood that confusion will occur as is the degree of care and attention they devote to the decision to purchase your product.[24]

Your counsel will review your particular situation by asking the following questions:

1. Who has superior rights (use, registration, assignment)? If you haven't registered, your counsel will have to analyze whether your competitor might also have superior rights in a limited geographic area, based on innocent adoption and use.
2. Is there a likelihood of confusion as to the following?
   a. Similarity of marks (appearance, sound, similar shape of packaging, artwork, and lettering)
   b. Similarity of goods or services (and the nature of the goods)[25]
   c. Similarity of distribution channels
   d. Similarity of communications mix employed
   e. Similarity of trade dress
   f. Strength of the respective marks
   g. Purchasing audience
3. Was there wrongful or innocent intent in the appropriation of the mark?
4. What defenses might another user have to defeat your claim of infringement?

In *most* cases you will want to enforce your mark by a cease and desist letter from your counsel, followed by litigation, if necessary.

LICENSING YOUR MARK

An increasingly lucrative form of income, especially in these days of brand image, is subsidiary rights from licensing your mark. A trademark license is the key to most franchise agreements.[26]

You may begin to license your mark once it is registered on either the *Principal Register* or the *Supplemental Register.* In addition to franchises, there is a whole host of options to consider. This is another area of teamwork between the marketing and legal departments. One emerging area is merchandising properties as "status" properties, "personification" properties, "popularity" properties, and "character" properties.

Status properties. These properties involve status symbols used on merchandise such as Jordache. These are bought for quality but more importantly as "ego merchandise." The other properties in this list are more likely associated with low-priced, "impulse" products.

Personification properties. These merchandising properties create demand by association, for example, "Be a Pepper, Drink Doctor Pepper." For some reason people aspire to associate with certain commercial efforts (e.g., the "Pepsi generation"). Playboy has always capitalized on its sex and fantasy mystique to successfully license and market products bearing the Playboy emblem.[27]

Popularity properties. These result from mass media hype given to movies such as *Annie* or *E.T.,* sports events, and other highly publicized items.

Character properties. If you wore a Beatle wig, a coonskin cap, or mouse ears at one time in your life, you have an idea what character properties are.

Ownership rights to these properties vary. If you own one of these properties, review with your counsel whether you should approach these as distinctive marks or immediately develop a strategy for developing evidence of a secondary meaning. This secondary meaning can result from licensing efforts and the extent of the popularity of the particular property.[28] You will also have to be alert to others developing confusingly similar properties, such as when Columbia Pictures successfully opposed the registration of the mark "Clothes Encounters" of clothing, based on its movie *Close Encounters of the Third Kind* and its own merchandising program.[29]

It is important to review your merchandising program early, both for the obvious product-line potential (as well as spin-offs into the ancillary properties discussed) and to be sure that the legal requirements of trademark-licensing agreements are adequately carried out. Your in-house trademark program is a key essential in developing all these properties.

CONCLUSION

Trademarks communicate information about your product by providing consumers with a handy reference which summarizes their past experience and information obtained about brands using the same mark. Your mark acquires meaning over a period of time by associations formed in the minds of the public about the quality standards identified with the mark. Repeat purchases eventually build up a positive reputation for your brand as consumers come to associate it with satisfaction of their needs.

Without a favorable reputation, no promised benefits will sell well. Therefore, prior good publicity is important to any marketing campaign. Such publicity reflects on your key communications headliner, the trademark. If your firm enjoys a good reputation and your product's name is associated with high quality, by all means *use that name.* As the old saying goes, if you've got it, flaunt it. However, the new saying goes, if you've got it, protect it! A trademark can be an incredibly useful device if you're vigilant and don't allow your competitor to abscond with it when your guard is down. The information in this chapter will enable you to ask the proper questions and create a mark which will more easily pass a final legal review.

REFERENCES

1 A "trade name" refers to the name of a business. There is a well-recognized distinction between the term "trade name" and the terms "trademark" or "brand," which refer to the product sold by the business. Phillip **Morris** v. Imperial Tobacco Co., 282 F. Supp. 1931 (1967).

2 15 U.S.C. sec. 1127. A trade name need not be affixed to your product. It is a name which has been used long and intensely enough so that the public associates it with your product. A trade name, like a trademark, can be a valuable asset in your communications strategy.

3 Mishawaka Rubber and Woolen Mfg. Co. v. S.S. Kresge Co., 316 U.S. 203, 205 (1942).

4 15 U.S.C. sec. 1127.

5 Procter & Gamble Co. v. Johnson & Johnson Inc., 485 F. Supp. 1185 (1979).

6 Abercrombie and Fitch Co. v. Hunting World, Inc., 537 F.2d 4 (1976). *See also* Raigh v. Southland Corp., 591 P.2d 985 (1978) (why a "hoagie" is a generic name for a sandwich).

7 DuPont Cellophane Co. v. Waxed Prods. Co., 85 F.2d 75 (2d Cir.), *cert. denied,* 299 U.S. 601 (1936).

8 Bayer Co. v. United Drug Co., 272 F. 505 (S.D.N.Y. 1921).

[9] Kellogg Co. v. National Biscuit Co., 305 U.S. 111, 116 (1938). ("shredded wheat" is a generic term).

[10] Finkler v. Shlussel, 469 F. Supp. 674, 678 (1979).

[11] *Id.* at 679.

[12] W.E. Bassett Co. v. Revlon, Inc., 435 F.2d 656 (1972).

[13] Sheraton Corp. of America v. Sheffield Watch, Inc., 103 F.2d 917 (C.C.P.A. 1939); Lever Bros. Co. v. Nobio Prods., Inc., 103 F.2d 917 (C.C.P.A. 1939). Note that while the use of a trademark in advertising ordinarily provides no protectable trademark rights, the use of a service mark in advertising constitutes valid service mark use and creates a protectable interest. *See* 15 U.S.C. sec. 1127.

[14] American Footwear Corp. v. General Goodware Co. and Universal Studios, Inc., 609 F.2d 655, 663 (1979). *See also* Proctor & Gamble Co. v. Johnson & Johnson, Inc., 485 F. Supp. 1185, 1197 (1979) and Ball v. United Artists, 214 N.Y.S.2d 219 (1939).

[15] 15 U.S.C. sec. 1114(1)(a).

[16] Household Fin. Corp. of Del. v. Household Fin. Corp. of W. Va., 11 F. Supp. 3 (1935). *See also* Roto-Rooter Corp. v. O'Neal, 513 F.2d 44 (1975) and Puritan Furniture Co. v. Lomerc, Inc., 519 F. Supp. 56 (1981).

[17] Reddy Communications v. Envtl. Action, 477 F. Supp. 936, 947 (1979) (a case holding that the use of a caricature was incidental to the sale and did not result in confusion).

[18] 15 U.S.C. sec. 1127. *See also* 15 U.S.C. sec. 1115(b)(2). Dawn Donut Co. v. Hart's Food Stores, Inc., 267 F.2d 358 (1959). *See also* Interstate Brands Corp. v. Way Baking Co., 403 Mich. 479, 270 N.W.2d 103 (1978) (intermittent periods of nonuse and reduced use do not constitute "abandonment" of a trademark).

[19] Other notices are "Registered in U.S. Patent and Trademark Office" or "Reg. U.S. Pat. & Tm. Off.", which can be rather obtrusive in ad copy. If you use these notices, they can be footnoted.

[20] Taylor v. Quebedeaux, 617 P.2d 23 (1980).

[21] Black Hills Jewelry Mfg. Co. v. LaBelle's, 489 F. Supp. 754 (1980).

[22] Johnson & Johnson v. Quality Pure Mfg., Inc., 484 F. Supp. 975, 980 (1979).

[23] United Artists Corp. v. Ford Motor Co., 483 F. Supp. 89 (1980). *See also* Volkswagenwerk Aktiengesellshaft v. Rosevear Enters., Inc., 592 F.2d 1180 (1979) and Burger Chef Systems, Inc. v. Sandwich Chef, Inc., 608 F.2d 875 (1979).

[24] Proctor & Gamble Co. v. Johnson & Johnson, Inc., 485 F. Supp. 1185 (1979).

[25] Here issues as to audience sophistication are taken into account, but if the goods can have a dangerous effect (e.g., medical products), the courts will exercise greater vigilance. *See* Morgenstern Chemical Co. v. G.D. Searle & Co., 253 F.2d 390 (1958). For a related case of interest see Aircraft Novelties Corp. v. Baxter Lane Co. of Amarillo, 685 F.2d 988 (1982).

[26] This is another area to review with your counsel before signing any agreements. Two issues to consider are (1) whether you can ensure that your franchisees

are "related companies," that is, those on which you can impose quality control and other standards and (2) whether at the same time you can avoid a potential conflict with antitrust laws (e.g., see Chapter 6).

27 See Shawn Tully, "Playboy Makes the Boss's Daughter Boss," *Fortune*, August 23, 1982, pp. 105–118. I'd venture a guess that Christie Hefner will not be a success once her father leaves. Playboy is basically an autobiographical sketch of the father that stimulates male fantasies. Since Ms. Hefner cannot replace the fantasy, she'll be a victim of reverse image marketing.

28 *See* American Footwear Corp. v. General Goodware Co. and Universal Studios, Inc., 609 F.2d 655, 663.

29 Columbia Pictures Indus., Inc. v. Miller, 211 U.S.P.Q. 816 (1981).

FOUR
THE LAW YOU SHOULD KNOW AFFECTING CHANNEL POLICY __

Your product is now designed and produced, and millions of consumers are eagerly waiting to buy it. How do you get it to them? Designing your channels-of-distribution strategy requires as creative a marketing effort as any other aspect of marketing your product. An ineffective distribution system is like a weak link in a chain and can mean the failure of an otherwise great product.

Conversely, the efficient and creative use of various channels of distribution can spell success for a product that wouldn't make it otherwise. In certain industries the great strategic question is the channel, namely which one will best show their label and enhance brand loyalty. One example of the strategic role of the channel was the introduction of the Timex watch in 1950. The traditional channel (jewelry and department stores) objected, and so unconventional channels (drug and hardware stores) were used. Twenty years later 50 percent of the watches sold in the United States were Timex!

Sometimes in reading various business texts, one gets the feeling that machines rather than humans are interacting during the complex marketing process. But it's important to remember that every step of the way you're dealing with other people, which can naturally lead to conflict. Personal or managerial conflicts can be resolved, often to the satisfaction of both parties. However, in making your channels decisions, the conflicts which arise will often be of a legal nature. It will help you tremendously if you know *in advance* the legal ramifications of the channel decisions you make.

This section addresses major legal issues which may arise from the decisions you make regarding the channels you'll employ. The first two chapters will examine areas of antitrust law: Can you use territorial restrictions? Will there be problems if you terminate a distributor? Are tie-ins always illegal? Channel planning is important to avoid other legal problems. For example, you must get the correct quantity of your advertised special to the correct store, or deceptive advertising problems (discussed in Section 5) might develop. Believe it or not, this is an *exciting* and dynamic field—witness IBM and Xerox breaking with their long-standing tradition by selling office automation products in retail outlets.

In times of high interest rates you are made painfully aware that channels mean inventory, warehousing, transfer of ownership, choice of carrier, and so on. From experience you know that business executives get much of their work done by knowing whom to trust, making oral agreements without a contract, and talking the language peculiar to managers. The law will facilitate these transactions where possible. Chapter 4 offers a nonjargon guide to the law of sales.

Finally, we'll go beyond traditional sales areas and discuss certain aspects of direct marketing. Whether you use mail, telephone, or interactive cable, you should be familiar with some of the salient legal issues affecting this dynamic and rapidly growing channel.[1]

REFERENCES

[1] Robert J. Posch, *The Direct Marketer's Legal Adviser,* McGraw-Hill, New York, 1983.

CHAPTER

FIVE

ANTITRUST ISSUES IN CHANNEL DISTRIBUTION___

In designing your channel distribution strategies, you will make marketing decisions every step of the way. Your objective is to design the distribution systems that give the best return on your dollar. In pursuing these objectives, remember that many decisions you make should promote—*not* inhibit—competition.

In this chapter we'll take a look at restrictive distribution systems employing vertical restraints, an area which has been the subject of much antitrust literature. Then we'll discuss the often thorny legal ramifications of terminating your distributor. You *can* do it without causing antitrust problems, provided that you understand the rules.

Remember that your understanding of these antitrust issues is essential to the entire marketing process. Although this is not the most thrilling subject, shelling out a large sum of money (from your personal or your corporate piggybank) as a fine is a lot *less* thrilling! Even *less* enticing is the thought of designing all your wonderful marketing strategies from your own exclusive prison cell!

DISTRIBUTION PLANS WITH VERTICAL STRINGS ATTACHED ___

Managers often wish to include distribution and territorial restrictions in their marketing plans. These restrictions may include limits which a supplier may impose on its distributors or retailers as to pricing, product, quality control, and the geographic market in which they may sell.

Any proposed restrictions must be reviewed by counsel, lest your firm leave itself open to unnecessary litigation. This doesn't mean that you can't consider any kind of restrictions in your distribution plan, but you should have a working notion of what is legally feasible. Knowledge of the present state of the law and of the direction in which it is heading will enable you to blueprint distribution plans that will get a green light from your own counsel, thereby saving time, energy, and costs for all concerned.

WHAT YOU MAY NOT DO

Allocation of market territory between horizontal competitors—that is, between competitors at the same level of the market structure—is so patently anticompetitive that it violates the Sherman Act without proof of unreasonableness.[1] Such agreements reduce competition between direct competitors. This is fairly straightforward.

Just as illegal but more subtle is a vertical agreement initiated by distributors to impose territorial restrictions. A vertical agreement is an agreement among persons at different levels of the market structure, for example, between suppliers and distributors or wholesalers and retailers. These agreements are also illegal, even when a supplier is nominally a party to the agreement.[2]

THE NONPRICE VERTICAL
TERRITORIAL OPTION

When the production processes are completed, your product is ready for distribution to the consuming public. The type of good determines whether the supplier desires an intensive or selective distribution.

The distribution systems available range from dealing with independent distributors to the supplier's development of a complete, vertically integrated system for merchandising the product. Trade-offs involved include the costs and benefits of the available delivery mechanisms and the degree of control the manufacturer needs or wants to retain over the product. In general, costs to the manufacturer increase in proportion to the greater control exercised. Therefore, suppliers have sometimes sought the advantages of vertical integration without the disadvantages of the required capital investment and ensuing operational costs by arranging contractually a variety of vertical restrictions.

Vertical restrictions on distributors are limits which a channel member at one level of the distribution system (usually the supplier) imposes on a channel member at a different level of the distribution system (such as a wholesaler or retailer). The four most common examples of such contractually arranged restrictions are:

1. Location agreements, which limit the distributor's resale operations to a specified physical site
2. Territorial sales restrictions, which limit a distributor to sales within a defined territory and which often include an agreement by the supplier to prohibit other distributors from selling within that area
3. Areas of primary responsibility, which give a particular distributor primary responsibility for selling in an assigned territory
4. Customer restrictions, which restrict a distributor's choice of customers, such as when the supplier rather than the distributor sells and services to a large national customer

Basically, there are three types of vertical distribution relationships: exclusive-dealing relationships, independent sales contracts (franchising, or any contracted long-term distribution arrangement), and full vertical integration. The most efficient distribution relationship is generally defined by your marketplace. However, regrettable abuses have occurred which have resulted in the enactment of legislation primarily designed to guide rather than to define marketplace conduct. The inherent tension between the manager's desire to maximize efficiency and profit in distribution and society's attempts to maintain the antiquated nineteenth-century concept of atomistic "free" competition has acted as a major constraint on short- and long-term distribution strategies.

Congress began seeking to resolve the tension of varied competing interests almost a century ago. Recognizing the increasingly dynamic economic environment of the day, it sought a legal posture which would evolve with the marketplace without constraining it. Since we are only a few years from the centennial of the famous Sherman Act, it is obvious that these laws usually work well.

With competitive markets, the consumer benefits from lower prices and a greater selection of goods accomplished by mass economies of scale as well as by efficient and economical distribution. History has demonstrated that marketplace competition thrives when efficient firms are permitted to enjoy the fruits of their superior planning, organizational, and capital investment skills. The need to maximize efficiency often encourages a firm to control its distribution through vertical territorial restrictions for both economic and social reasons.

Economically, the modern firm requires specialist expertise, a large capital investment, increasingly sophisticated technological resources, and marketing know-how to stay competitive. Years of research, development, and planning may be invested before an item is ready to be produced. To reduce risk, the firm seeks some advantage over its competition, such as a more desirable product, more appropriate positioning, the right degree of segmentation, loyal customers and wholesalers, and so on. One way of gaining this advantage lies in controlling the firm's distribution system so that the firm can reduce *intrabrand* competition in the interest of succeeding against *interbrand* competition. Interbrand competition is competition among producers of a generic product, for example, competition among producers of washing machines. Intrabrand competition is competition among retailers to sell a specific brand of washing machine. The costs the firm incurs in production will be constant regardless of which distribution system is employed. Therefore, the distribution system will generally be a key variable. Its proper selection and creative structure can significantly affect your bottom line.

By imposing nonprice territorial restrictions (that is, restrictions which do not result in price restraints) on where and how a distributor can sell its product, the supplier maintains a degree of control over the distribution without assuming the distribution function. The supplier enjoys the expertise of the distributor and its client contact while avoiding the cost burden of establishing its own distribution system through vertical integration. In addition, by choosing territorial restrictions instead of vertical integration, a manager may retain a necessary local flavor by taking advantage of the knowledge of the distributor's sales personnel concerning local demands, desires, and needs. The imposition of vertical territorial restrictions on the distributor can be especially beneficial to the supplier when the supplier is entering new markets, in inducing higher levels of distributor service and in encouraging distributors to provide a full product line to a full range of customers. Nevertheless such nonprice territorial restrictions may still be a violation if the restraint is an unreasonable one.

The key legal question is: At what point do the actions of free marketplace choices become unreasonable restrictions on free commerce? The courts have addressed this dilemma through two approaches: by adopting "per se" rules of illegality and by using a "rule of reason" approach which analyzes each case on its merits. Understanding the distinction between these approaches is important, since these terms appear throughout your antitrust reading in all texts and trade journals.

PER SE VERSUS RULE OF REASON

Violations of the antitrust laws traditionally have been classified into two specific categories and subjected to different treatment by the courts. Certain business agreements, conduct, or other interaction (such as price fixing, boycotts, agreements to retard technological development, horizontal territorial restrictions, and many tie-ins) are so inherently anticompetitive as to be considered illegal per se (in and of themselves) without any inquiry into the reasonableness of the activity involved or their actual effect on competition.

Violations of this nature are usually proven by circumstantial evidence, one example of which is a meeting between competitors followed by actions leading to restraint of trade. Any facts which show communications between direct competitors and which indicate some restraining effect are admissible as evidence. Courts are influenced by patterns of contact among competitors, so you must be alert in your conversations and contacts with your competitors, even at informal lunches and trade association meetings. When in doubt, don't talk—talk to your lawyer first.

Although the courts use per se rulings, the more common and increasingly preferred standard is the rule of reason. Using the rule of reason, a court inquires into the purpose of the activity, its socially redeeming virtues (for example, if the practice actually promotes interbrand competition by allowing a new competitor to enter or a failing competitor to remain solvent), and the existence of practical but less restrictive alternatives. The court proceeds to weigh each fact presented to determine its overall reasonability and therefore its legality.

The case which effectively enshrined the rule of reason approach was *Continental TV, Inc. v. GTE Sylvania, Inc.*[3] *Sylvania* represented a growing awareness by the Supreme Court that the marketplace is a dynamic forum and not a closed zone to be refereed by a few judges. It preserved the competitive spirit of the Sherman Act while reflecting on the particular activities of the industry involved. The crucial factors to analyze are:

1. The market power or dominance of the company imposing the restraints
2. The extent to which the restraints impede intrabrand competition
3. The justifications asserted for the restraints in terms of promoting interbrand competition

The drawback most often cited by critics when referring to the rule of reason is the ensuing increase in litigation. This, however, can be minimized by a working knowledge of the checklist set forth in the conclusion of this chapter. But first, we'll briefly review some sticky issues involved in terminating your distributor.

TERMINATING YOUR DISTRIBUTOR

Your right to unilaterally conduct your business in a manner you see fit and to choose customers with whom you wish to deal is acknowledged.[4] However, once you've freely elected to do business with a distributor, terminating that distributor can be a bit risky—unless you've done your homework. And "homework" in law means *documentation*.

First, you must show a legitimate business reason for the dissatisfaction, such as the distributor's lack of cooperation with your marketing plans or poor payment record or your own internal reorganization. Many states now require a showing of "just cause" and a period of advance written notice—specific areas you must review with your counsel. Second, remember the terminated distributor usually knows a lawyer—a bad combination for you.

However, if you have a poor distributor, don't be intimidated—see your counsel. The trend is that fewer and fewer terminated distributors are satisfying this burden of proof (that's legalese for they're losing most of the time). Since the distributor must prove that the termination had an anticompetitive effect, how do you deprive the distributor of possible proof?

Document all your business reasons for termination. Check your files, letters, and contracts, and review any significant conversations. Then examine your own motives. Is the termination based on emotion or price (e.g., a discounter), or is the termination based on sound business judgment?[5] You may terminate for two reasons:

1. To reduce the number of your dealers, especially if an alternate supply of your product is available to the terminated distributor.[6]
2. To end a relationship that has grown uneconomic. This might mean that even though the distributor's sales have not fallen off, its failure to enthusiastically adopt your new or current marketing strategy might be enough to terminate.[7] In addition to the distributor's failure to adequately promote the product line, the distributor's policy of late payments "plus more" may be sufficient grounds for just cause to terminate.

Finally, your case is greatly improved if your terminated distributor cannot show that the termination lessened competition or created an "unreasonable restraint of trade" in the affected industry.[8] In general, courts won't compel a manufacturer to renew a dealership if there is no public harm even if the distributor is hurt. This rule will hold even where the court recognizes that subjective hostility might be involved, for example, when former employees compete with you.[9]

Again, a thorough interview with your counsel is essential before termination—particularly if pricing motives are even partly involved in your termination decision.

TO WRAP UP THE DISTRIBUTION AREA . . .

The following checklist (with particular emphasis on post-*Sylvania* cases) will enable the manager employing or considering a restrictive distribution system to review it in light of the current judicial climate. You must review with your counsel the relevant court cases for any of the points which are applicable to your company and/or your distribution plan. Although the rule of reason enhances flexibility in designing channel strategy, in leaving open areas of interpretation it presents the possibility of adverse interpretation. As usual, however, a text or checklist is a general planning aide but is no substitute for a counsel who knows your unique needs.

1. *Can I create or participate in a horizontal territorial allocation of the market under any circumstances?* No—not even if you can show it will bring "stability." Market sharing limits aggressive well-run firms and protects less efficient ones.

2. *Could a complainant objectively demonstrate in a challenge that a portion of the relevant market is being effectively eliminated by the distribution plan?* Vertical territorial distribution restrictions may be valid even if they make distributor sales outside of assigned territories economically unattractive, provided that they do not totally bar such sales and can be shown to be reasonable to the maintenance of an efficient distribution system. Note that the exclusion of a portion of the relevant market may also be justified in the wake of *Sylvania* if necessary to safeguard unique quality standards. Again, before you pursue any of your ideas, it is important to review the specifics of your restrictions with your counsel.

3. *Could a complainant objectively demonstrate in a challenge that the distribution plan has substantially lessened interbrand competition or has tended to create a* *monopoly?* The reviewing court will judge harshly any plan which tends to have a monopolistic effect and to stifle competition. An important issue here will be whether you have sufficient market power in the relevant market.[10]

4. *Could a complainant objectively demonstrate in a challenge that prices are becoming artifically high as a result of a decline in intrabrand competition?* This area is fraught with peril and any such plan should certainly be reviewed by counsel.

5. *Can we demonstrate that the success of a challenge to our plan would result in incentives to vertically integrate our industry fully, thereby diminishing interbrand competition?* We should be able to demonstrate without complex economic analysis that the restraint in question will promote interbrand competition in the relevant market while minimizing a decline in intrabrand competition. In the wake of *Sylvania,* such an argument would be judged by the rule of reason; the vertical restrictions inherent in the plan would be considered preferable to full vertical integration which increases marketplace concentration.[11]

6. *Do we possess monopoly power?* The necessary ingredients for monopoly power are the percentage of market share controlled by the firm, the number and strength of firms already established in the market, and the ease of entry into the market by potential competitors. In general, the more monopoly or market power (i.e., the ability to raise and sustain prices above the prevailing competitive market price) a firm has, the more likely that its vertical territorial distribution plan will be challenged.[12]

7. *Is our monopoly power the result of purpose or intent to exercise that power through anticompetitive conduct?* To prove unlawful practices, the firm must have both the power to control prices and the *intent* to exclude competition in the relevant market.[13] If the firm's actions show that it means to keep and does keep a complete and exclusive hold on the market, it is monopolizing the market, no matter how innocently it may otherwise proceed.

8. *Is our monopoly power the result of a superior product, business acumen, or historic accident?* These would be considered mitigating factors in determining the question of unlawful practices, providing that the firm did not deliberately retain exclusive control of the market subsequently. A firm will not be penalized for growth or development as a consequence of a superior product, business acumen, or historic accident.[14]

9. *To what extent do we actually enforce any written restrictions?* Written restrictions which are firmly and resolutely enforced and which result in securing compliance with "suggested" prices are illegal.[15]

10. *Are we a new entrant into a highly competitive market?* If so, the use of vertical restrictions to gain a foothold in the marketplace might survive a rule of reason test, because any decrease in intrabrand competition would be more than compensated for by an increase in interbrand competition.

11. *Are we an established seller struggling to survive?* The arguments in favor of vertical restrictions for a failing firm are the same as those for a new entrant into a competitive market (see point 10).[16]

12. *Is our market share declining or increasing?* If the firm's market share is declining, the arguments for vertical restrictions are improved insofar as those restrictions will enable the firm to survive in the marketplace and will increase interbrand competition.[17] If, however, the firm's market share is increasing, it must be able to prove an increase in interbrand competition as a result of such restrictions.

13. *How does our absolute size compare to the size of the distributor on whom we're imposing our restrictions?* The smaller the firm's absolute size is in relation to the size of the distributor's, the less likely the firm's ability and intent to monopolize. Conversely, the larger the firm is compared with the distributor, the greater the burden of proof. Each case will be judged accordingly under the rule of reason.[18]

14. *Is there any presence of a direct or indirect relationship which could be conclusively presumed unreasonable and therefore constitute a per se violation (i.e., a naked restraint of trade with no purpose except stifling of competition) such as*:

a. *Price-fixing?* Managers should be very wary of instituting illegal practices in regard to price-fixing. This area is reviewed in depth in Section 5. Price-fixing is generally a naked restraint of trade, and as such is a per se violation of the Sherman Act. However, there are certain limited exceptions you should review with your counsel.[19] As a general rule, *any* attempt to influence prices, regardless of the market power of the group, will be illegal.[20]

b. *Group boycotts?* These involve concentrated efforts to avoid competitors and would be considered per se illegal.[21]

c. *Horizontal division of markets?* Agreements between competitors producing the same generic product to price fix or to impose horizontal territorial restrictions (i.e., to divide up the market geographically) are per se illegal. The effect is to stifle interbrand competition, and no such plan would be upheld in court.[22]

d. *Allocation of business by collusive bidding?* Again, there are no reasonableness factors to consider, and such practices are per se illegal.

e. *Tying arrangements?* The lower courts increasingly review many of these devices by a rule of reason analysis, although the Supreme Court still takes a dim view of tying devices. The crucial test involves whether the tie-in involves one product or service in which the company enjoys substantial market power and whether the tie-in represents the firm's attempt to extend its monopoly power from one area into another. Any such arrangement should be reviewed carefully by your counsel.[23]

15. *Must we retain distributors as long as they return a profit?* You must consult with your counsel as to whether the particular state involved has passed a law requiring that good faith and just cause be shown before a distribution agreement may be terminated. However, the refusal of a distributor to go along with a reasonable marketing plan not involving price-fixing or other anticompetitive requirements is sufficient grounds to terminate.[24] As stated earlier, you need solid documentation of your reasons. Then do the following:

   a. Give the proper notice required by your contract; if length of notice is not specified in the contract, give the longest reasonable notice.

   b. Consider whether to give objective reasons for the termination to document your just cause or to give no reason, relying on your contract provisions.

   c. Allow the distributor to complete all short-term agreements on which it acted in reliance. Show you're attempting to minimize any financial losses for the distributor.

16. *Is our product inherently dangerous?* The uniqueness of a product may justify vertical restraints. Restrictions on resale of potentially dangerous products may be justified to protect the public from harm and to protect the firm from potential product liability (discussed in Section 3). For any exposure in this area you must consult your counsel.

17. *Is the product essentially safe with certain safeguards we must control?* Where health and safety concerns (as well as adverse publicity and legal exposure) can be clearly shown by the manufacturer, distributors and resellers may be required to carefully abide by the firm's specifications as to resale restrictions.[25]

18. *Is the product highly perishable?* Under a rule of reason analysis, vertical restrictions employed to protect the quality of a product (and therefore the commercial reputation of its producer), such as one which is highly perishable, would in the absence of anticompetitive intent most likely be upheld.

19. *Is the product protected by patent or trademark?* If so, the restrictions reasonably necessary to protect the integrity of the patent and/or trademark may be justifiable, as distinguished from collateral restrictions relating to price or other competitive factors.[26]

20. *Are there specific legal requirements as to the method of distribution?* Specific legal requirements as to the method of distribution (for example, under the Magnuson-Moss Consumer Products Warranties Act or as required by the Consumer Product Safety Commission) are compelling arguments for the particular distribution plan chosen. In general, this is applicable only in specialized situations involving licensed dealers, such as those who sell prescription drugs or alcoholic beverages.

21. *Are there any other relevant factors in the nature of our market?* Carefully analyze with your counsel your distribution plan in light of any particularly unique characteristics of the product and/or firm which would further justify the use of a distribution system employing vertical territorial restrictions. The need to ensure prompt and skillful after-sale service for machinery might be strong grounds to demonstrate that the restrictions had sufficient potential to improve interbrand competition.[27]

22. *Could we establish a consignment, agency, or franchise relationship to justify distributor restrictions nominally questionable in arm's-length transactions?* These arrangements must still, if challenged, be defensible under the rule of reason. Examine the various alternatives to determine which will best suit the needs of your firm and will survive a legal challenge.

23. *Have we detailed any necessary investment in capital or labor required by the retailer to market the product efficiently and safely, therefore necessitating our territorial restriction?* Although not yet a recognized defense, it might be helpful to argue that in order for your firm to protect its investment, it was necessary to create a distribution system employing vertical territorial restrictions. Keep detailed and accurate records of all such investments as well as the marketing strategy necessitating the restrictions in anticipation of any litigious challenges.

CONCLUSION

The foregoing checklist is not meant to be a comprehensive study of the legal implications of vertical territorial restrictions. Rather, it provides food for thought and a brief overview of the major factors examined when a distribution program employing such restrictions is tested using the rule of reason. You should design the program to be cost-effective as well as efficient. However, since this area historically is fluid and subject to differences of persuasion, any distribution program incorporating territorial restrictions should be reviewed by your counsel, preferably annually and certainly when modifications are undertaken.[28]

REFERENCES

[1] Timken Roller Bearing Co. v. United States, 341 U.S. 593 (1951). *See also* P. Stone, Inc. v. Koppers Corp., 631 F.2d 241 (1980).

[2] United States v. Sealy Inc., 388 U.S. 352 (1967).

[3] Continental T.V., Inc. v. GTE Sylvania, Inc., 433 U.S. 36, 53 (1977).

[4] United States v. Colgate & Co., 250 U.S. 300, 307 (1919).

[5] R.E. Spriggs Co. v. Adolph Coors Co., 156 Cal. Rptr. 738, 94 Cal. 3d 419 (1979).

[6] Excello Wine Co. v. Monsieur Henri Wines, 474 F. Supp. 203, 210 (1979).

[7] Muenster Butone, Inc. v. Stewart Co., 651 F.2d 292 (1980).

[8] Oreck Corp. v. Whirlpool Corp., 563 F.2d 54 (1977). *See also* Daniels v. All Steel Equipment, Inc., 590 F.2d 111 (1979).

[9] Blair Foods, Inc. v. Ronchers Cotton Oil, 610 F.2d 665 (1980).

[10] Donald B. Rice Tire v. Michelin Tire Corp., 483 F. Supp. 750 (1980).

[11] Continental T.V., Inc. v. GTE Sylvania, Inc., 433 U.S. 36, 53 (1977).

[12] United States v. Aluminum Co. of America, 148 F.2d 416 (1945).

[13] Greyhound Computer Corp. v. IBM, 559 F.2d 488, 492 (9th Cir. 1977).

[14] United States v. Grinnell Corp., 384 U.S. 563 (1966).

[15] Adolph Coors Co. v. FTC, 497 F.2d 1178 (10th Cir. 1974), *cert. denied*, 419 U.S. 1105 (1975).

[16] Continental T.V., Inc. v. GTE Sylvania, Inc., 433 U.S. 36, 53 (1979).

[17] *Id.*

[18] United States v. O.M. Scott & Sons Co., 303 F. Supp. 141 (D.D.C. 1969).

[19] Eastern Scientific Co. v. Wild Heerburgg Instruments, Inc., 572 F.2d 833 (CA–119781), *cert. denied* 439 U.S. 833 (1928).

[20] United States v. Socony—Vacuum Oil Co., 310 U.S. 150 (1940).

[21] Klor's Inc. v. Broadway-Hal Stores, 359 U.S. 207 (1959).

[22] Timken Roller Bearing Co. v. United States, 341 U.S. 593 (1951).

[23] United States v. American Can Co., 87 F. Supp. 18 (N.D. Cal. 1949). *See also* Northern Pac. Rys. Co. v. United States, 365 U.S. 1 (1958).

[24] Excello Wine Co. v. Monsieur Henri Wines, 474 F. Supp. 203, 210 (1979).

[25] Clairol, Inc. v. Boston Discount Center of Berkeley, 608 F.2d 1114 (1979).

[26] United States v. General Elec. Co., 358 F. Supp. 141 (D.D.C. 1969). *See also* Adolph Coors Co. v. FTC, 497 F.2d 1178 (10th Cir. 1974), *cert. denied*, 419 U.S. 1105 (1975).

[27] Copy-Data Sys., Inc. v. Toshiba America, Inc., 1980–1 Trade Cas. (CCH) para. 63, 757 (1980).

[28] For a short article on point, see Robert J. Posch, Jr. and Saul Sands, "Legal Ramifications of Vertical Territorial Restrictive Distribution Plans for the 1980s," *Journal of Marketing*, Summer 1982, pp. 38–43.

CHAPTER
SIX
HOW TO AVOID GETTING TIED UP WITH TIE-INS

When you were young, did your parents ever tell you that you could go to the movies only if you took your pesty little brother? Since this was your only alternative if you were to see the film, you decided to go—brother and all. Your parents were using a tie-in when they insisted that you take your brother (the "tied" product) if you wanted to go to the movies (the "tying" product)! In this chapter we'll examine the legal issues that may arise when you use a tie-in.

WHEN IS A TIE-IN JUSTIFIED?

For our purposes, a tie-in is an agreement by a party to sell one product *only* on the condition that the buyer also purchases a different (or tied) product or at least agrees that she or he will not purchase the product from any other supplier.

Let's look at an example from creative marketing history. You may have heard of the town of Lansford, Pennsylvania. This town, nestled in Carbon County, was once unable to receive television signals through the use of conventional equipment because of its location. Milton Shapp, president of Jerrold Electronics, set up a community antennae television (CATV) system on a nearby hilltop, and a new direct marketing channel was born.

Jerrold Electronics sold its CATV systems on the condition that the purchaser accept its installation and maintenance services. This condition was elaborately detailed in the contracts. Due to this and other related contractual requirements, the Justice Department filed a complaint charging that these provisions constituted illegal tie-in sales.

The lower court recognized that the tie-ins were utilized "in the launching of a new business with a highly uncertain future."[1] The Supreme Court had generally held that "tying arrangements serve hardly any purpose beyond the suppression of competition."[2] However, here the Court did approve the restraint of an engineering service contract for highly complex equipment, during the early stages of a business, when technology was advanced but not yet proven. The Court was also impressed by the fact that a large capital expenditure was involved. Jerrold, unlike its limited competition, lacked the resources of a diversified business. Therefore, an initial tie-in requirement actually enhanced competition.

Thus a tying arrangement which is otherwise illegal under the federal antitrust law may sometimes be justified in limited circumstances during the development period of a new industry. Knowing the dynamics of a tie-in issue are important to all business professionals, particularly those involved in finding new markets and channels in the technological world of today.

GENERAL TIE-IN PRINCIPLES

In general, a tying arrangement exists when the sale of one product (the tying product) is conditional on the purchase of another (the tied product). The courts have generally recognized that these contracts suppress competition in that they involve the use of economic power in one market to achieve dominance in other markets. Buyers are forced to surrender their independent judgment as to whether to purchase the tied product. This does not further the goal of antitrust policy, which is the efficient allocation of economic resources through free and unfettered competition.

When do you have an illegal tying arrangement? There are four elements of tying violations:

1. There must be a tying arrangement between two distinct products or services.
2. The defendant must have sufficient economic power in the tying market to impose significant restrictions in the tied product's market.
3. The amount of commerce in the tied product market must not be insubstantial.
4. In general, the seller of the tying product must have an interest in the tied product.

In some, but not all, situations, a modicum of coercion may be present.[3]

THE TYING ARRANGEMENT

A formal tie-in can be formed by an express contract (such as Jerrold practiced), or the agreement can be inferred from the conduct of the parties. Any formal or informal arrangement which will involve two or more products or services in a package or a desired product with a less desired product should be reviewed with your counsel for tie-in exposure.

The issue as to separate and distinct products can be subtle. If there is a conflict, marketplace reality and not the intent of the parties is what controls. A left and right shoe are individual shoes, but one product, that is, a pair of shoes. Obviously the lack of two separate markets will tend to show a single product. Likewise, package deals involving the sale of two or more products as a single unit are not tie-ins when the buyer is in fact free to purchase each product separately.

The existence of dual markets is one way to determine the separateness of the products. Another way to view the separate-product issue is to examine whether the item is normally purchased as a distinct whole (for instance, an automobile manufacturer requiring its own engine to be installed) or whether the products are accessory and capable of being purchased as distinct products from other suppliers. For example, can they be returned separately for credit?

Here a commonsense test comes into play: often the tying product is simply less desirable. One example was the former practice of block booking of movie licenses; to get certain desired pictures, you were forced to also license less desirable ones. These arrangements were found to be illegal.[4] Any artistic or literary property is a unique product, and compelling the purchase of one property with another constitutes a separate product for tie-in purposes. At other times an "assortment" of bookings may result in a favorable discount. Because of the often narrow distinctions involved, consult your counsel when you approach these issues (as a buyer or a seller) especially *before* you sign any agreements.

Another interesting area is credit. Credit has been held a product separate from the sale involved; the extension of credit on favorable terms can be considered sufficiently unique to render it a tying product. The key question is "whether the seller (offering the credit terms) has the power within the market for the tying product to raise prices or to require purchasers to accept burdensome terms that could not be exacted in a completely competitive market. In short, the question is whether the seller has some advantage not shared by his competitors in the market for the tying product."[5]

Under this analysis, if you are offering terms to your customers, ask yourself if other competitors offer the same distinctive product. Only if other suppliers of credit cannot meet credit terms competitively does an illegal tie-in result from your extension of credit on favorable terms. Any contract you enter in which you *require* that your firm finance the product you're selling should be carefully reviewed with your counsel before it is presented to the buyer.

SUFFICIENT ECONOMIC POWER

The crucial test of sufficient economic power is whether the tie-in involves one product or service in which the company enjoys substantial market power. In other words, does the tie-in represent an attempt by a firm to exert leverage so that its economic power in one market may be extended to another? Economic power here does not mean monopoly or even dominant power. The test is whether the firm "has sufficient economic power with respect to the tying product to appreciably restrain free competition in the market for the tied product."[6]

In addition to dollar power in a market, economic power can be inferred from the tying product's desirability, its uniqueness, or even its consumer appeal. Economic power is presumed if you possess a legal monopoly such as a patent or copyright. Here a competitor cannot have access to the property except through a license by the owner, and requiring additional purchases to license this product can invite antitrust exposure.

A trademark can also confer the presumption of economic power. However, it must be shown that the trademark is a distinctive representation of product quality or that it possesses requisite goodwill and public acceptance unique to it to restrain competition in the product market. A trademark representing only origin (see discussions in Sections 3 and 6) lacks this power.

This problem often arises in franchising. For example, ice-cream retailers brought suit against their franchisor, alleging maintenance of an illegal tying arrangement, illegal horizontal-market allocations, and wholesale price-fixing. The appellate court held that, since the *trademark served to identify the ice cream, and thus the trademark and the ice cream were not separate products, the tying rules were inapplicable.* Rather than identifying a business format, the trademark only represented the end product marketed by the system. The desirability of the trademark, therefore, was *utterly dependent on the perceived quality of the product it represented.* Therefore, in the court's view, tie-in doctrine had no application because the *prohibition of tying arrangements is designed to strike solely at the use of a dominant desired product to compel the purchase of a second undesired commodity.* In addition, the desirability of the trademark and the quality of the product it represented were so inextricably interrelated in the mind of the consumer as to preclude any finding that the trademark was a separate item for tie-in analysis.[7]

You've no doubt eaten at a franchised "chain" restaurant at some time—possibly because of the goodwill of the franchisor's name. The franchisor may license its trademark (origin) and contract to sell any items unique to its particular operation. However, it may negotiate to sell but may not *require* you to purchase from it other items readily available in the open market from other competitors. For example, Howard Johnson's may not require its franchisees to purchase HoJo Cola, although through negotiation it may make it beneficial for the franchisee to do so. Again, think one product or distinct products. If the items are sold as a unit in the marketplace, there is only one product. If they are sold as separate items, then the trademark and franchise are tying products, and other required products are tied products and probably illegal.

Finally, in the form of a catch-22, the very fact that the seller could successfully impose a tying arrangement on an undesirable product demonstrates its economic power in the market.

EFFECT ON COMMERCE

A principal problem the courts have with tie-ins is that they deny competitors free access to the market for the tied product, not because the tying product is of better quality or at a lower price, but simply because of leverage in another (and possibly unrelated) market.

Interstate commerce consists of sales across state lines. A "substantial" amount is a subjective issue. A key point here is that the market in question and not merely gross sales will be the controlling factor. In one case, an amount of $60,800 was found to be a substantial amount of dollar volume affecting the market involved.[8]

SELLER MUST HAVE AN INTEREST IN THE TIED PRODUCT

When the seller of the tied product requires the buyer to do business with a specific firm to effectuate the contract, the requirement itself is the tying product. For example, a franchisor required that a restaurant be built by a particular contractor.[9] The franchisee sued, claiming that this was an illegal tying arrangement.

The franchisor won! It was found that it had no financial or other interest with the contractor (including rentals). The franchisor believed that this contractor would erect a better building than its competitors. However, as we mentioned when discussing credit-financing requirements, be careful whenever you require an additional, separate, and distinct purchase to do business.

SHOWING OF COERCION

Buyers must prove that they were *coerced* and not merely persuaded to buy an allegedly tied product. If you have an express provision in your contract, no coercion need be proven, since coercion is implied.

If you are attempting to demonstrate coercion by implication, look for the following. Have other buyers accepted similar such burdensome terms? Some concrete inference is important because a seller may have the economic power in your market, but, unless it actually employed its economic power in a *coercive* manner to force the purchase of the tied product, you may not be able to prove a tie-in.

SELLER'S DEFENSES

None of the following is a guaranteed defense but all could be helpful. Consult your counsel *in advance* about the specific details of a possible tie-in arrangement.

1. Demonstrate that the alleged tie-in is a single product.
2. Demonstrate that you are a new entrant or an infant industry.[10]
3. Demonstrate that goodwill and/or quality control is essential.

However, the Supreme Court has said that this last justification fails in the usual situation, because specifications of the type and quality of the products to be used in connection with the tying product is protection enough.[11] On the other hand, this view is becoming dated in light of the direction the courts are setting. Increasingly courts and commentators view these arrangements as vertical and judge them according to a true rule of reason analysis. There will be a realistic assessment of market power and a rule of reason analysis as to whether there really is any interbrand competitive effect of the tying arrangement.

EXCLUSIVE DEALING ARRANGEMENTS

An exclusive dealing arrangement normally requires the buyer to purchase exclusively from one supplier for an agreed-on time. This may exclude competitors from a substantial market. A court's analysis will center around the degree to which the supplier's competitors are foreclosed from customers or distribution outlets and whether the agreement improves overall interbrand competition.

Both exclusive dealing and tie-ins involve the attachment of terms and conditions to the purchase of a given product. However, the courts will generally uphold exclusive dealing agreements which were freely entered into by both parties to serve a legitimate economic need and not to foreclose competition. For example, if a new business uses this agreement to gain a foothold in the market, thereby improving competition, the agreement will in all likelihood be upheld.

CONCLUSION

The crucial test in a tying arrangement is whether the tie-in involves a product or service in which your firm enjoys significant economic power. Ask yourself whether reasonable appearances would indicate that you are attempting to exert leverage so that your monopoly power in one area (the tied product) may be extended into another (the tying area). This is particularly important for those engaging in franchising.[12]

REFERENCES

[1] Robert J. Posch, Jr., "How to Avoid Getting Tied up with Tie-Ins," *Direct Marketing*, August 1982, pp. 104–106.

[2] United States v. Jerrold Elecs. Corp., 187 F. Supp. 545 (E.D. Pa. 1960), *aff'd per curiam*, 365 U.S. 567 (1961).

[3] Standard Oil Co. of Calif. v. United States, 337 U.S. 293 (1949).

[4] United States v. Loew's Inc., 371 U.S. 38 (1962).

[5] United States Steel Corp. v. Fortner Enters., Inc., 429 U.S. 610, 615 (1977).

[6] Northern Pac. Ry. Co. v. United States, 337 U.S. 293 (1949).

[7] Krehl v. Baskin-Robbins Ice Cream Co., 1982-1 Trade Cas. (CCH) para. 64,449 (1978).

[8] Anderson v. Home Style Stores, Inc., (D.C. Pa.) 58 F.R.D. 653 (1st Cir.), *cert. denied*, 368 U.S. 931 (1961).

[9] Dehydrating Process Co. v. A.O. Smith Corp., 292 F.2d 653 (1st Cir.), *cert. denied*, 368 U.S. 931 (1961).

[10] *See* Jerrold electronics discussion as well as Posch, *supra* ref. 1.

[11] Standard Oil Co. v. United States, 337 U.S. 293 (1949).

[12] *Provisions of Franchise Agreement as Constituting Unlawful Tying Arrangements under Federal Antitrust Laws*, 14 A.L.R. Fed. 473 (1973).

CHAPTER

SEVEN

WHAT YOU NEED TO KNOW ABOUT PHYSICAL-HANDLING RELATIONSHIPS_____

You should be concerned about the safe storage and warehousing of your goods during the distribution process. This chapter will take a short look at bailments, so that you can spot legal issues and discuss them with your counsel before they spell trouble and before you have to be bailed out of a tight spot!

WHAT KIND OF TRANSFER IS YOUR TRANSACTION? _____

You've heard the term "bailment." Is a bailment a contract? Yes. Is it a sale? No. Bailments are important in the warehousing and storage of your goods at every stage of the distribution process. For your purposes, a bailment is the relationship created by the transfer of *possession* (not title) of an item of *personal* property by one, the bailor, to another, the bailee, for the accomplishment of a particular purpose.[1] Whenever you transfer, lend, or store personal property to or for another, think bailment.

Your best clue as to whether a bailment relationship exists is whether the identical article is to be returned in the same or in an agreed-on altered form. If another thing of equal value is to be returned, the transaction is a sale. Examples of bailments include your product stored in a warehouse pending sale or a dairy farmer's transferring milk to receive back milk or cheese.

BAILMENTS IN YOUR PERSONAL LIFE

It sounds complicated? You probably engage in these transactions daily in your personal life. You are a bailor and your bank a bailee each time you place an item in your safe deposit box. The last time you left your watch for repair at the jeweler's or your suit at the cleaners, you entered a bailment relationship.

Remember the last time you went on a pleasure outing to the city? Hunt as you might, it was impossible to find a parking spot. Finally you found a parking lot, and you were grateful just to dump the auto with the attendant and proceed on to your restaurant or show. Yet, what took place upon parking? If you parked your car in a parking lot, you may be merely renting parking space or you may be a bailor! Did you retain your keys? If so, you are probably renting space. If the attendant (bailee) retained your keys, then you have a bailment. The bailee is expected to exercise the degree of care over your car which a reasonable owner of such automobile would exercise under the same circumstances for its protection. Further, there is a similar obligation of care as to all items reasonably expected to be in your car (such as a spare tire or jack) but not as to items not expected to be in a car (such as a coat).

What if the small print on the back of your ticket exempts the garage or lot from negligence? In many states this will fail if the parking facility has the capacity to park four or more vehicles.[2] However, the owner might not be liable to you for theft by an employee of the parking facility.[3]

If you skipped the lot and pulled up to your restaurant and gave the keys to the attendant, you had a bailment. You entered the restaurant, sat down, and hung your coat on a hook in close proximity to your seat. There was no bailment, since you could take the coat at any time and the restaurant owner exercised no control over it. This is true even if your waiter helped you remove it and hung it up for you.[4] But, if the owner operated a checkroom to which you delivered your coat and received a receipt, a bailment was created, although liability might be limited by statute.[5] This protection may be less for an owner who allows a private concessionaire to operate the checkroom.[6]

BAILMENTS IN YOUR BUSINESS LIFE

Now that you know what a bailment is and how it operates in your personal life, let's review some common bailment relationships your product may pass through between your firm and your customer.

WAREHOUSE

Warehousing is a business engaged in storing goods for hire.[7] As you will note throughout this book, society grants greater legal protection to an individual consumer, and seeks to product those with unequal bargaining power.[8] In a warehousing relationship, the law will presume parity of arm's-length bargaining. Therefore, your warehouse representative may try to limit its duty of care. Without such a limit, the warehouser must exercise such care as a reasonable person would under such circumstances but, *unless otherwise agreed,* "is not liable for damages which could not have been avoided by the exercise of such care."[9] Your warehouse may also limit its liability for other damages in writing in the receipt or storage agreement. However, you have the right to request in writing that the warehouse increase its liability on all or part of your goods. The warehouse must honor this written request although it has the right to increase its rates based on the increased valuation.[10]

Therefore, do not treat the receipt or storage agreement as a non-negotiable "boilerplate." Carefully review the small print with your counsel. Discuss the minimum protection you need (consider your current insurance protection), and have your attorney draft an agreement accordingly. The added psychological value, plus stressing the goods' value and your desire to protect them, might in and of itself encourage greater vigilance at the warehouse.

If you end up with a warehouse full of merchandise, financing costs alone may doom you! However, don't expect any indulgences from your warehouse owner since he or she faces the same interest rate problems.

Before the goods have been stored, be prepared to pay in advance (unless otherwise agreed to in writing) to have your goods released to you or placed on a carrier. Again, the agreement controls. The warehouse owner has a legal right or lien to retain your goods until storage, transportation, insurance, labor, or other agreed-on charges in relation to the goods are paid for.[11] The warehouse will be loathe to release the goods to you because the lien is lost upon voluntary delivery to you.[12] You probably wouldn't even consider going to the dry cleaners to pick up your suit if you didn't have the necessary cash to pay for it! In addition to this lien, the warehouse has all other legal remedies afforded to a creditor against a debtor.[13]

Finally, remember that in all bailment relationships, the bailee is not an agent. You as bailor are not a principal. There is no delegation of control. Unless they undertake further services, bailees are merely depositories of your goods as per your agreement.

COMMON CARRIERS

A common carrier[14] takes goods from anyone in return for payment.[15] This is distinguishable from a private carrier, which may be more selective as to users. The liability of a private carrier is limited to negligence. The common carrier, however, is an insurer of your goods upon their receipt, with certain exceptions.[16] It is liable for a missing shipment of your goods irrespective of any exculpatory language in the bill of lading. Further, it can't exempt itself if another connecting carrier causes a loss or damage to your goods. The carrier is held to the degree of care a reasonable person would exercise in like circumstances both as to carriage and to the delivery date.

An important document in this relationship is the bill of lading. The bill of lading serves a threefold purpose: receipt of goods, contract for their carriage and delivery, and as a document of title.[17] You want to be sure you receive a "clean bill of lading" from your carrier. This signifies that the goods as delivered were in good order and condition. This clean bill of health puts you in a strong recovery position in the event of damage to the goods while in transit *and* until your buyer assumes control.

The carrier can become a bailee in a number of ways. Two important instances are when it holds the goods pending orders to ship [18] or when, after timely notice of arrival is given, the goods are not picked up by the buyer or consignee.[19] As with the warehouse operator, a carrier (common or private) has a lien on the goods covered by the bill of lading for charges subsequent to the date of its receipt of the goods for storage or transportation and for expenses necessary for the preservation of the goods incident to their sale pursuant to law.[20] As with the warehouse lien, the carrier lien is lost on any goods voluntarily delivered.[21]

Finally, the telegraph and telephone companies are carriers whose efficient service can be vital to you. If you are injured in your business dealings as a result of their foul-ups, you may not have to simply swallow it. Consult with your counsel. A telegraph company may be liable for mis-wording your message; their outright failure to deliver improves your chances for recovery. The telephone company is liable for gross negligence or willful misconduct. If you've been hurt, see your attorney.

CONCLUSION

When you surrender custody and control of personal property to another but you do not sell it, think bailment. Then ask yourself:

1. Did an actual or constructive delivery by the bailor to the bailee take place?
2. Did the bailee take possession with *intent* to possess it (think of who controls the car keys in the parking example)?
3. Was custody and control—but not title—transferred? If so, you have a bailment. If not, think contract.

REFERENCES

[1] Personal property is defined in the Glossary.

[2] *See, e.g.,* N.Y. Gen. Oblig. Law sec. 5-325 (Consol. 1982).

[3] Castorina v. Rosen, 49 N.E.2d 521, 290 N.Y. 445 (1943) (theft by an employee is outside the scope of the employee's employment).

[4] Wieler v. Silver Standard Ins., 263 A.D. 521, 33 N.Y.S. 2d 617 (App. Div. 1942).

[5] *See, e.g.,* N.Y. Gen. Oblig. Law sec. 201(1) (Consol. 1982). Patrons should be aware that they may have no redress where no check tickets are given out and certain signs are conspicuously posted informing the public that the management assumes no responsibility for loss or theft.

[6] Aldrich v. Waldorf-Astoria, 343 N.Y.S.2d 2830 (1973).

[7] U.C.C. sec. 7-102(h).

[8] For example, U.C.C. sec. 2-302 (unconscionable contracts or clauses), dismissed in greater detail *infra.*

[9] U.C.C. sec. 7-204(1).

[10] U.C.C. sec. 7-204(2).

[11] U.C.C. sec. 7-209(1).

[12] U.C.C. sec 7-209(4)

[13] U.C.C. sec. 7-210(7)

[14] These relationships are not always bailments. However, they often result in this form of relationship. Either way they can be an important factor in your channel decision (e.g., whether to mail by United Parcel or the U.S. Postal Service). The duties of a carrier will be specified in the bill of lading. If the transaction is intrastate, Article 7 of the UCC governs. If it is interstate, the Federal Bill of Lading Act (U.S.C. tit. 49) governs.

[15] A common carrier takes goods *or* persons. However, there are distinctions made between the two.

[16] Act of God, act of state, act of public enemy, or negligence of shipper (e.g., bailor who improperly packs the goods or damages them due to the inherent nature of the goods themselves). Frosty Land Foods Int'l Inc. v. Refrigerated Transps. Co., 613 F.2d 1344 (1980).

[17] U.C.C. sec. 7-104. The document lists the goods received by the carrier and states the agreed destination for the goods and the terms on which the carrier undertakes to deliver them.

[18] Liability is the same as that of a warehouser.

[19] This is a traditional bailment relationship.

[20] U.C.C. sec. 7-307(1).

[21] U.C.C. sec. 7-307(3).

CHAPTER
EIGHT
SALIENT ISSUES IN
SALES LAW

If you have a good to sell, you should familiarize yourself with the law of sales. In designing your channel strategy, this knowledge will give you the working overview of certain commercial practices that our society expects from a sophisticated manager. Reading this chapter is not intended to substitute for specific legal advice from your company's lawyer. However, it should alert you to the salient issues, so that you'll be aware of a legal issue in advance.

To have a thorough grasp of this area, your attorney must know some sophisticated distinctions and construction language, but this chapter will not place a premium on vocabulary; rather it will get you through this area with a minimum of pain and with some practical examples.

SELLING YOU ON THE UCC

Article 2 of the UCC (Uniform Commercial Code) applies to all *commercial* (not consumer) "transactions in goods."[1] Anything else (services, real estate, etc.) involves traditional contract law. For example, you wish to paint your office. The paint is a *good*—covered by the UCC. The painter is a *service*—covered by contract law. When you have a "mixed transaction," the main thrust of the transaction will determine whether it is covered by the UCC or by contract law.

Once you've determined that you are covered by the UCC, you'll want to answer these four questions:

1. What does your agreement consist of?
2. Is it an enforceable agreement?
3. If it is enforceable, what is the extent of the performance I'll receive (or have to provide)?
4. If I fail to receive performance (or fail to perform), what are my respective remedies (or penalties)?

We'll review these questions as they relate to the UCC and look at some representative cases. Although the UCC is not the most thrilling reading in the world, your perseverance will be rewarded when you find that you can apply your understanding of the UCC to your daily business transactions.

GENERAL PRINCIPLES OF THE UCC

The UCC is the constitution of the commercial world.[2] The writers of our Constitution intended it to be dynamic and to grow and mature with our nation. Likewise, the UCC provides "its own machinery for expansion of commercial practices. It is intended to make it possible for the law embodied in this Act to be developed by the courts in the light of unforeseen and new circumstances and practices."[3] Further, it was intended to coordinate commercial dealings in interstate commerce to produce one national marketplace with a set of common rules that all participants could understand. A number of key themes run throughout the UCC; read the following twice to get a good feel for the underlying principles of sales law:

Executed Sale. An executed sale is a sale which is final and complete in all contractual terms.

Executory Sale. The executory sale is a sale in which all terms and conditions were definitely agreed upon but which has not yet been carried into full effect in respect to some of its terms or details (e.g., price, quantity, delivery).

Good Faith. As a professional who reads books such as this, you are making a good-faith effort to stay on top of all areas of your profession. The UCC expects all your competitors to live up to similar standards. Good faith is simple honesty in fact. For merchants this means observance of commercial reasonableness and fair dealing in their trade. *Every* contract or duty under Article 2 of the UCC imposes an obligation of good faith in its performance and enforcement. Even if all parties agree at arm's length, they may not waive or disclaim the obligation of good faith.[4]

Goods. In general, goods are all things except real property and personal services, including specially manufactured goods, which are movable at the time of *identification* to the contract for sale. "Identification" means the designation of specific goods as the ones to be delivered under your contract. For example, "we designate these goods to be shipped as per the contract."[5]

Material Term. A material term is one that, when included in the contract, would make a difference as to whether you'd agree to the contract.

Merchants. Merchants are held to higher standards or skill concerning the goods involved as well as business practices in their particular fields. Who is a merchant? As defined by the UCC, merchants are those who deal in goods of the kind or otherwise hold themselves out as having knowledge peculiar to the practices or goods involved in the transaction.[6] Merchants *impliedly warrant* their goods as merchantable. As discussed in Section 3, this implied warranty means that the merchant's goods must at least pass without objection in the trade. As a business professional, you're probably being held to the merchant standards.

Payment. Payment can be rendered in any manner current in the usual course of the business. If the seller demands payment in legal tender, the seller must grant a reasonable extension of time to enable the buyer to procure it. No credit terms are *ever* assumed—such terms must be specified.

Reasonableness. This word or a variation of same is a theme of the article. No specific definition is given so that it can be used with flexibility in varied transactions. A negative limit exists in the term "unconscionability," which we'll get into more a little later.[7] On the whole, it may be said that if you're acting in good faith, you're acting reasonably.

Sale. A sale is a contract by which title passes from the seller to the buyer for consideration. Note that bailment is not a sale; it transfers possession, not title. A gift transfers title without consideration.

In summary, if you're a good person and a responsible professional, and you act accordingly in your transactions to buy and/or sell goods, the UCC is on your side.[8] If your competitor did likewise and yet you both made a few errors or omissions in evidencing agreement (which shouldn't happen if you properly consult your attorney from the beginning!), the UCC will help you. Let's see how and address those questions we mentioned a bit earlier.

WHAT DOES YOUR AGREEMENT CONSIST OF?

A written business transaction agreement between two commercial enterprises dealing on an equal basis which states that it is the exclusive statement of the terms of the agreement will have priority over the UCC.

The courts will not use the UCC to create a result contrary to the clearly understood intentions of the parties. Further, the parties are generally free to agree to terms not encouraged by the specific UCC provisions. However, few contracts are this clear-cut.

The UCC provisions are designed to assist two parties achieve the benefit of the arm's-length bargain they sought. Under the UCC, the agreement for the sale of goods may be made in any manner sufficient to show agreement, including conduct by both parties which recognizes the existence of a contract. Such conduct is sufficient to establish a contract for sale even though the parties' writings don't. The contract will not fail for indefiniteness if the UCC can provide for the "missing links."[9]

The courts will accept testimony as to custom and usage in your trade, and they will examine whether there was a pattern of prior dealings between the parties.[10]

IS YOUR AGREEMENT ENFORCEABLE?

The most important idea underlying the discussion of Article 2 is that the UCC will work to assist all parties in realizing their good faith commercial expectations. For example, the "common law" formalistically (that is, by looking at form over substance) has defeated valid contractual expectations in two ways.

An offer is effective when communicated and accepted. In many states the offer is effective when accepted in an *authorized* manner. In general, this means that, absent any indication to the contrary, the offeror authorizes the acceptance only if communication of the acceptance is performed in the same manner which he or she used. For example, if you received the offer by mail, your acceptance must be by mail. If the acceptance is by mail, it is accepted when *sent*. However, if a telegram or other vehicle was used, the acceptance is effective only when *received*.

The UCC permits acceptance in any manner and by any medium reasonable under the circumstances, unless the offeror unambiguously indicates how acceptance is to be made.[11] Communication of acceptance can also be accomplished by conduct: If your buyer orders 200 widgets, you may indicate acceptance by immediately shipping goods conforming to the order.[12]

Another common-law exception applies to *merchants*. Contract law requires that "firm offers" be sustained by some valid consideration to bind the offeror. Again, the UCC is flexible in light of commercial realities. An offer by a *merchant* to buy or sell in a signed writing which gives assurance that it will be held open needs no consideration to be irrevocable for a stated time. If no time period is stated, then the period of irrevocability may extend to 90 days.[13]

CONFLICTING WRITINGS

Conflicting writings constitute a common problem in your everyday ordering. Your business transactions are often conducted by phone, followed by a standardized form. After your phone conversation you receive a form from the buyer, but things don't exactly jell; some terms are open, and others are at variance. Under the UCC you'll work out a contract provided that you have a specified *quantity term* on which the courts can build and which will help fill in the gaps. The courts will proceed under the overall spirit of the UCC as well as the general formation section, which states that "even though one or more terms are left open a contract for sale does not fail for indefiniteness if the parties have intended to make a contract and there is a reasonably certain basis for giving an appropriate remedy."[14]

However, merchants have special privileges to facilitate the contract formation process. The UCC recognizes that the realities of business life make it impossible for every routine sales transaction to be accompanied by proposals which agree on all terms. Therefore, a written confirmation sent to your buyer within a reasonable time operates as an acceptance, even if it states different or additional terms to those offered originally. Between merchants such terms become part of the contract unless (1) the offer expressly limits acceptance to the terms of the offer, (2) the merchants materially alter it, or (3) notification of objection to them has already been given or is given within a reasonable time after notice of them is received.[15] These exceptions help to resolve the often-quoted "battle of the forms." The first and third exceptions are fairly obvious. A *material* alteration may vary depending on the trade in which you are marketing. In general, a *material alteration* is an addition to or change in the contract which would result in surprise or hardship if incorporated into the contract without the express awareness of the other party. The "choice of law" your attorney places in your contract is generally not a material alteration, even if the first proposal sets forth a different state from the one in which you're negotiating the agreement.[16]

A clause negating standard warranties of merchantability or fitness for a particular purpose usually is a material alteration. Arbitration is less clear, and it's determined on a state-by-state basis.[17] Most states follow the "New York rule," which declares that for purposes of this section of the

UCC, the unilateral insertion of an arbitration clause is a material alteration of the contract.

Review all additional proposals with your counsel—both those you send
and those you receive. As to the former, you may not wish to offer your
buyer an "out" without knowing all legal consequences. If you are the
recipient, your counsel will explain your legal exposure if you fulfill the
agreement as is. Whether the additional term is material is a matter for
your counsel; if you want out, you should immediately direct your counsel
to draft a letter that complies with the *prompt* notification of objection
described in the third exception.

Finally, even if you don't believe your writings are a contract, conduct by
both you and your buyer which recognizes the existence of a contract will
establish a contract: "In such case the terms of the particular contract
consist of those terms on which the parties agree, together with any
supplementary terms incorporated under any other provisions of this
Act."[18] The latter may include custom or evidence of course of performance. These will be considered and weighed on a priority basis. Express
contractual terms control over all else. Course of performance controls
over evidence of both course of dealings and usage of trade.[19]

INSUFFICIENT WRITING— THE ORAL CONTRACT

We've reviewed the areas of too many writings and of how the UCC
attempts to sort them out. What about too few writings? Take the case of
the classic order over the telephone: You receive a bid from XYZ supplier
over the phone for the $8000 worth of merchandise necessary for your
fulfillment of a lucrative contract. You accept the bid, hang up the phone,
and come up with your total cost after considering XYZ's bid, your costs,
and a reasonable profit. You then call your buyer, B, who accepts immediately. You're elated. Three days later a quick memo arrives from B,
confirming the conversation and stating the agreed-on quantity ordered.
Three weeks later you call XYZ, and they can't honor the bid. Can you sue
XYZ? Can you opt out of your agreement with B?

You can't sue XYZ. Except for some exceptions which we'll discuss later,
a contract for the sale of goods for the price of $500 or more is *voidable*
unless in writing signed by the party to be charged for its fulfillment.[20]
The contract is voidable rather than void, because your supplier still has
the option to fulfill its moral obligation on the oral agreement. But, your
supplier is not legally bound to fulfill without a written confirmation.[21]

You won't be able to avoid your contract with B—even if your lawyer found it missing a material term such as the price or even if it wasn't signed by you or by B (unless you can prove that availability of your supplies from XYZ is a material term). A contract for the sale of goods need not contain *all* material terms (just the quantity term), and the material terms need not be precisely stated. The only requirement is that the writing afford a basis for believing that there is a real transaction resulting from the oral evidence—the phone calls plus the memo from B.[22] The memo need not have been signed! A memo containing B's letterhead, quantity designation, and other identifying criteria is a sufficient writing confirming the contract.[23]

Again, there is a special section for merchants. You didn't have to sign an acceptance to B's letter. If you as the party to be charged are a merchant and you receive a writing in confirmation of your oral sales contract, this confirmation binds you unless you *object within 10 days*.[24] If you had seen your attorney concerning this matter, you'd have been told to follow up your conversation with XYZ; if XYZ didn't object within 10 days, you could hold it to the agreement as B is holding you.

Other exceptions to the statute of frauds are:

1. Partial acceptance and/or partial payment for the goods. The goods that are paid for are not covered by the statute, but the balance of the unpaid goods is.[25] However, the acceptance of part of any commercial unit is an acceptance of the entire unit. A commercial unit is a unit which by commercial usage is a single whole for the purpose of a sale, depending on the relevant market.[26]
2. An admission by the party against whom enforcement of the contract is sought and *only* to the extent of the quantity of goods admitted.[27]
3. A substantial beginning in manufacturing or procurement of special goods for the buyer before you receive a notice of repudiation from the buyer. In this case, the contract is enforceable despite the lack of a writing.[28]

PAROL EVIDENCE RULE

In your contracts you'll often seen the familiar "integration clause," which generally states that "this instrument contains the entire agreement between the seller and buyer and no statement, promise, or inducements made by either party or agent of either party that is not contained in this written agreement shall be valid or binding; and this agreement may not be enlarged, modified or altered except in writing signed by both the seller and the buyer and endorsed hereon." This may or may not be to your advantage. If it is, then your written agreement is the complete and exclusive statement of the terms of the agreement. If the wording of the integration clause is not in the agreement, then the agreement is not to be taken as including all matters agreed upon. You may be able to later get in evidence of prior written or oral agreements or consistent additional terms as well as the opportunity to explain or interpret by oral evidence your current terms bv demonstrating usage of trade, course of dealings, or course of performance.[29]

Discuss this subject carefully with your attorney. If you need a narrow contract, your attorney will carefully negate the permissible introduction of anything but that within the contract. If you need greater flexibility now or anticipate that you might as your marketing effort develops, advise your attorney accordingly.

UNCONSCIONABILITY

Another way of challenging the validity of a contractual clause or perhaps even the entire contract is to demonstrate, in cases of "extreme overreaching," that the matter in question is unconscionable. The basic test is whether, in the light of the general commercial climate then existing and within the framework of a particular transaction, the clauses involved are so one-sided that they are unconscionable as of the *time of making the contract*.[30]

This time qualification is important, because the UCC is not interested in propping up poor negotiators or someone who simply blew a deal. For example, making a too-low bid due to miscalculation isn't enough—the court won't rescue you from a negligent mistake which may not be initially apparent but which becomes obvious as the transaction proceeds.[31]

A court wants to see real pain suffered in a situation of disparate bargaining posture. This setting can defeat the necessary mutuality of agreement and obligation. A good working definition of a rule of thumb is contained in the court's decision in a case involving a *consumer* who couldn't speak English, much less read and understand the fine-print terms: "the doctrine of unconscionability is used by the courts to protect those who are unable to protect themselves and to prevent injustice. . . . Unequal bargaining powers and the absence of meaningful choice on the part of one of the parties, together with contract terms which unreasonably favor the other party *may* spell out unconscionability."[32]

Whenever you wish to preserve the general contract but have reservations about any clause, discuss with your counsel adding in a paragraph such as "The doctrine of severability shall be applied to this agreement. In the event that any term of this agreement is declared illegal, void, or unenforceable, such declaration shall not affect or impair the other terms." A court may second-guess you on a particular clause; if it is severable, it may be able to save the rest of the contract. The downside is, of course, that if you don't want the contract without that paragraph, then you don't want the severability option included.

SOME CONTRACTUAL GAP FILLERS

We've emphasized the UCC's flexibility as well as its desire to uphold the intent of the parties. As you know from experience, it is a rare sales contract which satisfies every term which might come back to haunt you. The following are a few more ways the UCC will step in and help once it has established that all parties have an "agreement to agree."

Open price. When your contract is silent as to price it is assumed that both parties intended a reasonable price at the time of delivery.[33] If the price is to be fixed by the seller or buyer, then such price must be set in good faith.[34]

Open quantity terms. As we discussed earlier, a contract must specify the quantity you're selling or purchasing to satisfy the statute of frauds. However, the quantity need not be specified in numerical figures. An agreement that your buyer will purchase all requirements from you for a defined period is a "valid requirements contract."[35] Likewise, your buyer may agree to take *all* goods produced by you from a specific production unit during a given period of time. This is a "valid output contract."[36]

Single lots. If the parties are silent in their agreement, the UCC requires them to make delivery in a single-lot shipment. Note that a commercial unit is a single whole for purposes of a sale. For example, the seller ships a commercial unit of 10 watches; the buyer returns 4. The seller need not accept, because if the buyer accepts any item in a commercial unit, the buyer accepts *all* the items in the unit.[37]

Place of delivery. If the parties are silent and delivery by carrier is *not* an issue,[38] the place of delivery is the seller's place of business or, if none exists, the seller's residence.[39]

Time of delivery. If the parties are silent then a reasonable time for delivery is implied. Such reasonable time must be determined by the good-faith commercial standards of your industry.[40]

Time of payment or credit. If the parties are silent, payment and delivery are concurrent conditions. Payment is due at the time and place at which your buyer is to receive the goods, that is, where your buyer takes physical possession of the goods.[41] If delivery is authorized and made by documents (e.g., bills of lading or warehouse receipts)[42] then payment is due at the time and place that your buyer receives the documents.[43] The credit period begins to run from the date of shipment, subject to verifiable delays.[44]

Open shipping arrangements. If the parties are silent, the duty to make shipping arrangements falls on the seller.[45]

Although the courts will read these significant gap fillers into an agreement when it appears that the parties intended an enforceable contract, sloppy work on your part or your failure to review your agreement with counsel is not encouraged. The more gaps you permit, the more difficult establishing a bona fide contractual intent will be.

If you are reading this chapter en toto, refer back to Section 3's chapter on warranties (Chapter 3), which discusses UCC requirements.

COMMERCIAL DELIVERY OBLIGATIONS

Your invoices may contain myriad shipment terms. For nonmaritime contracts the leading shorthand you'll see is FOB (free on board).[46] There are varied uses for the term, but the most common are the following:

FOB point of shipment. If this is specified in the contract, the seller must bear only the risk and expense of bringing the goods into the possession of the carrier.[47] The seller does not bear the expense of loading.[48] As a seller this is the wording you want.

FOB carrier. This wording means that the seller is obligated to bear the expense and risk to have the goods loaded on board.[49]

FOB destination. This wording obligates the seller to bear the expense and risk of having the goods brought to the point of destination. This is the language your buyer wants.[50]

If the agreement is silent, the UCC will read in a point-of-shipment contract. If you don't want this, make sure you specify what you want in your contract. Remember that at all times the parties are free to prescribe terms and conditions of delivery which are controlling.

As a seller one final protection you might like to have your counsel draft into your contract is a "no arrival, no sale" clause, which means that you promise to ship conforming goods but you assume no obligation for the actual arrival of the goods, unless you are responsible for their nonarrival.[51]

"SALE ON APPROVAL" AND "SALE OR RETURN"

In a sale on approval, you deliver your goods to a potential purchaser for examination. This is a bailment relationship; the bailee (seller) has the option to purchase. Title to the goods does not pass until the option is exercised by an indicated approval or until the expiration of a reasonable time, when a time limit for approval has not been agreed upon. This presupposes both an actual receipt by your buyer as well as a reasonable opportunity to inspect the goods. This is a tricky area. For instance, a coin dealer sent his samples to a customer by registered mail. A so-called unknown person signed the receipt. The coin dealer argued that the buyer received them and that registered mail was adequate protection. Not so, said the court—a buyer must actually take delivery *and* accept.[52]

In a purchase subject to return, the goods belong to the buyer until she or he acually returns them. Any loss or damage to the goods while in the buyer's possession falls on the buyer. If the buyer elects to return the goods, they must be returned in their original condition with the buyer bearing risk and expense.[53]

SELLER'S PERFORMANCE OBLIGATIONS

The doctrine of substantial performance does not apply to a contract for the sale of goods[54] except when specifically modified.[55] If the goods or tender of delivery fail in any respect to conform to the contract, "the buyer may reject the whole, accept the whole, or accept part and reject part."[56]

To satisfy proper delivery, the seller must put and hold goods conforming to the contract at its buyer's disposition as well as give the buyer any notification reasonably necessary to enable the buyer to take delivery.[57] If the seller's original tender of the goods is rejected as nonconforming and the time for performance has not yet expired, the seller may promptly notify the buyer of an intention to "cure" and then, within the contract time for performance, make a conforming delivery.[58] This option is available even when the seller has taken back the nonconforming goods and refunded the purchase price.

You also have the right to cure after expiration because of a "surprise rejection," when the seller's tender was nonconforming but the seller had good reason to believe it would be accepted. The reasonable grounds might be prior course of dealings or trade usage. Also, there is good-faith common sense, such as where the buyer ordered an older model hearing aid. The seller sent the new model, believing the buyer would want it. Upon rejection, the seller may cure even after the expiration date.[59] Make sure that you retain your insurance coverage for the goods during the cure effort.[60]

Unless specified otherwise in your contract, the buyer has a right to inspect the goods before payment or acceptance unless the goods are sent COD (cash on delivery) or the buyer pays against an order bill of lading. Inspection expenses are borne by the buyer but will be recovered from you (the seller) if the goods don't conform and are rejected.[61]

BUYER'S REMEDIES UPON BREACH

We've discussed your buyer's rights upon improper delivery, but there are other rights you should be aware of.

EXERCISE THE RIGHT OF REJECTION. Notification to the seller of rejection must be done within a reasonable time after delivery or tender. An exercise of ownership by the buyer is wrongful and destroys the effect of the rejection if the seller decides to treat it as an acceptance. If rightfully rejected, the buyer's duty to pay never arises, the goods remain the seller's property, and risk of loss also remains with the seller. The buyer is required to hold the goods with reasonable care at the seller's disposition for a time sufficient to enable the seller to remove them (the buyer is now a bailee for the seller).[62]

If the seller fails to provide reasonable instructions to the buyer, the buyer may store the goods on the seller's account, reship them, or resell the goods for the seller's account. At all times the buyer has a security interest in the goods to the extent of the down payment. However, the buyer must maintain records in case the seller demands an accounting.[63]

REVOKE PRIOR ACCEPTANCE. When revoking prior acceptance, the original acceptance might have been on documents. On inspection the buyer notices a latent, substantial, or material defect not observable sooner. The buyer must immediately notify the seller, and the content of such notification should identify the particular goods revoked, setting forth the nonconformity in detail.[64] A buyer who so revokes has the same rights and duties with regard to the goods as if they were rejected outright. Here the risk of loss is on the seller only to the extent of any insurance deficiency of the buyer.

EXERCISE THE RIGHT TO COVER. The buyer may in good faith and without unreasonable delay make a reasonable purchase of or contract to purchase goods in substitution. The buyer may receive as damages the difference between the cost of cover and the contract price together with incidental and consequential damages.[65] The cost of cover applies even if the buyer makes a substitute purchase that wasn't identical to the goods originally ordered.[66]

SUE FOR WARRANTY BASED ON BREACH OF CONTRACT. This option is available after the goods have been accepted and the time for revocation of acceptance has elapsed. The buyer may recover for the difference of the value of the goods accepted and the value they would have had if they were as warranted.[67]

RECOVER THE GOODS. When the seller repudiates or fails to deliver or when the goods are unique, the buyer may obtain specific performance or replevy the goods designated as the ones to be delivered under the contract of sale.[68]

SELLER'S REMEDIES UPON BREACH

The following are significant remedies available to the seller.

WITHHOLD DELIVERY OF GOODS.   If the buyer wrongfully rejects or revokes, then the seller may withhold any of the undelivered goods.[69]

RESELL AND RECOVER DAMAGES.   Resale is to be done in good faith in a commercially accepted reasonable manner. The seller may recover the difference between the resale price and contract price plus incidental damages *less* expenses saved because of the buyer's breach. If the goods were of the inventory type (cars or other goods of an "unlimited inventory"), the seller may be entitled to lost profits. If you regularly deal in goods of any kind (assuming you aren't selling a one-of-a-kind Picasso), discuss with your counsel whether you can recover the profits you would have made if the contract had been completed.[70]

RIGHTS INHERENT TO BOTH PARTIES

Whether you be a buyer or seller, the following remedies may be available to you.

RIGHT TO ADEQUATE ASSURANCE OF PERFORMANCE.   With bankruptcy courts doing a booming business, you don't want to be left holding the bag as a general creditor. The UCC also does not want the commercial world to slow down anticipating insolvency by their counterparts in sales transactions.

When reasonable grounds for financial or credit insecurity arise with respect to your buyer *or* seller, you may demand adequate assurance of due performance. Until you receive such assurance, you may suspend further performance. If you don't receive a response within 30 days, you may treat this as an automatic repudiation of the contract. Any acceptance of an improper delivery or payment does not prejudice your right to demand adequate assurances of future performances. As between merchants, the courts will look to what assurances are customary in the trade.[71]

If the seller *first* learns of the buyer's insolvency while the goods are in transit (including those in the possession of any bailee), the seller may stop such goods and also reclaim the goods upon demand within 10 days (or possibly 90 if the buyer had misrepresented solvency in writing) after their receipt by the buyer. Henceforth the seller may refuse to send all deliveries except for those made for cash.[72]

ANTICIPATORY REPUDIATION. An unconditional repudiation by either party as to its future performance is a breach of the contract. The aggrieved party has three options:

1. To await performance by the repudiating party for a commercially reasonable period of time.[73]
2. To resort to *any* legal remedy even while awaiting the repudiating party's retraction.
3. In either case to suspend performance. If the aggrieved seller is in the process of manufacturing to the buyer's order, the seller may complete the manufacturing process and identify the goods for the contract or cease manufacture and resell for salvage value.[74]

CONCLUSION

This chapter has given you a brief look at the dynamics that affect various physical handling relationships and commercial arrangements entered into on a regular basis. The law will definitely impact a manager's strategic channel decisions. The references provide valuable follow-up.

An informed professional understands the need to consult with experts in particular fields. These transactions require a counsel who is familiar with your firm, its trade (e.g., reference as to trade, custom, and usage), and the law. No guidebook can do you a better service than to urge you to consult with counsel as you enter these transactions to avoid the varied problems that can result. If problems result anyway, you have an expert familiar with the transaction since its inception.

REFERENCES

[1] U.C.C. sec. 2-102.* Hereafter all references to the U.C.C., unless otherwise specified, refer to U.C.C. Article 2—"Sales as defined in 2-101." The sale itself consists in the passing of title from the seller to the buyer for a price, U.C.C. secs. 2-103(1)(a), -103(1)(d), -106(1). *See also* Bonebaker v. Cox 499 F.2d 951 (1974).

[2] The U.C.C. has been adopted by 49 of the 50 states (Louisiana is the exception).

[3] U.C.C. sec. 1-102 comment 1.

[4] U.C.C. sec. 1-102(3).

[5] U.C.C. sec. 2-105, which should be read with sec. 2-107. *See* U.C.C. sec. 2-105(1) (when "identification occurs" if you don't have an "explicit agreement" between the parties evidencing same).

[6] U.C.C. sec. 2-104(1).

[7] U.C.C. sec, 2-302.

[8] In general, this discussion assumes that you're marketing or selling, so that the discussion is from a seller's perspective.

[9] U.C.C. secs. 2-204, -207(3), -311(1).

[10] A proper reading of a sales contract requires a full review of the general trade background (U.C.C. sec. 1-205) and the particular trade dealings between the buyer and seller (U.C.C. secs. 1-205, 2-208). These realities, not merely a written contract, will structure the agreement. *See also* U.C.C. secs. 1-201(1) and -201(3).

[11] U.C.C. sec. 2-206(1)(a).

[12] U.C.C. sec. 2-206(1)(b).

[13] U.C.C. sec. 2-205.

[14] U.C.C. sec. 2-204(3).

[15] U.C.C. sec. 2-207(2). *See also* Trust Co. Bank v. Barrett Distribs. Inc., 459 F. Supp. 959 (1978). As a practical matter, be aware that many of your buyers have "magic language" in their purchase forms which *automatically* objects to additional or different terms.

[16] Coastal Indus., Inc. v. Automatic Steam Prods. Corp., 654 F.2d 375, 378 (1981). Note: Where both parties are merchants, nonmaterial terms are accepted by silence. However, if the terms are material, silence is not an acceptance.

[17] *Id.* at 379. *See also* Fairfield-Noble Corp. v. Pressman-Gutman Co., 475 F. Supp. 899 (1979).

[18] U.C.C. sec. 2-207(3). Again, the clear pattern and intent of article 2 is to recognize and uphold a contract where there is evidence of intent to contract. *See also* Clifford-Jacobs Forging Co. v. Capital Eng'g & Mfg. Co., 437 N.E.2d 22 (1982).

[19] U.C.C. secs. 1-205, 2-208(2).

[20] U.C.C. sec. 2-201(1). Note the emphasis on the tangible price. The UCC does not look to the more intangible "value."

[21] C. G. Campbell & Son, Inc. v. COMDEQ Corp., 586 S.W.2d 40 (1979). Note: The social policy for the statute of frauds is to prevent fraud or perjury on claims of substance.

---

*Note that all references to the U.C.C. are to the official text. In drafting your agreements, your counsel will also consult applicable state law that contains local variations of these sections

[22] U.C.C. sec. 2-201. *See also* Iandoli v. Asiatic Petro Co., 57 A.D.2d 815, 395 N.Y.S.2d 15 (1977).

[23] Alarm Device Mfg. Co. v. Arnold Indus. Inc., 417 N.E.2d 1284 (1979).

[24] U.C.C. secs. 2-104(1,3), 2-210(2).

[25] U.C.C. sec. 2-201(3)(c). *See* Starr v. Freeport Dodge 54 Misc. 2d 271, 282 N.Y.S.2d 58 (1967). Part payment for an automobile constitutes payment for the *entire* automobile.

[26] U.C.C. secs. 2-105(6), 2-201, 2-606.

[27] U.C.C. sec. 2-201(3)(b).

[28] U.C.C. sec. 2-201(3)(a).

[29] U.C.C. sec. 2-202. A writing intended as the final expression of the parties' agreement cannot be contradicted but may be explained or supplemented by consistent additional terms, course of dealings, usage of trade or business, or prior course of performance.

[30] U.C.C. sec. 2-302. *See also* Industralease v. R.M.E. Enter., 58 A.D.2d 482, 396 N.Y.S.2d 427 (1977).

[31] Tierney, Inc. v. T. Wellington Carpets, Inc., 392 N.E.2d 1066 (1979). For a decision on how to get out of a mistake, see Confrancesco Const. Co. v. Superior Components, Inc., 371 S.W.2d 821 (1963). At a minimum you'll have to demonstrate a nonnegligent unilateral mistake accompanied by other facts, such as a typographical error of price which is both out of line and obvious to the other party, *and* that the other party is not injured by the cancellation.

[32] Brooklyn Union Gas Co. v. Jiminez, 82 Misc. 2d 948, 951, 371 N.Y.S.2d. 289, 292 (1975). (Emphasis my own).

[33] U.C.C. sec. 2-305(1).

[34] U.C.C. sec. 2-305(2). A proper reading of a sales contract always requires a full review of the general trade background (U.C.C. sec. 1-205) and the particular trade dealings between buyer and seller (U.C.C. secs. 1-205, 2-208).

[35] U.C.C. sec. 2-306(1).

[36] U.C.C. sec. 2-306(1).

[37] U.C.C. sec. 2-307.

[38] *See* U.C.C. sec. 2-504 which controls, not 2-308.

[39] U.C.C. sec. 2-308.

[40] U.C.C. secs. 1-203, 1-204, 2-103, 2-309. *See also* Capital Steel Co. v. Foster and Creighton Co., 574 S.W.2d 256 (1981).

[41] U.C.C. sec. 2-310(a).

[42] U.C.C. sec. 2-103(1)(c).

[43] U.C.C. sec. 2-310(c).

[44] U.C.C. sec. 2-310(d).

[45] U.C.C. sec. 2-311(2).

[46] For "F.A.S.," "C.I.F.," or "C & F," see U.C.C. secs. 2-319(2), -320.

[47] Carrier obligations were discussed earlier in this chapter.

[48] U.C.C. sec. 2-319(1)(a).

[49] U.C.C. sec. 2-319(c).

[50] U.C.C. sec. 2-319(1)(b).

[51] U.C.C. secs. 2-324, 2-613.

[52] U.C.C. secs. 2-326(1)(a), 2-327(1)(a)–2-327(1)(c) and First Coin Investors v. Coppola, 88 Misc. 2d 495, 388 N.Y.S.2d 833 (1976). Sale on approval has similarities to consignment sales. As to consignments, see Glossary.

[53] U.C.C. secs. 2-326(1)(b), -327(2)(a), -327(2)(b).

[54] "Substantial performance" requires a buyer, under certain circumstances, to accept something less than perfectly conforming tender. *See* Moulton Cavity & Mould, Inc. v. Lyn-Flex Indus. Inc., 396 A.2d 1024 (1979).

[55] U.C.C. sec. 2-612 (substantial performance permitted in installment sales contracts).

[56] U.C.C. sec. 2-601.

[57] U.C.C. sec. 2-503(1).

[58] U.C.C. sec. 2-508(1).

[59] U.C.C. sec. 2-508(2); Bartus v. Riccardi, 55 Misc. 2d 3, 284 N.Y.S.2d 222 (1967).

[60] U.C.C. sec. 2-509(3); Ramos v. Wheel Sports Center, 96 Misc. 2d 646, 409 N.Y.S.2d 505 (1978).

[61] U.C.C. sec. 2-513(1)(b).

[62] U.C.C. secs. 2-510(1), 2-602. Again, you must be careful as to your position in these areas, since the UCC prefers to uphold contracts. Carefully review any rejection agreements with your counsel before acting to your possible prejudice.

[63] Kleiderfabrik v. Peters Sportswear Co., 483 F. Supp. 1228 (1980). U.C.C. secs. 2-602, -604, -706(6).

[64] U.C.C. secs. 2-106(2), -606(1)(b), -607, -608. *See also* Lynx, Inc. v. Ordance Prods. Inc., 327 A.2d 502 (1974). Note: If the use of the goods is necessary to allow proper evaluation of them, such use does not constitute acceptance (U.C.C. secs. 2-606, -608. *See also* United Airlines, Inc. v. Conductron Corp. 387 N.E. 1272 (1979).

[65] U.C.C. sec. 2-715; Lowes Glove Co. v. Acme Fast Freight Co., 54 Misc. 2d 429, 282 N.Y.S.2d 869 (1967). *See also* U.C.C. secs. 2-712(1), 2-712(3); American Carpet Mills v. Grinny Corp., 649 F.2d 1056 (1981).

[66] U.C.C. secs. 2-711, -725; Thorstenson v. Mobridge Iron Works Co., 208 N.W.2d 715 (1973).

[67] U.C.C. sec. 2-714.

[68] U.C.C. sec. 2-716. *See also* sec. 2-502.

69 U.C.C. sec. 2-609, -610, -703(a).

70 U.C.C. sec. 2-706.

71 U.C.C. sec. 2-609 (defines insolvency).

72 U.C.C. sec. 2-702(1)(b).

73 Such party can retract its anticipatory repudiation, subject to U.C.C. sec. 2-611.

74 U.C.C. secs. 2-610(a)–2-610(c), 2-704(2).

CHAPTER
NINE
YOUR GUIDE TO DIRECT-MARKETING LEGAL COMPLIANCE___

Electronics and computer science will so revolutionize the art of direct marketing that this channel will dominate marketing in the next century. What is direct marketing? Who is a direct marketer? Henry R. Hoke, Jr., who runs a leading think tank in the field, sets forth a flowchart in each of his magazines.[1] Specifically, "direct marketing is an interactive system of marketing which uses one or more advertising media to effect a measurable response and/or transaction at any location." Hoke has defined a direct marketer as "one who owns and maintains a mailing list, used to support any and all methods of selling. The list is the cornerstone."[2]

Detractors often dismiss this channel as "junk mail." It's a little more than that, of course, encompassing interactive cable, videotext, 800 numbers, etc. By 1988 you'll see $250 billion in marketing growth.

More important, however, is its ability to enable entrepreneurs with a little capital to rapidly enter national markets. One graphic way to demonstrate the power of direct mail is to look at its influence in politics. The conservative movement's unique mastery of the art of political communication through direct mail enabled it to dominate politics during 1977 to 1980. As the leading creative genius in the field, Richard Viguerie, stated:

> Direct mail has been our basic form of communication. The liberals have had control not only of all three branches of government, but of the major universities, the three major networks, the biggest newspapers, the news

weeklies, and Hollywood. . . . Fortunately, or rather providentially, a whole new technology has become available just in time—direct mail, backed by computer science, has allowed us to bypass all the media controlled by our adversaries.[3]

This channel's potential is unlimited, but you must know the rules. We'll review here a few rules of the most interest which form a vital core to managers using this channel. For a more in-depth study, see Robert J. Posch, Jr., *The Direct Marketer's Legal Adviser.*[4] After you read it, place it into the hands of your associates who need to know the basics of legal compliance.

THE MAILSTREAM OF COMMERCE

Direct marketers have less difficulty than most in determining the length of the product-marketing channel needed to reach their markets. No matter how rapidly your customer registers the desire to purchase your product or even pays (e.g., instantaneous electronic fund transfer), you must contend with the delivery constraints of the U.S. Postal Service or a private carrier.[5] Intermediaries are few, although drop shippers may be used. Once the direct marketer was mainly concerned with postal regulations and costs and with physical distribution management. Recently, however, four major areas of compliance have arisen: The 30-day rules, the unordered-merchandise statutes, "dry testing," and merchandise substitution.

With increases in costs for almost all aspects of mail-order selling (e.g., postage, printing, and the goods themselves), most firms have cut back on inventories. As a result, they can't always fill incoming orders promptly. Further, some marginal companies caught in the vise of inflation have sought interest-free, or "dry," loans, that is, holding their cash flow vis-à-vis fulfillment for as long as possible.

The FTC and many states have enacted 30-day rules or laws.[6] These state laws must be consulted, especially the laws of the state in which your corporation is located. Note 5 of the FTC rule specifically states that the FTC does not wish to preempt consistent but narrower state laws on point. Therefore, you may find that your firm must comply with a narrower state law. For our purposes, we'll focus on the FTC rules.[7]

THE 30-DAY RULE

The FTC's mail-order rule was adopted in 1976; it will be enforced literally, and penalties up to $10,000 may be issued for each violation.

Since it is only 3½ pages long, it is worth your time to review it. It is written for the layperson and avoids legalese. It boils down to three key areas:

1. Initial solicitation requirements
2. First-delay and multiple-delay notification
3. Internal procedures

INITIAL SOLICITATION.   It is an unfair or deceptive act to solicit *any* order through the mails unless you have a reasonable basis (arrived at in good faith, with objective substantiation) to believe you can fulfill the order within the time you specify or, if no time is specified, within 30 days after the receipt of a *properly completed* order from your buyer.

What is reasonable is reflected by the variables of your industry, product, and market—an issue affected by the interplay of many considerations. We all know the value of a dollar in hand and the retention of same. The FTC also understands the "float" value of money and doesn't want your customers providing you with interest-free loans. Your best protection as to your good faith and reasonable expectations at the time of solicitation is to maintain an organized system of written, internal records which will objectively validate your expectations.

Remember, however, that *you* elect to become involved with the 30-day aspect of this rule. You can insulate yourself from the problems here if you state at the outset a date you can live with clearly and conspicuously on your promotion piece. You might state "90 days from receipt of order" or "allow 13 weeks for shipment." Then there is no first-delay problem until 90 days have elapsed—not 30. The trade-off here might be a loss of "spontaneity," since customers might be discouraged by a long wait. The choice is yours.

You also elect to come within the provisions of this rule by accepting cash orders. An alternative is to bill only by outside credit cards (may help your bad debt, too) or by a system of internal credit adjustments or even COD. In none of these cases will you bill before delivery, and, therefore, in none of these cases will you be affected by the 30-day rule. Further, if you don't use the mail, the rule does not apply. For example, orders made by telephone and charged to a credit card account after shipment are *not* covered since the mail is not used to finalize the sale.

Finally, there are ways to decrease potential legal problems as well as customer dissatisfaction. A customer complaint to the FTC, a state attorney general's office, or better business bureau is not helpful even if totally unjustified. Such complaints attract unwanted attention to your firm and may accumulate. Examine the following as possible ways to decrease complaints:

1. Don't wait until checks clear. The 30-day meter is running. Test whether this delay is resulting in 30-day shipment problems. If so, does the trade-off vis-à-vis your bad debt picture justify this practice?
2. Test different post offices or even the time of day that you ship (if this option is available to you). Your legal requirement is to ship—not deliver—within 30 days. Legally, your customer must then contend with the inherent delays in the U.S. Postal Service or some other system of distribution you employ. However, your customer only knows that he or she is waiting. Maximizing your deliveries by finding the best post office (and they vary) will enhance goodwill and avoid complaints to the regulatory agencies.
3. Remember that the 30-day meter only begins after you receive in-house a *properly completed order*. The order is properly completed when you receive payment and all the information you need to fill the order. If you write back to your customers, make sure you keep a record. You'd be wise to retain a copy of the incomplete order and to refrain from cashing any checks. Customers may forget that the initial delay was not prompted by you but by them. When they complain to you or any agency, it will satisfy that you both filled the order and shipped it within the required time once a properly completed order was returned.

The rule applies to *all* mail-order transactions; this includes transactions between businesses as well as consumers.

FIRST-DELAY SITUATIONS. The reality of any marketplace is that unanticipated delays occur, such as a welcome deluge of orders or a simple delay by your supplier. When you are unable to ship the merchandise within the applicable time (i.e., the specific time you stated in your promotion or 30 days if no time is specified), you have the option to cancel the agreement and to so inform your buyer or attempt to preserve the sale.

To preserve the sale, you must send a *postage-paid* return option notice to the buyer as soon as you first become aware of the shipping delay. The option notice must clearly and conspicuously offer the buyer the choice either to cancel the order and receive a full and prompt refund or to extend the time for shipment to a revised shipping date. The notice must inform your buyer that nonresponse is considered consent to the delay. You must have a reasonable basis on which to base this revised shipping date. Tactically, you have an advantage here, since inertia is in your favor.

If the buyer does not answer at all, you get up to an additional 30-day delay.

What if you are unable to provide a revised shipping date? If you simply don't know when the goods will be available for shipping, your notice must state that you cannot determine when the merchandise will be shipped. It must also state that the order will be automatically canceled unless (1) you do not receive your customer's cancellation before shipment (within 30 days of the original shipping date) or (2) you receive within 30 days of the original date your customer's consent to the delay.

This is also required if the definite revised shipping date is more than 30 days after the original date. When you are unable to provide a revised shipping date, you must inform your customers of their continuing right to cancel the order by notifying you prior to actual shipment.

Don't attempt to improve upon the prepaid reply device (postcard or letter). You may feel an 800 number is more spontaneous and actually a greater benefit in facilitating the customer's response, but the standards you must meet in compliance are much tougher. Further, you've lost some of the "inertia" advantage, and the free and immediate access to an 800 number may encourage more cancellations. The postage-paid factor is very important, since buyers must not have to exercise their rights at the penalty of even a first-class stamp!

MULTIPLE-DELAY SITUATIONS. You may obtain as much as 60 days grace in fulfilling an order unless the buyer specifically returns the postage-paid notice requesting a refund. The buyer's silence is construed as an acceptance of the delay.

If, after 60 days, there remains some unanticipated delay (e.g., a strike), you might still be able to save the order. The 30-day rule will allow further delays in certain limited circumstances.

You must notify the buyer of the additional delay. You may request the buyer's permission to ship at a certain specified future date or even a vague, indefinite date. The renewed-option notice (again prepaid postage) must inform customers that they must respond or their order will be canceled. Your buyer may then cancel or may agree to extend the time for delivery. At this time you must also notify buyers that if they consent to the delay, they may still cancel at any subsequent time by notifying the seller prior to the actual shipment. The buyer may then cancel or agree to extend the time for delivery.

This renewed-option notice situation is most distinguishable from the first-delay option notice insofar as silence by the buyer cannot be construed as acceptance. If the buyer remains "silent" (that is, fails to return the postage-paid card), then you must treat the order as canceled and return a refund promptly to the buyer.

What is a prompt refund? This depends on the payment option elected. If the buyer sends cash or a check, the buyer is entitled to have mailed first class a refund in full within 7 business days. If a credit card or other form of credit adjustment is required, then you have a full billing cycle from the date on which the buyer's right to a refund begins. All refunds are to be sent by first-class mail and returned in the form received where practical, that is, if cash was received, a return check would be permissible and prudent. Under no circumstances are credit vouchers or scrip permitted.

INTERNAL PROCEDURES.   The mail-order rule stresses the need for adequate systems and procedures to create a presumption of a good-faith effort to satisfy customer inquiries and/or complaints. These systems and procedures should also be adequate to establish the basis of your good-faith business judgment upon which to solicit the initial order to request a delay. The lack of such systems and procedures creates a rebuttable presumption that your firm failed to comply.

The rule does not apply to negative option forms of selling governed by the FTC's negative option rule or to magazine sales (except for the initial shipment), COD orders, orders for seeds and growing plants, mail-order photo-finishing, or credit orders where the buyer's account is not charged before you ship the merchandise.

DRY TESTING

As discussed, the social policy behind the mail-order merchandise rule was to discourage the practice of dry loans. We also stressed that the FTC considers it an unfair or deceptive act to solicit an order through the mails unless you have a reasonable basis to believe you can fulfill the order within a certain time. In light of all this, can you still "dry test" (i.e., solicit for a product before it even tangibly exists)? Interestingly, the answer is yes—in certain circumstances.

There is limited law on point, but you should be aware of FTC advisory opinion no. 753 7003:[8]

> [T]he Commission does not object to the use of dry-testing a continuity book series marketed by mail order as long as the following conditions are observed:

1. No representation, express or implied, is made in advertisements, brochures, or other promotional material, which has the *tendency or capacity* to mislead the public into believing that the books have been or will definitely be published, or that by expressing an interest in receiving the books a prospective purchaser will necessarily receive them.
2. In all solicitations for subscriptions and other promotional material, *clear and conspicuous disclosure* is made of the terms and conditions of the publication, distribution, and other material aspects of the continuity book series program. Such disclosure must provide adequate notice of the *conditional nature* of publication of the book series, i.e., the fact that the book series is only planned and may not actually be published.
3. If the decision is reached to not publish the book series, due notice is given to persons who have subscribed, within a reasonable time after the date of first mailing the solicitations for subscriptions. The *Commission considers four months or less to be a reasonable time,* unless extenuating circumstances exist. If the decision whether or not to publish the book series has not been made within that time period, persons who expressed a desire to subscribe should be notified of the fact that a decision has not yet been reached, and should be given an opportunity to cancel their order.
4. There is no substitution of any books for those ordered.[9]

UNORDERED MERCHANDISE

The problem of unordered merchandise involves a person who receives something that he or she *didn't* order.[10] The law[11] on mailing of unordered merchandise is short and should be read by anyone in the field.[12] This law forbids not only blatant sending of unordered merchandise but also sending of merchandise on approval without your "customer's" prior permission. The FTC specifically warned the mail-order stamp industry of this in 1979.[13]

The only two kinds of merchandise that may be sent through the mails without prior consent are (1) free samples (which must be clearly marked as such) and (2) merchandise mailed by charitable organizations.

However, merchandise mailed by charitable organizations is sent on approval and need not be paid for. Your customer may return it or keep it but need not pay for it.

When in doubt, don't dun. If an innocent error is made (e.g., computer mislabeling), write off the order. The customer won't complain unless an effort is made to compel payment. Your dunning for unordered merchandise can be the trigger for unwanted involvement with the Federal Trade Commission or a state attorney general or simply bad customer relations. Dunning accomplishes this in two ways: (1) the billing or dunning for unordered merchandise is, itself, an unfair trade practice and (2) many customers do not complain to a regulatory body until dunning begins, because they were not aware of the problem and/or violation.

What is the rule concerning the mailing of unordered merchandise and how can you avoid problems with it? We shall review it paragraph by paragraph and then discuss its exceptions.

MAILING OF UNORDERED MERCHANDISE

(a) Except for (1) free samples clearly and conspicuously marked as such, and (2) merchandise mailed by a charitable organization soliciting contributions, the mailing of unordered merchandise or of communications prohibited by subsection (c) of this section constitutes an unfair method of competition and an unfair trade practice in violation of section 45(a)(1) of Title 15 [of the United States Code].

This paragraph quite clearly makes it a per se violation of the unfair trade laws to ship unordered merchandise which is defined as "merchandise mailed without the prior expressed request or consent of the recipient."[14] The only ambiguity here was the reference to "mailed."

Because the original pronouncement referred to the Postal Reorganization Act, some thought that enforcement would be limited to those using the U.S. Postal Service. The FTC clarified its position in 1978 by stating that all unordered merchandise was included whether shipped by mail, United Parcel, other private alternate delivery, or any other carrier.

(b) Any merchandise mailed in violation of subsection (a) of this section, or within the exceptions contained there, may be treated as a gift by the recipient, who shall have the right to retain, use, discard, or dispose of it in any manner he sees fit without any obligation to the sender.

It should be noted that it is a *separate* violation (apart from the initial sending itself) for anyone to mail unordered merchandise without attaching a clear and conspicuous statement informing the recipients that they may treat the merchandise as a gift.

(c) No mailer of any merchandise mailed in violation of subsection (a) of this section, or within the exceptions contained therein, shall mail to any recipient of such merchandise a bill for such merchandise or any dunning communications.

It is a third violation of this statute for any sender of unordered merchandise (including correctly marked free samples and merchandise sent by charitable organizations) to send the recipient any bill or dunning communication (or suggestion of one) in connection with such unordered merchandise.

Again, when in doubt, don't dun. A customer complaint to a regulatory body or a private action (discussed further later) will rarely occur unless an effort is made to compel payment.

Now that we've reviewed the text of the law, a number of questions remain. For example:

1. *What are the penalties?* The penalties for both firms and individuals are up to $10,000 per violation. State laws may carry varied penalties and also may be drawn more narrowly. Review the law for each state in which you're doing business and routinely monitor legislation and regulations in such states.

2. *Must the consumer obtain remedy by complaint to an agency?* No. Congressional intent was to permit consumers to protect themselves under the terms of the unordered-merchandise statute. Among the consumer's remedies is the right to treat the merchandise as an outright gift, with no return obligation.

3. *What if your customer denies the existence of an agreement?* You are in a strong posture if you have a signed order that unequivocally states the contractual relationship to which the individual is subscribing. If the signature was a forgery and/or was contested by the recipient in good faith, you would be on firm ground to request that the customer return the item at your postal expense.

Prior course of dealings, such as a call with follow-up shipment, is not a valid argument when dealing with a consumer on a one-shot basis. Under the UCC (which we discussed in the last section), two merchants can develop such prior course of dealings, but this UCC defense is *not* applicable to this situation. The fact that you have shipped before and the customer has paid for similar items by check or otherwise really proves nothing in this particular instance of shipment.

If you dun, expect problems if the recipient complains to a public body. Your common-law implied contract would probably not be compelling to the FTC or a state regulatory body—although by all means argue it, since it might establish good faith.

The weakest position of all is that of the telephone marketer making "cold call ordering," whereby, without a prior business relationship, the seller ships on order with no confirming documents.[15] There is little possibility of enforcing such a call against a complaint filed under the unordered-merchandise statute. You have no acceptable proof at all of an order. Some ways you might consider protecting yourself include:

a. Send all orders COD so that unordered merchandise might be rejected up-front.

b. Send a postage-paid envelope with the order to encourage those recipients who receive unordered merchandise to return such goods immediately, at no cost to themselves, thereby saving the merchandise itself.

c. Comply with the cooling-off provisions as worded or provide your customer with a follow-up written confirmation which could be responded to in a positive or negative option manner (the former response would probably negate any problems as to cold calls).

d. Follow up all orders with a subsequent phone call confirming the original order. This is still weaker protection (because it is oral) than following points a and b, but if routine, it may prove to an agency that you employ bona fide methods to avoid unordered merchandise problems.

No matter what safeguards you employ, an oral order is *not* a provable order, and this must be considered at all stages—especially before you dun.

4. *How does this statute affect negative option plans?* During the commitment period and at all subsequent times, there is an ongoing business relationship subject to the FTC's rule on point.

Further, the negative option rule permits the sender to ask for its return (but not bill) this one time.[16] Any subsequent shipments constitute unordered merchandise.

5. *What about a continuity plan?* Your rights are less clear as there is no rule on point. You could use a similar approach as to the one isolated shipment after cancellation, but don't dun.

6. *What about substituted merchandise?* The entire area is fraught with peril, even if the substitution is of *equivalent or superior quality*.[17] Artistic property by its very nature is too unique to ever substitute. If a seasonal surge or other unanticipated ordering deluge is overwhelming your inventory reserve, get expressed consent in writing before you substitute. This will save your sale as well as satisfy customers who prefer the substitution to nothing when they need the item by a given date. Substitution without the prior expressed consent or request of the recipient falls within the literal terms of the statute and is considered an unfair trade practice. Finally, where a valid substitution is offered, your customer must be afforded the opportunity to return the item at no postage penalty.

SUMMING UP UNORDERED MERCHANDISE. The federal law on unordered merchandise is short and is written in uncomplicated language. Most states have similar laws on their books, and some such state laws are more narrowly drawn.

Whenever possible, coupons or order forms authorizing the shipment of merchandise to a consumer should be signed and clearly laid out in separate and distinct paragraphs. All wording should be in layperson's English, and the merchandise or purchase plan should be described in detail.

When a serious doubt arises as to the validity of your efforts to recover payment—don't dun.

BEFORE WE HANG UP . . .

This last heading may be a bad pun, but it helps introduce a brief discussion of telephone marketing. Unlike the direct marketer's screen media (cable, teletext, videotext, etc.),[18] the telephone marketer's legal environment is fairly well defined, although this definition wasn't accomplished without a major lobbying and legislative effort by various interested parties![19]

The FTC has a specific cooling-off period rule for door-to-door sellers.[20] Most states have adopted similar language, and many have incorporated telephone sales in their home solicitation sales laws. We have itemized most of the laws in the References.[21] You should review with your counsel the specific wording and impact of these laws. The other area of significant note concerns states regulating automatic dialing devices. Again, the References constitute a wealth of knowledge on point and should be consulted.[22]

REFERENCES

[1] See under "Departments" the "Direct Marketing Flow Chart/Explanation" in each issue of *Direct Marketing*.

[2] Henry R. Hoke, Jr., "Editorial," *Direct Marketing*, July 1982, p. 238.

[3] Richard Viguerie, "Ends and Means," *The New Right Papers*, Robert W. Whitaker (ed.), St. Martin's, New York, 1982, p. 31.

[4] Robert J. Posch, Jr., *The Direct Marketer's Legal Adviser*, McGraw-Hill, New York, 1983.

[5] Robert J. Posch, Jr., "The U.S. Postal Service: Dinosaur or Dynamic Carrier?," *Direct Marketing*, March 1982, pp. 128–131 and Posch, "New Postal Legislation: More Power to the Postal Service," *Direct Marketing*, June 1983, pp. 114–116.

6 For example, review N.Y. Gen. Bus. Law sec. 396(m).

7 See also Robert J. Posch, Jr., "The 30 Day Mail Order Rule: Satisfying FTC, Customers," *Direct Marketing*, December 1981, pp. 84–87.

8 "Dry Testing" and "Bulk Loading" a Continuity Book Series by Mail Order, 85 F.T.C. 1192–97 (1975) (emphasis my own).

9 *Id.* at 1193–94. For a discussion of how to obtain "your own" advisory opinion from the FTC, see Section 6.

10 See also Robert J. Posch, Jr., "Avoiding the Pitfalls of Unordered Merchandise," *Direct Marketing*, January 1982, pp. 98–101.

11 39 U.S.C.S. sec. 3009. New York direct marketers might wish to review N.Y. Gen. Oblig. Law art. 5-332 (McKinney's: 1982).

12 As usual, your reading and familiarizing yourself with a rule of law is no substitute for professional legal advice in a given situation.

13 FTC press release, May 24, 1979.

14 39 U.S.C.S. sec. 3009(d).

15 Such marketer should note that more than 10 states have incorporated such calls into their respective Home Solicitation Laws, requiring a 3-day cooling-off period (see Ref. 21).

16 16 C.F.R. sec. 425.1(b)(1)(iii).

17 For example, see N.Y. Gen. Oblig. Law secs. 396-m(3)(z)(i)–(ii).

18 This area has yet to be completely "shaken out" as to franchising, taxes, obscenity, defamation, and list rental or retrieval. Certain cable advertising areas will be discussed in Section 6. See also Robert J. Posch, Jr., "Cable Marketing Not Yet in Focus," *Direct Marketing*, October 1982, pp. 202–204, and Posch, *The Direct Marketer's Legal Adviser*, McGraw-Hill, New York, 1983.

19 Robert J. Posch, Jr., "Telephone Marketing—It Survived and Prospered!," *Direct Marketing*, September 1982, pp. 106–109.

20 Cooling-Off Period for Door-to-Door Sales, 16 C.F.R. sec. 429. For an interesting discussion of door-to-door regulations in general, *see In re* Encyclopedia Britannica, Inc., 87 F.T.C. sec. 421 (1976).

21 The social policy of the 3-day "cooling-off period" was to allow an individual to reflect after signing a "hard sell" personal contract. State statutes which have acted to cool off the telephone's spontaneity include:

a   Ariz. Rev. Stat. chap. 80, amending secs. 44-5004, -5992, (no threshold amount).

b   Ark. Stat. sec. 70-914 et. seq. (threshold more than $25 in sales).

c   Ind. Code sec. 501 1C 24-4.5-2-501 (applies to consumer *credit* sales in any amount).

d   La. Rev. Stat., Louisiana Consumer Credit Law, tit. 9, sec. 3516, para. 17 (similar to the above although it excludes catalog credit sales).

e   Mich. Comp. Laws sec. 445.111 (threshold figure is sales of *more* than $25).

f   N.D. Cent. Code secs. 51-18-01–51-18-07 (all telephone sales).

g   Ohio—*see* Brown v. Martinelli, 66 Ohio St. 2d 77 (1981) discussing Ohio Rev. Code sec. 1345.21 (telephone solicitation sales must have cooling-off period for all sales *over* $25).

h   Or. Rev. Stat. secs. 83.710, 646.608 (affects sales of $25 or more with certain qualifications).

i   Wyo. Stat. sec. 40194-251 (sales of $25 or more).

There are local ordinances, for example:

a   Sheffield, Ala., Code sec. 18-51.1 (1965).

b   Carlsbad, New Mexico, Ordinance 727 (1972).

c   Bedford, Ohio, Ordinance 4788-78, sec. 719.01(b)(1)(c) (1978).

d   Bedford Heights, Ohio, Ordinance 76-45, sec. 1, para. 733.02 (1976).

e   Alabama Law Enforcement Officers, Inc. v. City of Anniston, 131 So. 897 (1961) [declaring that a municipality (Anniston, Alabama) may declare "unwanted" telephone calls a nuisance].

There are a few select FTC consent orders requiring cooling-off periods for specific firms:

a   United States v. Neighborhood Periodical Club, Inc., Civ. C-2246 (S.D. Ohio 1980) (for various reasons, the defendant was, among other things, fined $150,000).

b   *In re* Commercial Lighting Prods., Inc., 95 F.T.C. 750 (1980).

c   *In re* Perfect Film & Chem. Corp., Perfect Subscription Co. and Keystone Readers' Serv. Inc., 78 F.T.C. 990 (1980).

Finally, at least one state has voluntary guidelines on point: For a booklet detailing same, contact the Virginia Telephone Solicitation Ethics Council, P.O. Box 10011, Richmond, Virginia, 23240. *See also* Va. Code sec. 40.1-112 (regulating the solicitation of book and magazine contracts).

22   a Alaska Stat. secs. 45.50.472(a), .472(b), .472(c) (banning a "telephone call made for the purpose of advertising through the use of a recorded advertisement").

b Arkansas Act 947 of 1981 prohibited the use of automatic dialing systems with recorded messages to make telephone solicitation calls except when initiated by the receiver.

c Cal. Pub. Util., Code, ch. 10 arts. 2871–2875 (certain qualifications placed on "automatic dialing-announcing devices").

d Colo. Rev. Stat. tit. 18, art. 9, pt. 3 (generally bans "cold calls" employing the use of automated dialing systems with prerecorded messages soliciting a purchase of goods or services).

e Fl. Stat. Ann. sec. 365.165 (bans the "use of an automated system for the selection and dialing of telephone numbers and the playing of a recorded message when a connection is completed to the called number").

f Md. Ann. Code art. 78, sec. 55c, (banning the use of automated dialing).

g Mich. Comp. Laws Ann. art. 445.111(a) (bans cold calls using recorded messages).

h Neb. Rev. Stat. sec. 87-302 (requires a permit to make these calls).

i N.C. Gen. Stat. sec. 75-30, ch. 75, sec. 1, art. 1 (regulates but does not ban commercial calls).

j Unlawful Use of Telephone, Va. Code art. 6, sec. 18-2-425.1 (requiring any recorded call to terminate as soon as the receiver hangs up).

k Regulation of Trade, Wis. Stat. Ann. sec. 134.72 (requiring prior consent for prerecorded messages).

FIVE
THE LAW YOU SHOULD KNOW AFFECTING PRICING POLICY___

You have now selected your product, and your distribution channels are in place. The latter will be included in considering your pricing strategy, depending on the markup. Now the price is selected in light of your strategy, and the law.

Economic activity is at its root cooperative, but the antitrust rules are written so that things don't get too cozy. You are expected to set prices and make deals at arm's length. When you meet with friends from other firms or attend trade association meetings, you must always remember that the law goes with you. Penalties for price agreements include fines and jail sentences. People *do* go to jail, and fines are not deductible. Even a suspended sentence can kill a career of otherwise admirable achievement.

In this section we'll examine price-fixing. Then we'll join a hypothetical trade association meeting and see how unwary participants can become involved in antitrust activity through their words, actions, and *lack of* actions. From there we'll proceed through the myriad areas of the Robinson-Patman Act to learn how the law will look at your discriminatory pricing policies. An overview of deceptive pricing will conclude this section.

CHAPTER
TEN
ANTITRUST ISSUES AFFECTING PRICE-FIXING

This chapter addresses issues you will undoubtedly encounter in your career. For a lucid in-depth saturation of the field, I recommend that you read Richard Calkins's fine work.[1] Your best guide to everyday legal compliance is to remember the underlying social policy. Antitrust policy remains rooted in the assumption that free competition will promote optimal economic performance. Therefore, whenever you spot a potential antitrust issue in your career, ask yourself whether the activity you are undertaking will add to or diminish market concentration.

PRICE-FIXING

Price-fixing is an *agreement* among two or more parties on the prices which they will charge for their product or service.[2] The traditional definition is any combination formed for the purpose of and with the effect of raising, depressing, fixing, pegging, or stabilizing prices.

However, it is not necessary to show explicit promises, commitments, or the existence of a written agreement to establish unlawful collusive activity; rather, the term "agreement," as used in antitrust law, means no more than adherence to or participation in a common scheme. Any mutual understanding of this nature, written or oral, explicit or tacit, is illegal. This can include "gentlemen's agreements" and off-the-record conversations as well. Moreover, it is not essential in establishing a violation that the parties actually perform the agreement.

Proof of collusion or agreement can be based on seemingly isolated facts which, when viewed together, present a chain of circumstantial evidence from which an agreement or conspiracy may be inferred. Any discussion or agreement among any parties which would dilute traditional arm's-length bargaining should alert you to possible price-fixing situations. One question to ask is whether price uniformity is developing among competitors, customers, or suppliers. Be aware, also, that not just prices, but any factor influencing prices, such as warranties, discounts or credit, and shipping terms, may not lawfully be the subject of an agreement among competitors.

The following are some questions which frequently confront managers.

1. *What is horizontal price-fixing?* This is a price-fixing agreement or other agreement limiting price competition among competitors on the same (horizontal) level of competition. For example, a horizontal price-fixing conspiracy may be aimed at the elimination of discounters and the raising of prices at which consumers purchase goods.

2. *What is vertical price-fixing?* This is a price-fixing or other agreement limiting price competition with a firm in your distribution channel (for example, a supplier or a wholesaler). For instance, here the conspirators might agree with intermediaries to set resale prices to be charged to third parties.

3. *Will the law treat violators differently?* No. Whether you engage in vertical or in horizontal price-fixing, the penalties will be the same.

4. *What are the penalties?* Section 1 of the Sherman Act is straightforward:

> Every person who shall make any contract or engage in any combination or conspiracy hereby declared to be illegal *shall be deemed guilty of a felony and, on conviction thereof, shall be punished by fine not exceeding one million dollars if a corporation, or, if any other person, one hundred thousand dollars, or be imprisoned not exceeding three years, or by both said punishments,* in the discretion of the court. [Emphasis my own.]

5. *What if I intentionally engage in price-fixing to benefit the consumer?* Any agreement to fix prices or reduce price competition is illegal. This includes agreements which fix prices at lower than market levels, even if the agreement would mean lower prices for the consumer!

6. *What about agreements concerning credit terms among competitors?* It is unlawful for competitors not only to set maximum or minimum prices but to enter into any agreement affecting or relating to credit terms. Again, the key here is "agreement." Exchanges of credit information with competitors are permissible provided that there is no agreement to adopt common credit policies or to refuse to extend credit to any customer.

7. *What if I don't deal directly with competitors?* Your exposure is more limited, but you're not immune. Be alert to your intracorporate activities; there are definite restrictions which limit the freedom with which you can conduct intracorporate matters. The doctrine of intracorporate conspiracy, for purposes of Section 1 of the Sherman Act, treats as separate actors members of the same corporate family, either a parent and its subsidiary or affiliated companies which have a common parent.[3]

The Supreme Court has held that "the fact that there is common ownership or control of the contracting corporations does not liberate them from the impact of the antitrust laws."[4] The courts have held that since you've availed yourself of the privilege of doing business through separate corporations, common ownership (generally) could not save you from any of the obligations that the law imposes on separate entities. There can be an exception if all corporations involved are owned and controlled by one person who makes all decisions for them. A conspiracy involves two or more people. One person acting alone cannot have the requisite "meeting of two or more minds."[5] This exception is commonly referred to as the "sole decision maker rule."

Another area of risk not involving *your* competitors could be multiple customer or franchisee arrangements, in which the courts will deem a horizontal constraint to exist by reason of the acquiescence of the intermediaries for whom you are the source of a common pricing or other distribution policy.

8. *What if we use divisions?* No problem! Divisions are *not* separate legal entities capable of conspiracy. This distinction and the intracorporate conspiracy idea in general have been criticized in legal literature.[6]

9. *Who enforces these laws?* The primary responsibility for enforcing the federal antitrust laws lies with the Antitrust Division of the Department of Justice and the FTC. There is state action under state antitrust laws and some enforcement authority under the federal laws. In addition, private rights of action in injunctions or treble damages are provided, and criminal fines and penalties are covered.

10. *Can consumers sue?* Yes, a private consumer can sue under the antitrust laws. The law states that the illegal conduct must inflict injury directly on the consumer's business or property. If a consumer can demonstrate that he or she paid higher prices because of violations of antitrust laws, then that consumer suffered injury to property (i.e., money) and may have grounds to sue.[7]

11. *What about fair trade laws?* Formerly these laws permitted a manufacturer under certain conditions to establish a minimum resale price for its products. These agreements are now illegal.

CONSPIRACIES AND MONOPOLIES

A conspiracy isn't something that just takes place in a novel, nor does a monopoly mean controlling Boardwalk and Park Place. A look at the Sherman Act in a little more detail explains what constitutes conspiracy and monopolization violations.

A conspiracy has always had an odious connotation in the law, because it establishes that the offense has moved beyond the random act of an individual to an organized group of calculating individuals or institutions. This ability to magnify a violation through a larger body of participants demands that the law act swiftly and punitively. If a price conspiracy is agreed on among competitors, nothing further need be proven to establish a violation of the Sherman Act.

To establish a *conspiracy* in violation of Section 1 of the Sherman Act, your accuser must establish that you and at least one other party conspired to impose unreasonable restraints on interstate commerce. To prove a conspiracy, it must be proved that you and one or more other parties combined to accomplish some unlawful purpose or to accomplish a lawful purpose by unlawful means. The kind of agreement or understanding which existed as to each defendant must also be established. To prove that the parties were involved in a conspiracy in unreasonable restraint of trade, your accuser must show either that any conspiracy that is proved falls within one of the categories of per se offenses (such as price-fixing, group boycotts, or division of markets or customers) or that any such conspiracy is unreasonable when tested by the rule of reason. (For a detailed analysis of these terms, see Section 4, Chapter 5).

The law does not look with favor on overwhelming monopoly power which is consciously acquired, as opposed to monopoly power which is thrust on a firm or is a rational response to underlying economic forces such as scaled economies. *Unlike conspiracy,* monopoly power can be acquired by one firm with an intent to monopolize. No evidence of a conspiracy with other firms is necessary. Monopoly power enables a firm to fix prices on its own initiative without the "need" to depend on or seek out others to achieve this goal through a conspiracy. Overwhelming monopoly power, consciously acquired, necessarily runs afoul of the Sherman Act.

To establish a *monopolization* violation of Section 2 of the Sherman Act, your accuser must establish the existence of a relevant product and geographic market. It must also be shown that you and one or more other parties possessed monopoly power within that relevant market and that you willfully acquired or maintained this power with the intent to monopolize. To establish an *attempt* to monopolize in violation of Section 2 of the Sherman Act, your accuser must establish the existence of a relevant product and geographic market. It must also be proved that you and one or more other parties had the specific intent to acquire monopoly power within that market, that you and the others took steps to achieve that purpose, and that you and the others posed a dangerous probability of success in obtaining monopoly power.[8]

THE COLGATE DOCTRINE

The Colgate doctrine is often argued by those involved in price-fixing. The Colgate case attempted to reconcile the prohibition on agreements between manufacturers and distributors to fix prices with the freedom of a manufacturer to sell to whom it chooses. The Supreme Court observed that a manufacturer may freely exercise its own independent discretion as to the parties with which it will deal and may announce in advance the circumstances under which it will refuse to sell.[9]

However, cases setting forth what does violate the Sherman Act indicate that as a practical matter, price-fixing will rarely be sustainable under Colgate. The manufacturer may not enter into agreements with its customers obliging them to sell at fixed prices or use any other form of coercion, including termination and possibly even the threat of termination.

One example was the *Coors* case. Coors argued the Colgate doctrine in defense of the termination of its distributor. The distributor argued that the "suggested prices" were enforced. The court noted that

> Coors' ideas about proper prices at the wholesale and retail level may only have been couched in terms of suggestions, but having in mind Coors' relative economic clout, particularly its power to cancel valuable distributor franchises almost at will, it seems clear that there is evidence that Coors engaged in price maintenance through suggestions which the distributors could not refuse.[10]

If you fix prices or enforce suggested prices you are exposing yourself to Sherman Act enforcement. One suggestion to help you protect yourself is to print "suggested price" immediately adjacent to the preprinted price, and don't do any arm-twisting to enforce the suggested price.

RECIPROCAL AGREEMENTS

Although collusion between competitors constitutes the most obvious and the most dangerous violation of the antitrust laws, violations may be found in restrictive arrangements with customers and suppliers. Unlike price-fixing, which is per se illegal (i.e., absolutely illegal without regard to the reasonableness of the activity involved), a reciprocal agreement is judged by the rule of reason. Often reciprocal agreements are a naked abuse of market power and will be viewed as such. You must review all such agreements or arrangements in advance with your counsel.

Reciprocity is when you use your purchasing power with a supplier to achieve a coercive or voluntary agreement that "I will buy from you if you buy from me." Reciprocity is generally considered an anticompetitive practice, because it denies competitors an equal opportunity to sell on the basis of price, quality, and service. Such dealings are always unlawful when your company is using its strong market position and purchasing power to promote sales, that is, you only buy products from a supplier on the condition that such supplier buys from you.

As with price-fixing, an agreement or understanding to deal reciprocally may be proved by circumstantial evidence. To avoid even the appearance of this situation, document that each purchasing decision by your company is made independent of any consideration of whether the supplier is purchasing other products of your company. Demonstrate that profit maximization is your overriding goal. One way to decrease your exposure here is to prohibit marketing and purchasing personnel from dealing jointly with customers or suppliers. Likewise, do not keep statistical records which combine the sales and purchase activity of various suppliers or customers.

CONCLUSION

The exchange of price information among competitors has a chilling effect on the vigor of price competition. Regardless of whether they improve competition or even lower prices, actual price-fixing agreements among competitors are illegal.

Don't forget that areas such as warranties and credit terms are essential, bargained-for competitive assets which must not be fixed any more than price. Watch "suggested price," and don't enforce resale prices after you've sold an item. If you want better pricing control, explore with your counsel a consignment relationship. Here you will retain title as well as risk of loss until the item is purchased by the ultimate buyer.

Finally, watch your intracompany statements and memoranda. Such communications may one day be analyzed by government investigators or private litigants as possible evidence in antitrust litigation. Will an outsider misconstrue certain statements against you? For example, if you are preparing an analysis of market data, including pricing or other competitive elements, specify your information source and internal research purpose to prevent the misapprehension that you resorted to illicit communication with your competitors.

Stay alert—your career is on the line. When in doubt consult your attorney at once. It will almost always be a false alarm, but here your counsel can give you a few "but fors" on how close you might have come to adverse exposure.

REFERENCES

[1] Richard M. Calkins, *Antitrust Guidelines for the Business Executive*, Dow Jones-Irwin, Homewood, Illinois, 1982.

[2] For purposes of this discussion, assume that all transactions are in interstate commerce.

[3] *Every* contract, combination in the form of trust or otherwise, or conspiracy in restraint of trade is declared illegal.

[4] Tinker Roller Bearing Co. v. United States, 341 U.S. 593, 598 (1951). *See also* United States v. Yellow Cab, 322 U.S. 218 (1947), Kiefer-Steward Co. v. Joseph E. Seagram and Sons, Inc., 340 U.S. 211 (1951), Perma Life Mufflers, Inc. v. International Parts Corp. 392 U.S. 134 (1968), and Minnesota Bearing Co. v. White Motor Corp., 470 F.2d 1323 (8th Cir. 1973).

[5] Harvey v. Fearless Forris Wholesale, Inc., 589 F.2d 451, 457 (9th Cir. 1979). *See also* Galardo v. AMP Inc., 1982-1 Trade Cas. (CCH) para 64, 468.

[6] Handler and Smart, *The Present Status of the Intracorporate Conspiracy Doctrine*, 3 Cardozo L. Rev. 23 (1982).

[7] Kathleen R. Reiter v. Sonotone Corp., Trade Cas. (CCH) para. 62,688 (1979-1). A state law on point for example is Michigan's, specifically, Mich. Comp. Laws sec. 445.711, Mich. Stat. Ann. sec. 28.38 (Callaghan 1983.)

[8] Eliason Corp. v. National Sanitation Found., 485 F. Supp. 1062, 1075 (1977).

[9] United States v. Colgate and Co., 250 U.S. 300 (1919). *See also* FTC v. Beech-Nut Packing Co. 257 U.S. 441 (1922) (Although this decision was decided on the basis of Section 5 of the FTC Act, rather than the Sherman Act, the Court's opinion indicates that it viewed the manufacturer's practices as violating the Sherman Act as well). Another decision of interest here is Albrecht v. Herald Co. 390 U.S. 145 (1968).

[10] R.E. Spriggs Co. v. Adolph Coors Co., 156 Cal. Rptr. 738, 741, 94 Cal. 3d 419, *cert. denied* 444 U.S. 1076 (1979).

CHAPTER
ELEVEN
TRADE ASSOCIATION MEMBERS— COMPETITORS OR CONSPIRATORS?

You've most likely attended one or more trade association meetings; at almost all such meetings or any other type of similar meeting, you rub elbows with your competitors. These affairs can be socially useful, can provide information, and can assist an industry in self-policing. These affairs can also result in fines and prison terms for unwary participants.[1]

Trade associations have always been fraught with potential antitrust problems, because they constitute ready-made combinations of competitors. In this chapter we shall discuss how a trade association can create problems as well as avoid them. If you have any doubts as to any activity you might be involved in, consult your firm's counsel immediately.

Certain agreements, such as those concerned with the dissemination of general, relevant information, are lawful so long as there is no indication of a purpose to inhibit an individual firm's competitive decision making. Other agreements which directly (and often indirectly) involve price-fixing (depression, pegging, stabilizing, etc.), boycotts, standard industry contracts, product specifications, or allocation of customers and/or territories will (if discovered) probably involve you with the Antitrust Division of the U.S. Department of Justice. Their subsequent action against you may well result in severe, non-tax-deductible fines and/or in an undesired sojourn in a federal facility.

In between are the gray areas. Any agreement among competitors which limits their competition in some significant respect will prompt close scrutiny; these include gentlemen's agreements and those which "improve" competition. The following scenario takes you through some of the "gray area" issues that could arise at a hypothetical trade association gathering. As you read this, you might consider which resolutions you'd endorse, which resolutions you'd oppose, and when you would formally and physically withdraw from the meeting.

AT THE MEETING

In April a number of firms send representatives to attend a specially convened meeting of the Widget Trade Association. The attendance is large, because the industry has seen increased price competition in the face of declining demand. Some firms are threatened with bankruptcy while newer firms are entering the marketplace, further jeopardizing all concerned.

This disturbs all involved, since over the years the members have developed a pleasant rapport. All realize that those let go from the failing firms will enter a market which is not hiring. Individual careers will be destroyed, and no one's bottom line is being enhanced by the downward price wars. The general consensus is to reach some form of accommodation.

The meeting is called to order. Mary Lou, a financial analyst representing a New York City Widget firm, proposes that the association obtain and publish for the members average price data, so that the membership may have an idea of what is going on in the industry. The motion is carried, and the association designates one of its statisticians to set up a procedure immediately. However, Joe, an attorney for a Dallas firm, left the meeting claiming that this was price-fixing. To allay Joe's fears, a new motion was entertained and approved to retain an independent outside accounting firm to gather and disseminate the data in question. Informed of this action, Joe still refused to accept this policy.

Then George, a buyer of widgets for the eastern region, argued that all the price data in the world are useless, because they were comparing apples and oranges. Unless there was a uniform warranty for quality, different types of widgets could be sold. He cited numerous instances of widgets that varied from firm to firm and demanded that the trade association certify one standard widget to "protect" the consumer.

The association agreed to promulgate a set of standards and a certification procedure which would identify those widgets which meet a definable quality standard. A number of members argued that this was policing the industry. Counsel for the association stated that the standards would not be enforced by a boycott of noncertified products.

John, a legislative administrator for the association, then stated that they were spinning their wheels. He proposed that the association voluntarily raise a war chest to lobby Congress to bar any new firm from entering the market. Judith, another legislative expert for the association, protested that this could take years. John then proposed that they organize an initiative in California, since this was the most visible state and also the location of the larger widget employers, to get this issue before the voters. The vote in 7 months would receive national attention similar to Proposition 13; Congress would be impressed and act accordingly. Judith countered that any measure to bar competitors might be unconstitutional. Further, the high visibility they'd generate in attempting this effort to eliminate competition would invariably bring indictments before a vote could be taken.

Judith argued that the members' money would be better spent in an intimidation campaign of publicity against various key legislators. Judith's motion was defeated; before John's motion could pass, Judith asked that the minutes show she left before the vote. She left, and John's motion carried.

The members left the meeting generally pleased that they were finally doing something constructive. Later that night, Mary Lou, George, and John met at the home of the latter. They were a bit uneasy. Judith had phoned each one earlier, stating that she was glad she formally left and that they would wish they had done likewise. She accused them and the association of involving themselves in price-fixing, controlling prices, establishing a constructive boycott, and blatantly and unethically attempting to manipulate government bodies to legislate illegal laws. Was Judith correct?

PRICE-FIXING ISSUE

Price-fixing has been defined as "any combination formed for the purpose of and with the effect of raising, depressing, fixing, pegging or stabilizing the price of a commodity in interstate commerce."[2] Did the Widget Trade Association engage in price-fixing?

Probably not—the motion itself as carried was not price-fixing. However, the surrounding atmosphere could invite scrutiny, since the meeting was called to try to stabilize a chaotic price market. On close examination, the association's motion as carried appears to be an effort to circulate information pertaining to general, *past* industry pricing which would *not* identify specific parties or transactions. Further, and what is more important, we are not dealing with a concentrated market which might tend to stabilize prices based on this information.

In this case, the trade association is fulfilling one of its primary and necessary functions—that of providing general information to assist its members in more efficient competition. However, any exchange of information, whatever its nature or purpose, may be presumed to have an anticompetitive effect if prices *stabilize*. The association should note this in each information paper disseminated to its members and specify that there is no association commitment to comply with these prices and that in fact the association expressly discourages any such conformity. Finally, the association should (as it did here) retain an *independent third party* to collect and disseminate the data. Doing this internally invites investigations and other problems.

You should note that this is about as far as you should go, even in a highly competitive industry lacking oligopolistic tendencies. If the association had agreed to disseminate data relating to current prices or current production and/or relating to specific members, then a serious anticompetitive situation would have existed. Obviously, the association's publication of suggested prices and/or requiring the members to adhere to such prices would present a price-fixing situation.

In conclusion, the circulation of price information can give rise to an agreement to fix prices. However, general, average, dated, and unidentifiable industry price data collected and disseminated by an independent accounting firm should not present an anticompetitive problem, unless there is a tendency toward price stabilization or evidence that such exchanges were undertaken for the purpose of regulating prices.

CERTIFICATION OF STANDARDS

There were two issues here—one as to uniform warranties and one as to the formal adoption of standards. The former should be avoided. Generalized guidelines are probably lawful, but such guidelines have a tendency to promote uniformity. Uniform warranties by competitors are prohibited. The warranty can be an essential, bargained-for, competitive asset every bit as significant as a bargained-for price.

As to the proposed standard of minimum quality, this can present problems even though designed for the best of motives, that is, consumer protection and preserving the reputation of the industry from inferior product entrants. When there is any doubt, you should discuss with your counsel whether an advisory opinion rather than a set of standards would be preferable. Good intent, in and of itself, is no defense if it results in an unlawful restraint of trade.[3] However, this set of standards and certification procedure would probably survive because:

1. There is a statement expressly providing that no boycott or other restriction will be imposed on its members or others.
2. There will be no sanctions imposed on the members for a departure from the recommended standards.
3. Not stated, but necessary, is that the association will not attempt to restrict the activities of its members in any way relating to prices and/or conditions of sale.

If any of the three points is omitted, the standards and certification procedure would probably be proscribed. An example of the certification issue concerned a trade group's setting standards for refrigerators in the food service industry. A manufacturer who failed to qualify argued that the certification was an illegal restraint of trade. The court disagreed, stating that there was no direct or indirect boycott or evidence of price-fixing, division of markets, or division of customers. The court held the certification to be procompetitive:

> [T]he record demonstrates that the primary purpose behind the NSF standards program has been pro-competitive in attempting to promote uniform standards among public health jurisdictions, thereby minimizing the number of differing, even conflicting, requirements, reducing costs for all manufacturers, and increasing the number of manufacturers able to compete in each jurisdiction.[4]

In conclusion, an association should not adopt uniform warranties. An association may adopt a reasonable product standard and certification program provided that it does not effect a boycott, fix prices, exclude members or other competitors, and/or control production.

LEGISLATIVE CAMPAIGN

There is no doubt that the legislative campaign would seek official sanction for anticompetitive purposes. Ironically, it's most likely legal! Attempts by an association to lobby a government body are absolutely immune from antitrust liability according to the Supreme Court.[5] Specifically, "the Sherman Act does not prohibit two or more persons from associating together in an attempt to persuade the legislature or the executive to take particular action with respect to a law that would produce a restraint or a monopoly."[6]

In short, the association's purpose in seeking the political action is irrelevant. Further, the constitutional question raised by Judith is not controlling—an association is constitutionally protected in any activity that is a genuine effort to influence legislation. Once the genuine effort is established, the association is not obligated or expected to predict the results of a constitutional challenge in the courts. A subsequent declaration by the court of unconstitutionality will not expose the association or its members to antitrust penalties, regardless of their anticompetitive purpose.

These same principles govern attempts to influence the full gamut of political life: legislative, executive, administrative, and judicial bodies as well as attempts to legislate through the initiative process.[7] Ironically, Judith's lesser "cost and exposure" publicity campaign would probably come under the "sham" exception, that is, "[t]here may be situations in which a publicity campaign, ostensibly directed toward influencing governmental action, is a mere sham to cover what is actually nothing more than an attempt to interfere directly with the business relationships of a competitor and the application of the Sherman Act would be justified."[8] The sham exception comes into play when the participant is not seeking official action by a governmental body. A publicity campaign aimed at intimidation rather than concerted government action would probably result in the courts' imposing sanctions for an unlawful violation of the antitrust laws.

In conclusion, the First Amendment offers an association and/or its membership free and unlimited access to petition its government regardless of intent or purpose so long as its efforts are "genuine." A mere publicity campaign not undertaken for the purpose of influencing government action would probably not be protected and, therefore, could result in antitrust sanctions on the association and/or its members.

TO SUM UP

The problem of distinguishing between those trade association activities which serve to enhance competition by improving a member's knowledge and those which have as their purpose the elimination of competition is a difficult one.

As a general rule, any activity (such as price stabilization or allocation of territory or customers) which substitutes arm's-length competition for handshake cooperation is suspect. Obviously, as an informed professional, you are aware of your duty to consult with counsel if a question arises in this field. You also have a duty to anticipate activities or involvement which might place you in a compromising situation both for yourself and your firm. As a general rule you should avoid even being present at discussions of an improper nature. If nothing else, it reflects on your professional judgment.

If, however, you are unwittingly placed in a situation where you might be linked to the questionable acts of an association or its individual members, make every effort to demonstrate that *you* did not condone such acts. Once you are aware of even the inference of questionable conversation and/or proposals, immediately and formally disassociate yourself from the group and the meeting. If minutes are kept, have this disassociation reflected in them. Then immediately speak to your firm's counsel. Relate exactly what was said and/or ratified, exactly what steps you were involved in, and when you disassociated (if at all) yourself from the meeting. The conversation is confidential, and the advice will be specific and personally geared to your individual situation.[9]

We reviewed at length trade association exposure because the obvious accessibility of competitors in a congenial manner is fertile ground for even subtle understandings which may result in a felony conviction. However, an unwary individual can be just as vulnerable at a lunch setting or even over the phone. Prompt consultation with counsel in these circumstances could be the best career move you ever make.

ARE THERE OTHER EXCEPTIONS?

Yes. As we discussed, you are permitted to join with others to lobby for government action, even if the desired intent is to act with an anticompetitive purpose. Other exemptions include:

1. Organized labor (except where collusion with industry members is involved.[10]
2. Agricultural and fishing cooperatives.
3. Certain contracts necessary to the national defense.

4. Insurance industry. Congress has delegated the states the power to regulate and tax this industry.[11]
5. State action which, if done by private parties, would be illegal.[12]

FINAL COMMENT

You and those working under you should not hold membership in any trade association in which you don't actively participate. A "paper membership" may help your resumé, but it does prevent you from knowing what's going on. Without active participation you are not in a position to quickly disassociate yourself from a questionable course of conduct. Your attendance is also necessary to make sure a responsible and accountable officer of the association itself is in attendance. Finally, active participation includes a review of the agenda prior to the meeting. You should make it clear that you will not support any "informal" ad hoc groups or any meeting where an agenda has not been prepared in advance.

REFERENCES

[1] See also Robert J. Posch, Jr., "Permissible Conduct at Trade Association Meetings," *Direct Marketing*, April 1982, pp. 102–105.

[2] United States v. Socony Vacuum Oil Co., 310 U.S. 150, 221 (1940).

[3] Hydrolevel Corp. v. American Society of Mechanical Eng'rs, Inc., 635 F.2d 118. (1980).

[4] Eliason Corp. v. National Sanitation Found., 485 F. Supp. 1076 (1977).

[5] Eastern R.R. Presidents Conference v. Noerr Motor Freight, Inc., 365 U.S. 127 (1961) and United Mine Workers v. Burlington, 318 U.S. 657 (1965).

[6] Eastern R.R. Presidents Conference v. Noerr Motor Freight, Inc., 365 U.S. 127, 136 (1961).

[7] *See* Subscription TV v. Southern Cal. Theatre Owners, 576 F.2d 230 (1978).

[8] Eastern R.R. Presidents Conference v. Noerr Motor Freight, Inc., 365 U.S. 127, 144 (1961).

[9] The exception to this is if you actually engaged in criminal activity. If you did, the attorney will interrupt you immediately if it appears you are confessing to criminal wrongdoing. The attorney represents the company, and she or he will

inform you that you should retain your own lawyer. However, a competent in-house counsel should be able to refer you to a list of competent specialists in antitrust defense.

[10] 29 U.S.C. at 52 *et seq.*

[11] 15 U.S.C. sec. 1011–15.

[12] Parker v. Brown, 317 U.S. 341 (1943).

CHAPTER
TWELVE
PRICE DISCRIMINATION AND THE ROBINSON-PATMAN ACT

The Robinson-Patman Act is aimed at price and other forms of discrimination, not conspiracy. Its intent is to prohibit preferential pricing, allowances, or services which place the seller's customers or competitors at a significant economic disadvantage.

The Robinson-Patman Act originated in a period in which price uniformity was widely considered a positive value. During this same period legally supported resale price maintenance ("fair trade") began to take hold in various states.[1] An antitrust exemption for such statutes was enacted the following year, in 1937, and was to last until repeal in 1975.

Many critics have argued that Robinson-Patman encourages price uniformity. It may become an anachronism simply through decreased enforcement. Aggressive FTC enforcement is minimal at present, and the Department of Justice actually urged its repeal![2] Then the *Payne* decision was rendered in 1981.[3] Prior to this a company proving price discrimination was held by some courts to be entitled to "automatic damages," which provided that damages would be automatically allowed in an amount equal to the dollar value of the illegal discrimination experienced. The Supreme Court rejected automatic damages, thus raising a private litigant's burden of proof (and lessening chances of monetary recovery). Now you must prove specific injury as well as a violation of the act.

However, the small business lobbies are staunch advocates and will keep the act on the books, and they may eventually obtain greater enforcement.[4] They want and need to ensure hard competition in a free enterprise system. We'll look at each section of the act and explore in detail the sections of the act that concern discounts and allowances [secs. 2(d) and 2(e)], because they are the real meat of the act where today's manager is concerned.

SECTION 2(a)

There are six elements to a section 2(a) violation. First and most obvious, there must be *price discrimination*. An outright refusal to sell to one customer does not of itself constitute a Robinson-Patman Act violation.[5] You must be able to show a difference in prices charged by a seller to different customers for the same product. This can be any price concessions made to one competing purchaser and not another, such as free merchandise, preferred credit terms, and other similar competitive benefits. Then you must satisfy other criteria.

Second, the transaction must be in interstate commerce (across state lines). Although the Sherman Act includes transactions merely "affecting" commerce, Robinson-Patman is inapplicable unless the transactions complained of are actually in interstate commerce.[6]

Third, the seller must discriminate by price among two or more purchasers, that is, two or more actual sales reasonably close to each other in time must be made. No single sale can violate the act.

Fourth, the products sold must be *commodities* which are goods, wares, merchandise or other *tangible goods*. Commodities do not include real estate, services, or intangibles.

Fifth, the products sold must be of *"like grade and quality."* The interpretation of "like grade and quality" goes further than a requirement that the goods be absolutely identical. If a difference is not significant so that there is true interchangeability and substitutability with the same performance results for the proposed use, goods may be found to be of like grade and quality.

Elements to consider here are whether the physical and chemical properties of the products are the same: cross-elasticity of demand, substitutability, physical appearance, and identity of performance.[7] However, if there are substantial physical differences in products which affect consumer preferences or marketability (beyond mere brand packaging), they probably aren't of like grade and quality, and the act will not apply.[8] The advisable course is to emphasize product differentiation if you are charging different prices for basically similar goods.

Sixth, you must be able to demonstrate significant, *actual competitive injury*. To demonstrate competitive injury you must be able to show injury to competition, not just to yourself. The effect of the price discrimination must be to substantially lessen competition or create a monopoly in your market. You must be able to demonstrate this for cases involving primary-line competition (the seller's competition) and for cases involving second-ary-line competition (the buyer's competition).

DEFENSES TO ROBINSON-PATMAN VIOLATION

An absolute defense of changing market conditions is written into the act.[9] Here there are the obvious: perishable goods, seasonal goods, "going out of business" sales (honest ones, that is), and distress sales under court order. These areas are interpreted broadly. For example, cars may be considered seasonal goods, and wide latitude may be permitted in the normal change in a car model year.[10] Another example is remaindering— here books no longer in great demand (hopefully not this one) are sold for a nominal price and then discounted to the customer, often on those large table sales you see in certain bookshops. Check with your counsel in areas such as clothing, tools, and leisure goods.

Then there are the two better-known and more common defenses of cost justification and meeting competition. The cost justification defense is predicated on services performed and the purchasing practices of the customer. You are permitted price differentials if you can demonstrate legitimate cost justification. For example, if the selling or shipping ar-rangements with a buyer result in a substantial saving to you (the seller), the saving may be passed on to the buyer in the form of a discount. However, no more than the *exact* cost savings attributable to the saving may be passed on. Finally, quantity discounts are generally lawful if the dis-counts are available to all competing customers and if all customers can realistically buy in quantities required to obtain the largest discounts. However, quantity discounts must be distinguished from volume dis-counts (i.e., discounts based on cumulative purchases during a stated period) and rebates not based on cost savings which are price concessions reserved for large and powerful buyers.

Under the meeting competition defense, discriminatory prices other-wise unlawful under the act are defensible when you (the seller) act "in good faith to meet an equally low price of your *own* competitor" or any discounts, services, or facilities offered by your competitor. This is an absolute defense where justified. You should note that only a lawful lower price may be met.

Again, you are not required to meet competition. It is an option you elect. However, to justify this defense, you must demonstrate the following.

1. Good-faith belief (rather than an objective certainty) that your competitor is offering a certain lower price. The courts have viewed it as the "existence of facts leading a reasonable and prudent person to believe that the granting of a lower price would meet the equally low price of a competitor."[11]

2. Evidence of the competitor's price that you are seeking to meet. This evidence may not result from verification directly through the competitor; you may, however, obtain it from the customer in writing or from published sources. However, note that the Supreme Court has held that what would otherwise be an unlawful exchange of price information between competitors is *not* excused or defensible on the grounds that the supposed purpose of the exchange was to verify a buyer's claim of a lower competing offer and thereby establish a "meeting competition defense to price discrimination under the Robinson-Patman Act."[12]

The Court has recognized that casual reliance on unverified reports of buyers or sales representatives may be insufficient to establish that you acted in good faith in proving that your competitors were offering the same product for a lower price. The Court concluded that where you have "only vague, generalized doubts about the reliability" of a buyer's information, you are permitted to offer a competitive price to make the sale.[13] It was further recognized that where a customer's veracity or the accuracy of reports received by the seller may seriously be in doubt, the defense is likely to be unavailable should you grant a discriminatory price.[14]

The Court does not want direct verification as a defense to a Sherman Act price-fixing charge, because "the most likely consequence of any agreement to exchange price information would be the stabilization of industry prices."[15]

3. The reduction was made to meet an individual competitive situation. The decision to meet a competitor's price should be made on a case-by-case basis and should never be automatic, pursuant to an established policy or practice.

4. Only a lawful lower price may be met. This is common sense, since you can't have a "good-faith" argument of meeting competition if you have knowledge or reason to believe that the price being met is an unlawful one.

5. A meeting competition reduction may be granted and kept in place only as long as the competitive prices which initiated it persist. Consequently, you must periodically review price reductions to determine whether they are still justified by the realities of your marketplace.

BROKERAGE PAYMENTS AND ALLOWANCES—SECTION 2(c)

This section was enacted to eliminate discriminatory rebates granted large sellers under the guise of "brokerage fees" which were never actually earned. This occurs when seller's brokers yield to the economic pressures of large buying organizations to grant them preferences related to their size rather than to cost efficiency. As Congress stated in its legislative history:

> . . . it prohibits the direct or indirect payment of brokerage fees except for . . . services (actually) rendered. It prohibits its allowance by the buyer direct to the seller, or by the seller direct to the buyer; and it prohibits its payment by either to an agent or intermediary acting in fact for or in behalf, or subject to the direct or indirect control of the other.[16]

You will run afoul of this section if you reduce the brokerage fee received by the agent for *tangible* goods and pass the reduction on to the buyer in some form.

Whenever both the buyer and seller are in a brokerage relationship, or there is a third party performing services for either, you must carefully review your brokerage payment schedules with counsel to ensure that large buyers are not gaining discriminatory preferences over smaller ones solely by virtue of their greater purchasing power.[17] If you are employing brokerage commissions in this manner you are engaged in price discrimination regardless of your lack of intent or motive to discriminate or cause injury to competition.

PAYMENT FOR OR FURNISHING OF SERVICES OR FACILITIES—SECTIONS 2(d) AND 2(e)

Sections 2(d) and 2(e) are the heart of the act for most readers, and we'll review these sections in detail as well as refer to the applicable FTC guides on point.[18]

With the increasing costs of all forms of customer communication, many managers are expanding their involvement in cooperative promotions. Many hail the practice as increasing the flow of choice selection information to the consumer. Others, including one of cooperative promotion's inventors some 40 years ago, have deemed it a "pernicious influence" in advertising which "restricts the customer's freedom of choice, encourages greater standardization, and makes it less likely that the best can get a chance to reach the marketplace."[19] One of the reasons for strong reservations about cooperative advertising is the economic reality that firms that are better endowed financially have a big advantage in providing subsidies. This economic leverage could crowd out smaller firms which might have high-quality merchandise to offer but no cooperative advertising money to support a public awareness campaign.[20]

If you are involved or may be involved in cooperative promotions, you should know your rights and responsibilities in this area.

Sections 2(d) and 2(e) of the Robinson-Patman Act prohibit a seller from granting advertising and promotional allowances or services to customers unless they are available to all competing customers on proportionally equal terms. In section 2(d) the buyer supplies the services or facilities and the seller pays all or an agreed-on portion of the bill; in section 2(e) the seller supplies the services and facilities for the use of the buyer in facilitating resales. (For brevity's sake, the FTC guides on point have stated that the terms "services" and "facilities" have the same meaning.)[21]

For your cooperative promotional program to comply with sections 2(d) and 2(e) as well as the FTC guides, you must overcome three minimum hurdles[22]:

1. What must you do to make your promotion "available" and on "proportionally equal terms"?
2. To whom must you make your promotion available, that is, who are your actual competing customers?
3. How does this act affect issues such as credit granting, and what are the defenses available?

In the review of these questions that follows, keep in mind that the purpose of the law and the guides is to eliminate direct or indirect devices by which large buyers obtain discriminatory preferences under the guise of promotional allowances.

AVAILABILITY OF YOUR PROMOTIONAL PLAN

Section 2(d) requires the seller to make a promotional payment available to competing customers on proportionally equal terms. Section 2(e) requires the seller to offer a promotional arrangement on terms accorded to all buyers. The seller who intends to institute a promotional arrangement, therefore, must solve the problem of how to make that program proportionally available to competing customers.

The seller's obligation to make promotional arrangements available imposes the obligation to (1) inform all competing buyers that promotional programs are available to them and (2) offer a promotional plan that contains meaningful alternatives for all competing buyers.

How to inform is clearly spelled out in the relevant FTC guide, which provides that the seller should take some action to inform *all* its customers competing with any participating customer of the availability of its plan.[23] You might elect to use letters or mailgrams, or you may choose to publish notice of the availability and essential features of the promotional plan in a publication of general distribution in the trade.

For example, placing such a notice of the terms of cooperative advertising or other promotional allowances in a specific trade magazine should satisfy the seller's duty to inform.[24] Further, you might employ the direct mail channel "advising customers from accurate and reasonably complete mailing lists."[25]

Word-of-mouth publicity through your sales force is also a possibility, but receipt and retention of such notice isn't always provable.[26] The best way to be able to prove you actually informed *all* your customers is to follow the specific advice of the FTC:

> The seller can make the required notification by any means he chooses, but if he wants to be able to show later that he gave notice to a certain customer, he is in a better position to do so if it was given in writing.[27]

To summarize, detailed written notification to all your customers communicated in ample time for them to use the available promotional services will almost always satisfy your requirements to notify and inform.

After your customers are informed and understand the essential features of your plan comes the hard part—how can you tailor your plan to make it meaningfully available to all your customers? Again, the FTC is fairly emphatic that more than a minimal effort to proportionalize in good faith must be made:

> *The plan should be such that all types of competing customers may participate. It should not be tailored to favor or discriminate against a particular customer or class of customers, but should, in its terms, be usable in a practical business sense by all competing customers.* This may require offering all such customers more than one way to participate in the plan or offering alternative terms and conditions to customers for whom the basic plan is not usable and suitable. *The seller should not either expressly, or by the way the plan operates, eliminate some competing customers, although he may offer alternative plans designed for different*

customer classes. If he offers alternative plans, all of the plans offered should provide the same proportionate equality, and the seller should inform competing customers of the various alternative plans. [Emphasis my own.][28]

In one situation it was found that in lieu of a cooperative newspaper advertising program which precluded many smaller customers,[29] the firm in question could offer in-store promotional aids of display racks to satisfy the proportionally equal test.[30]

In the celebrated *A & P* case, a wholly owned subsidiary corporation published *Woman's Day* magazine solely for the competitive advantage of A & P retail stores.[31] The magazine was only available at A & P stores, *not* at newsstands or by subscription (except in Colorado, where A & P had no retail stores). The state wholesale grocers (none of whom owned a magazine) sued saying that the advertising dollars spent in *Woman's Day* were not available to all grocers on proportionally equal terms. The court of appeals held that grocery suppliers (here specifically General Foods Corporation, Morton Salt Corporation, and Hunt Foods, Inc.) who placed ads in *Woman's Day* violated section 2(d) unless they made similar payments available on proportionately equal terms to other grocery companies in competition with A & P.

WHO ARE THE RELEVANT COMPETING CUSTOMERS?

A seller who decides to make promotions available to a particular buyer must determine whether that buyer sells to other purchasers who compete with the buyer, since any promotional plan developed must cover *all* customers who compete with any customer participating in the plan.[32] Determining which buyers are subject to the act's protections involves problems which fall into these areas:

1. The geographic area of competition, that is, any area in which two competitive buyers are competing for a customer.[33]
2. Sales involving direct buying retailers and retailers buying through wholesalers.

Essentially, the seller should treat all purchasers who buy from wholesalers as if they were buying directly from the seller with regard to all promotional arrangements.[34] Also, the FTC warns that "The seller should be careful here not to discriminate against customers located on the fringes but outside the area selected for the special promotion, since they may be actually competing with those participating."

MISCELLANEOUS PROVISIONS

In addition to promotional allowances, sections 2(d) and 2(e) have been used to curb most other schemes by which large buyers are favored over smaller ones. These include discriminatory impact in warehousing and storage compensation and allowing credit for returns of merchandise.[35] However, the extension of credit itself is *not* within the purview of sections 2(d) or 2(e). Credit is too subjective a question because of differences in a borrower's financial strength, business expertise, and simply seat-of-the-pants judgment often needed in these decisions.

Finally, you may be displeased to know that one of the traditional defenses—cost justification, discussed earlier—is not available to you in a section 2(d) or 2(e) claim.[36] The guide on point states that "It is no defense to a charge of unlawful discrimination in the payment of an allowance or the furnishing of the service for a seller to show that such payment, service or facility could be justified through savings in the course of manufacture, sale or delivery."[37]

The defense of meeting competition remains a defense in this form of action.

BUYER'S INDUCING OR RECEIVING A DISCRIMINATORY PRICE— SECTION 2(f)

Sometimes it's natural to assume that antitrust problems are strictly the seller's realm. Section 2(f) covers all bases by prohibiting a buyer from *knowingly* inducing or receiving a discriminatory price unlawful under section 2(a) of the act.[38] The knowledge requirement can be satisfied by showing that the buyer possessed "trade experience" in the industry. The legal question posed is to what extent can a buyer bargain, and to what extent can the uncertain seller reduce a price, before there is Robinson-Patman exposure?

Short of outright fraud or the "lying buyer situation," a buyer is not liable under this section if the lower prices induced are within one of the seller's defenses (for example, meeting competition) or if the buyer does not know that the lower prices are not within one of these defenses.[39] The court has held that a precondition of finding an inducement or receipt of an illegal price was the granting of a discriminatory price by the seller.

This interpretation was tested again in 1979, and the court again held that there is no inducement of price discrimination by a buyer if the seller has a valid defense of meeting competition. The court left unresolved the question of a price induced by the buyer's fraud.[40]

CONCLUSION

If you're a seller and you don't offer discriminatory preferences—including price discounts, favorable credit terms, cooperative advertising promotions, and the like—to favored buyers, you should have no trouble avoiding adverse action under the Robinson-Patman Act. Nor should you encounter problems under this act if you're a buyer and you don't deceive your seller into granting you a discriminatory price not justifiable under one or more of the act's defenses.

As a word of warning, although enforcement of this act may be diminished at present, legal climates *do* change, and violations of any of the sections discussed above could come back to haunt you. As usual, consult your counsel.

REFERENCES

[1] For background see Schwegmann Bros. v. Calvert Distillers Corp., 341 U.S. 384 (1951).

[2] U.S. Department of Justice, *Report on the Robinson-Patman Act,* 1977.

[3] J. Truett Payne Co. v. Chrysler Motors Corp., 449 U.S. 1108 (1981). *See also* Crowl Distrib. Corp. v. Singer Corp., 543 F. Supp. 1033, 1035 (1982) (no automatic damages, but you must show actual injury to yourself attributable to something the antitrust laws were designed to prevent).

[4] *See* Calvani, *Effect of Current Developments on the Future of the Robinson-Patman Act,* 48 Antitrust L.J. 1, 692 (1929).

[5] Mullis v. Arco Petroleum Corp., 502 F.2d 290, 294 (7th Cir. 1974).

[6] Standard Oil Co. v. FTC, 340 U.S. 231 (1951).

[7] Checker Motors Corp. v. Chrysler Corp., 283 F. Supp. 876, *aff'd* 405 F.2d 319, *cert. denied,* 394 U.S. 999 (1968).

[8] Quaker Oats Co. 66 F.T.C. sec. 1131 (1964).

[9] 15 U.S.C. sec. 13(a).

[10] Valley Plymouth v. Studebaker-Packard Corp., 219 F. Supp. 608 (1963).

[11] Covey Oil Co. v. Continental Oil Co., 340 F.2d 993, *cert. denied*, 380 U.S. 964 (1965).

[12] United States v. United States Gypsum Co., 438 U.S. 422 (1978).

[13] *Id.* at 454, n. 29.

[14] *Id.* at 455–6.

[15] *Id.* at 457.

[16] H.R. 2287, 74th Cong., 2d Sess. 15 (1936).

[17] Woles Home Remodeling Co. v. Alside Aluminum Co., 443 F. Supp. 908 (10th Cir. Wisc. 1978).

[18] Robert J. Posch, Jr., "Cooperative Promotions: To Cooperate or Litigate, Legal Outlook," *Direct Marketing*, June 1982, pp. 146–149.

[19] Stanley Marcus, *Quest for the Best*, Viking, New York, 1979, p. 136. See also chapter 8, "The Seduction of the Buyer," in the same work.

[20] *Id.* at 133.

[21] Guides for Advertising Allowances and Other Merchandise Payments and Services, 16 C.F.R. sec. 240.5 (1981).

[22] Advertising is a service, but if it is involved with *commodities* (as we discussed earlier) you are covered by the laws on point.

[23] 16 C.F.R. 240.8. However, this is sufficient notice only if your customers ordinarily read this magazine. *See* Exquisite Form Brassiere, Inc. v. FTC, 301 F.2d 499 (1961), *cert. denied*, 382 U.S. 888 (1962).

[24] 16 C.F.R. sec. 240.8(b)(3).

[25] 16 C.F.R. sec. 240.8(b)(3)(C).

[26] Vanity Fair Paper Mills, Inc. v. FTC, 311 F.2d 480 (2d Cir. 1968).

[27] 16 C.F.R. sec. 240.8(a).

[28] 16 C.F.R. sec. 240.9(a).

[29] Surprise Brassierre Co. v. FTC, 406 F.2d 711 (5th Cir. 1969).

[30] For a discussion of the flexibility as to display racks, see Allen Pen Co. v. Springfield Photo Morent Co., 653 F.2d 17 (1981).

[31] State Wholesale Grocers v. Great Atlantic and Pacific Tea Co., 258 F.2d 831 (7th Cir. 1958), *cert. denied*, 358 U.S. 947 (1959).

[32] FTC v. Fred Meyer, Inc., 390 U.S. 341 (1968).

[33] FTC v. Simplicity Pattern Co., 360 U.S. 55 (1959).

[34] 16 C.F.R. sec. 240.12.

[35] There are FTC advisory opinions indicating that there is a limited exemption from Robinson-Patman under the Motor Carriers Act of 1980. This exemption is limited to "products sold primarily in grocery stores." If you deal in these products discuss this with your counsel. *See In re* Procter and Gamble Co. (CCH) para. 64, 422 (1981-2) and Nifty Foods Corp. v. Great Atlantic and Pacific Tea Co., 614 F.2d 832 (2d Cir. 1981).

[36] Covey Oil Co. v. Continental Oil Co., 340 F.2d 993, *cert. denied*, 380 U.S. 964 (1965).

[37] 16 C.F.R. sec. 240.17.

[38] 16 C.F.R. sec. 240.16.

[39] Automatic Canteen Co. v. FTC, 346 U.S. 61 (1953).

[40] Great Atlantic and Pacific Tea Co. v. FTC, Trade Cas. (CCH) para. 62, 475 (1979-1).

CHAPTER
THIRTEEN
HOW TO AVOID
DECEPTIVE PRICING___

How people do love a bargain, but oh, how they hate to be conned! Examples of deceptive pricing abound in everyday life: the so-called going-out-of-business sale where everything is marked way up before the "25 percent off everything" signs go up, comparisons between a fictitious "former price" and the new "sale" price, "sales" that never end. These deceptive pricing schemes are not only aggravating to the consumer, they're also illegal.

We'll focus on deceptive pricing as it relates to specific topics in other chapters.[1] When it comes to pricing, this area permits no latitude for puffery, and you may have to stifle your creative urge just a bit. Objective accuracy is at a premium. Unlike the more subjective claims of quality, when you stress price you are in an objective area of substantiation. Let's review a few common questions on point.

1. *What is deceptive pricing?* This is any unsubstantiated price claim which would materially affect the purchaser's decision to buy your product.[2]

2. *What if I don't intend to deceive?* Your intention to deceive is not a prerequisite to committing an unfair or deceptive trade practice. The test of a violation is the effect on the purchaser.[3] Further, although a false price may be obviously false to those in your trade, that is no defense if it deceives a particularly vulnerable group (e.g., children) or "that vast multitude which includes the ignorant, the unthinking and the credulous."[4]

3. *What if my price is the actual value of the product?* If you are selling a $35 grill for $35—no problem. However, if you had previously marked up the grill to $60 and then "cut" the price to $35 to advertise a "sale," you are engaging in deceptive pricing.[5]

4. *What former price comparisons may I use?* In making former price comparisons, you must have made bona fide sales at the advertised former price in the *recent* past. If the product was offered for sale but no sales were made at that price or any other price in the recent past, that fact must be disclosed in connection with any mention of the former price. This test is important: You must be able to demonstrate that the product was openly and actively offered for sale for a reasonably substantial period of time, in the regular course of business, honestly and in good faith. The product must have been offered for sale in the same trade area (e.g., geographically comparable over the entire market area), and not an "average" of all markets in general. If a savings cannot be substantiated over a significant geographic area, a disclaimer is advised. Sales records, checks, invoices, and even correspondence will be helpful here as objective evidence.

Finally, don't forget qualitative aspects. If you have diluted the quality of your product (e.g., using inferior ingredients), you may not create the impression that the original product is being offered at a reduced rate.[6] The standard of comparable product is a requirement for all price claims by you and your competitors.

5. *What about just stating my "regular" price?* This is OK if you use the word "regular" or other words of similar import and mean to refer to any price amount which is not in excess of the price at which any article, merchandise, or service has been sold or offered for sale in good faith by you for a reasonably substantial period of time in the recent, regular course of your business. Further, your business records must establish that this amount is the price at which your merchandise has been sold or is offered for sale in good faith by you for a reasonably substantial period of time in the recent, regular course of your business.

There are two points to keep in mind here; you must be able to demonstrate that you have a reasonable basis (scientific sampling) to substantiate that your sample is representative. Also, you must be careful that any sale prices do not exist for more than 6 months and that no more than 50 percent of the sales were at the sale price, because then the "sales price would become the regular price." If the same sale price is always maintained, the offer is merely deceptive advertising.

6. *What about manufacturer's list prices?* Use of manufacturer's list prices is acceptable *if* relevant to the area you do business in or the "trade area." The following are a few things to watch:

a. If an article is seasonal, don't compare a "substantial markdown" due to seasonal preferences to the in-season price.

b. Don't call yourself a "wholesaler" or imply that your large buying power enables you to eliminate the intermediary unless this is true or, in the latter case, such savings are *directly* passed on to the purchaser.

7. *May I charge more than list price?* Yes, but you might have to say so. Many states and municipalities have disclosure laws on point.

For example, a seller in New York City significantly marked up his calculators.[7] He was fined $2000 for violating the Administrative Code. The seller argued (correctly) that the higher rents in his area justified the higher price. He also alleged that his "customers are both willing and happy to pay its prices because of the store's convenient location and knowledgeable sales staff."[8]

Not good enough, said the court: "When a fact is material to a buying decision and consumers would not ordinarily discover that fact before buying, it is deceptive not to disclose such a fact. . . . To a consumer who wishes to make an informed choice, disclosure that the selling price far exceeds the manufacturer's suggested retail price is clearly material."[9] The court upheld the regulation on its merits insofar as it enhances comparative shopping and diminishes the vulnerability of the public. Check with your counsel about similar state and local laws on point.

8. *What substantiation is required in comparative pricing?* No comparisons should be made or implied between the price at which an article is offered for sale and some other reference price unless the nature of the reference price is explicitly identified and you have a reasonable basis to substantiate its accuracy. This substantiation must be undertaken *prior* to publishing the price comparison advertisement. It must be relevant to the area in which the audience will shop.

9. *What is "relevant" to my audience?* What is your geographic drawing power? Are you a national chain? If so, verification of prices is required using reasonable business methods in your trade, such as market surveys. If you are an independent, you should ascertain what prices are being charged at the principal retail outlets in the area.

10. *What about media life?* This can complicate a reference price for comparison purposes. For example, you target certain strategies as to media exposure life. Newspapers may last a day, *TV Guide* a week, cable guide a month, and your annual catalog may be retained and browsed through over an entire year! Here good faith and reasonable business practices are in order for the promotional vehicles with a longer life. Provided that the prices were substantiated as a reference at the time of publication, you will probably meet this hurdle.

11. *What if all my competitors are engaged in violations?* Sorry—no defense. You can be singled out. Even if all your competitors are *more* deceptive, this evidence is irrelevant to your defense.[10]

TO SUMMARIZE

The FTC will review and consider the following points:

1. The items you're comparing must be identical or substantially similar. For example, if you're comparing meats, they must be identical in cut and grade.
2. All price comparisons (your own prior claims or comparisons with a competitor) must be based on "actual, bona fide prices at which the article was offered to the public in the trade area on a regular basis for a reasonably substantial period of time."[11]
3. Geographic changes in pricing (if significant) must be accounted for or a disclaimer provided stating that such comparison prices do not mean that the consumer will always save by purchasing the item advertised.
4. Terms such as "wholesale" or "factory" prices should not be used unless you are selling at prices consumers would pay if they purchased directly from the supplier.[12]
5. In order to establish the objective validity of your claims through market research, competitors to be surveyed must be selected in such a way as to provide a valid basis for any generalizations made from the results.
6. All promotions must be conducted within the following guideline: "In every case act honestly and in good faith in advertising a list price and not with the intention of establishing a basis, or creating an instrumentality, for a deceptive comparison in any local or other trade area."[13]
7. All pricing promotions should be reviewed with counsel in a systematic way—especially any new "creative" concepts.

REFERENCES

[1] See the discussion of the pricing allowances earlier in this chapter; see Chapter 2 for discussion of the Fair Packaging and Labeling Act (15 U.S.C. sec. 1451); and see Section 4 for a discussion of bait advertising (16 C.F.R. sec. 238), free offers (16 C.F.R. sec. 251), and what a sale is.

[2] A material term provides information which an ordinary, reasonable consumer would consider when deciding whether to purchase the particular product you are offering.

[3] We're referring to the FTC here, particularly Guides against Deceptive Pricing, 16 C.F.R. sec. 233 (see distinction between guides and rules in the Glossary). However, most states have laws on point similar to or narrower than the guides. Consult with your counsel as to applicable laws for your promotion.

4 FTC v. Standard Education Society, 302 U.S. 113 (1937) and P. Corillard Co. v. FTC, 186 F.2d 52, 58 (1950).

5 16 C.F.R. sec. 233.1(c).

6 Royal Baking Co. v. FTC, 281 F. 744 (1922).

7 City of New York v. Toby's Elecs., Inc., 110 Misc. 2d 848, 443 N.Y.S.2d 561 (1981).

8 *Id.* at 566.

9 *Id.*

10 Spiegel, Inc. v. FTC, 494 F.2d 59, 65 (1973).

11 16 C.F.R. sec. 233.1(a).

12 16 C.F.R. sec. 233.5.

13 16 C.F.R. sec. 233.3(i).

SECTION

SIX

IMPLICATIONS OF THE CREDIT DISCLOSURE LAWS

This section is worth reading for personal as well as professional benefit. As to the former, these laws affect you every day in your daily purchases. You'll find it useful to update your knowledge of your rights from time to time. As to your professional benefit, in today's business environment, it is a dubious policy to assume that consumer credit laws are solely the province of your financial or credit departments. A serious marketing effort is impossible unless your customer has the ability to purchase. As was demonstrated in the period 1980 to late 1982, a lack of ability to borrow is a vital component in the consumer's purchase decision. Further, many payment options you offer are considered "credit." Therefore your credit policy is vital to your marketing effort. How your policy will benefit your consumer must be clearly conveyed both to boost sales and to avoid serious legal problems.

The FTC (which has a separate Division of Credit Practices to oversee enforcement by the commission) and other federal agencies have enforcement responsibilities in the area of credit regulations that affect you and your business.[1] The regulations involved have an increasing impact on situations and practices far removed from those generally thought to involve either consumers or credit. This agency (and its state compatriots) has adopted the policy of "caveat vendor" (let the seller beware) in its truth-in-lending enforcement as well as in its truth-in-advertising role.

Credit is a marketing decision variable, but a right decision about your markets can be a wrong decision legally. Anyone involved directly or indirectly in the extension of credit should have an overview of the prominent laws on point. The essence of compliance with these laws is proper *notice* and full *disclosure*. It is impossible within the scope of this book to make you a credit attorney, but seriously reviewing this section will make you familiar with the laws, their interpretations, and their terminology to assist you in integrating their requirements into your planning.[2] You should then obtain specific advice from your counsel, who will advise you of the specific intricacies that affect your business and your customers' credit needs.

REFERENCES

[1] The cast of administrative enforcers is legion. For example, the Truth-in-Lending Act assigns the administrative enforcement of its requirements to the following agencies: Federal Trade Commission, Federal Reserve Board, Comptroller of the Currency, Federal Deposit Insurance Corporation, Federal Home Loan Bank Board, Bureau of Federal Credit Unions, Civil Aeronautics Board, Department of Agriculture, and the Farm Credit Administration!

[2] If credit compliance is important to you or your business, you should subscribe to *Consumer Credit and Truth-in-Lending Compliance Report*, Warren, Gorham & Lamont, Inc., 210 South Street, Boston, Massachusetts, 02111.

FOURTEEN
TRUTH-IN-LENDING
ACT—REGULATION Z__

Understanding the Truth-in-Lending Act (Regulation Z) is useful to you personally as well as professionally since this law affects various aspects of your credit purchases.[1] The Truth-in-Lending Act was designed to improve disclosure of credit terms by creditors who regularly extend consumer credit, and the FTC was given the jurisdiction to enforce the act.

In enacting the Truth-in-Lending Act, Congress felt that the best marketplace decisions are made by an informed purchaser. Congress required that a consumer receive a full and detailed disclosure as to the full cost of consumer credit. Such costs to the consumer include the cash price, down payment, payment schedule, deferred-payment price, annual percentage rate, and other financial information. Each prospective purchaser of credit is to be treated on his or her merits without consideration of the economic bargaining power of such purchaser. The purchaser should then be able to comparison shop among the various credit options available and avoid the uninformed use of credit. To accomplish this fundamental objective, the act imposes a fairly complex and technical set of rules, which contain many pitfalls for the unwary.

MUST YOU COMPLY _____

The Truth-in-Lending Act does *not* govern every extension of credit; it is *limited to* an extension of credit where a finance charge is imposed for such

179

extension. The law likewise applies when there is no finance charge but payments will be made in *more* than four installments. To best understand this area, it is necessary to labor through a few important definitions. To come within the provisions of the act, the transaction must contain *all* four of the following variables:

1. The transaction must be a credit transaction (involving a credit sale), which is the right to defer payment of debt or the right to incur debt and defer payment.
2. The transaction must be a consumer credit transaction, which is credit offered or extended to a consumer primarily for personal, family, or household purposes. (It must not be for business or commercial purposes.)[2]
3. The consumer credit must be offered by a creditor. A creditor is one who regularly extends or arranges for the extension of credit. To be a creditor you need not extend credit but may merely "regularly arrange for the extension of credit." Regularly means extending credit more than 25 times during the preceding calendar year.[3]
4. Such arrangement or extention of credit must be payable by written agreement in more than four installments or with a finance charge.[4]

If all the preceding criteria are *not* met, the federal act does not cover you. If it does, you should not be myopic and focus only on the federal law. Consult state law, since Regulation Z will defer to substantially similar and *consistent* state laws. A "consistent" state law does not contradict current federal law.[5] Thus, the regulation leaves in effect state laws that require disclosures that the federal law no longer requires. For example, the federal law still requires disclosure of the amount financed, but it no longer requires any itemization of the components of the amount financed. A state law, modeled on the old federal law, will continue to require both, and creditors must continue to make both disclosures to satisfy state law. Review applicable state law requirements with your counsel.

In addition to keeping an eye on state law, you must determine whether you (as a creditor) are offering "open-end" credit or "closed-end" credit.

Open-end credit is consumer credit extended to a creditor under a plan in which:

1. The creditor reasonably expects the customer to make repeated transactions. This element of repeat transactions is based on good faith and your demonstration of your ongoing relationship with your borrower. (This would be easier for a financial institution to justify than a car dealer selling "one shots.")

2. The creditor may impose a finance charge from time to time on the unpaid balance. Note that your plan can meet the finance charge criterion even though most members actually pay no finance charge during their member life because they pay within 25 or 30 days (or whatever the time necessary to avoid finance charges) of billing. The only way a plan fails to meet this criterion is if there is no possibility that a periodic finance charge may be imposed on the outstanding balance.
3. As the customer pays the outstanding balance, that amount of credit is, generally, once again made available to the customer. This criterion contemplates a credit limit (reusable line) under which amounts repaid would generally be available for additional extensions of credit in the absence of individual credit problems.

Closed-end credit includes all consumer credit that does not fit the definition of open-end credit; it consists of both sales credit and loans. In a typical closed-end credit transaction, credit is advanced for a specific time period, and the lender and the customer agree on the amount financed, the finance charge, and the schedule of payments.

Now let's tie in these definitions with their practical impact on you—that is, what you must disclose. Credit decisions now affect not just legal compliance and your customer's ability to pay; they also impact a very real trade-off, copy space. If you comply with the Truth-in-Lending Act, you will sacrifice creative wording and copy space for required language and disclosures which must be printed clearly and conspicuously. Some of the disclosure areas are set forth in the following pages. However, make sure you review all copy text with your counsel.

OPEN-END CREDIT DISCLOSURES[6]

You must set forth your credit policy plan to your customers in a "clear and conspicuous" manner. The plan's wording must be in a reasonably understandable form. Such information must be furnished to your customer in a specific written disclosure statement prior to the consummation of the credit transaction. Your customer must be able to keep the full text of the disclosure form. The prominence you must give to the terms "finance charge" and "annual percentage rate" will vary depending on your particular communications vehicle. You *must* consult counsel before public circulation of your credit offer.[7]

Your disclosure need not be segregated from other material in your promotion. If a mailing is used, promotional or welcoming material may accompany the disclosure. The disclosures need not be located in a particular place, provided that they constitute an *entire, integrated* document. For example, you may use more than one page as well as the front and reverse sides. However, you cannot intersperse promotional material in your disclosures or send the disclosures in more than one envelope. Note that all previously mandated type-size requirements were eliminated.

TIME OF FIRST DISCLOSURE

The initial disclosure statement must be delivered *before* the first transaction under your plan and before your customer is obligated to the terms of the plan. Delivery of the disclosures is legally permissible at any time even if a membership fee or advance charge has already been posted, provided that your customer may, after receiving the disclosures, reject your plan with no further prejudice or obligation.

WHAT MUST THE INITIAL DISCLOSURE STATEMENT CONTAIN?

The initial disclosure must contain the following[8]:

1. All finance charge information must be included.
   a. When the finance charge accrues. (You need not state a specific date—a general one, e.g., "30 days from billing statement date" is sufficient.)
   b. What "free period" (before imposition of charges) your plan is extending.
   c. Each periodic rate, the range of balances to which it applies, and the corresponding annual percentage rate.
   d. An explanation of the method used to determine the balance subject to the finance charge.
   e. An explanation of how the finance charge will be determined by your plan, including the amount of any charge other than a finance charge that may be imposed (e.g., an additional "late fee").
   f. A statement outlining the creditor/member's respective rights and responsibilities under the Fair Credit Billing Act.

2. Any other material facts of significance to a reasonable consumer in his or her "comparison shopping" for credit must be included. A disclosure is material if "a reasonable consumer would find it significant in deciding whether to use credit."[9]

Later in the life of your plan, the following disclosures are necessary.

PERIODIC STATEMENTS. You must mail a periodic statement for each billing cycle for which there is an ending debit or credit balance of more than a dollar or on which a finance charge has been imposed.[10] The language and terminology of all statements must be the same as that used in the initial disclosure.

The statement must be sent at least 14 days prior to the end of any "free period" you granted in the initial disclosure. Failure to meet the 14-day period will forfeit the right to collect a finance charge in that cycle. In general, the periodic statement need not be sent if you have begun dunning. Each periodic statement you send must include the following disclosures:

1. Your customer's account balance at the beginning of the cycle.
2. An easy to understand identification of each transaction on your customer's account.
3. Each credit to your customer's account during the billing cycle, including the amount and date.
4. Each periodic rate, the range of balances, and the corresponding annual percentage rate.
5. The amount of each type (if more than one) of finance charge imposed during the billing cycle. These must be separately itemized.
6. All other account debits.
7. The closing date of the billing cycle and the outstanding balance on that date.
8. The address to be used for notification of billing errors. (See the in-depth discussion of the Fair Credit Billing Act later in this section).[11] A telephone number may also be given, but the number may *not* be in lieu of an address. Further, the number should be accompanied by a precautionary instruction that telephoning will not preserve your customer's rights. This latter instruction will also be stated in the initial disclosures.

OTHER SUBSEQUENT DISCLOSURES. Other required disclosures include:

1. *Annual Statement of Billing Rights.* Here you may elect to send out the same statement provided with the initial disclosure, or you may include

a shorter statement on or with each periodic statement. The annual statement is sent to all your credit-qualified active customers for the particular billing cycle in which the annual statement is mailed.
2. *Change in Terms.* The member must be notified (with certain exceptions) of any changes in credit features, terms, rates, etc.

OTHER COMPLIANCE REQUIREMENTS

You will be required to credit your customer's payment as of the date of receipt. For instance, payment by check is received on the date of arrival, not when the funds are collected.

However, you may require a "no cash in the mail" policy and that your customer include an account number on the check. If your customer's check is nonconforming, a reasonable in-house processing delay may result during which finance charges accrue.

You must comply with the treatment of credit balances (more on this later in the section). The law here has been clarified.[12] Whereas formerly the law spoke only of "payment balances," it now specifically includes balances resulting from *any* source, including returns. Also, the time to mail a refund specifically requested by a member has been extended from 5 to 7 business days.

Finally, you should retain records evidencing your compliance for 2 years from the date the disclosures are required to be made or actions are required to be taken.[13] A customer who catches you in violation of this act must sue you within 1 year of the alleged violation or be barred by the statute of limitations.[14]

CLOSED-END CREDIT DISCLOSURES

Disclosures for closed-end credit must be made clearly and conspicuously in writing and in a form that your customer may keep. You can make specific terms, such as "amount financed," "finance charge," and "annual percentage rate," more conspicuous by printing these terms in bolder type or in colors different from other disclosures, by underlining them, or by putting them between asterisks. The disclosures should be grouped and *segregated* from all other materials (in contrast to open-end credit). The itemization of the amount financed must be provided separately from your other segregated disclosures.[15] This segregation may be accomplished by any of the following:

- Outlining them in a box
- Using bold print dividing lines
- Using a contrasting color background
- Using different style of type (e.g., elite or pica)
- Placing them on a separate sheet of paper

However, there are exceptions to the group and segregate requirements which should be reviewed with your counsel.

CONTENT OF THE DISCLOSURES

As applicable, the following disclosures should be made for each closed-end credit transaction:

1. Identity of the creditor.[16] You should include your firm's name, address, and telephone number, although this is optional. All the law specifically requires is that you state your correct name.
2. The amount financed. The term "amount financed" must actually be used.[17] This must be accompanied by a brief description such as "the amount of credit provided to you or on your behalf."
3. An itemization of the amount financed.
4. The finance charge. The term "finance charge" must be used with a brief description such as "the dollar amount this credit will cost you."[18]
5. Annual percentage rate. This term must be used with a brief description such as "the cost of your credit at a yearly rate."[19] For variable rate transactions, this language may be modified.
6. Variable rate.
7. Payment schedule, including the number, amount, and timing of payments to repay the obligation. The repayment schedule should reflect all components of the finance charge, not merely interest.
8. Total of payments. Use this specific term along with a brief explanation, such as "the amount you will have paid when you have made all the scheduled payments." This must be disclosed unless it is a single-payment transaction. For variable rate transactions the phrase may be modified.
9. Demand feature, if any.
10. Total sale price. Use this specific term and a descriptive explanation (including the amount of any downpayment) such as "the total price

of your purchase on credit, including your down payment of $_____."
The total sale price is the sum of the cash price, finance charge, and
other items such as taxes, license fees, and insurance premiums that
have not been included in the cash price or finance charge.
11. Prepayment costs.
12. Late-payment charge.
13. The security interest the creditor may or may not acquire in the
property as part of the transaction.
14. Insurance.
15. Certain security interest charges.
16. Contrast reference.
17. Assumption policy.
18. Required deposit.

As you can gather from the varied nature of the areas reviewed, this is a
complicated area. Don't attempt to design the disclosure documents yourself without the assistance of counsel.[20]

CONSIDER A LATE FEE

If you demand a late payment and want to avoid the Truth-in-Lending
Act, make sure that your late fee is not a finance charge. A charge assessed
for late payment is distinguishable from a finance charge in that it is
imposed for an actual and *unanticipated* event. The specific citation on
point reads as follows: "A late payment, delinquency, default, reinstate-
ment or other such charge is not a finance charge if imposed for actual
unanticipated late payment, delinquency, default or other such
occurrence."[21]

To comply with the statutory exemption, your late fee plan must satisfy
the following:

1. The account must involve credit extended on a *single* occasion for a
specified sum.
2. The late charge may not be cumulative.
3. Your bill must offer your customer no choice but full and immediate
payment. I wouldn't stress a grace period if you offer one, since it
might dilute the immediacy of your payment demand. You want no
inference made that you are giving your customers any right to defer
payment. You expect it now, and you demand it now.
4. It can only be a one-time charge based on the amount of a monthly
payment due and *not* on any general balance.

5. Most important, your system must be one in which you can demonstrate that your late-payment charge assessment is not anticipated.

IMPLEMENTATION

State your payment policy up front, for example, "payment due on
receipt." Then no late fee should be assessed until you consider an account
in default and treat your customer accordingly (e.g., dunning). If you do
not regard your customer's account in default in the event of a late
payment but continue to service the customer, you will expose yourself to
a finance charge disclosure problem. You will definitely have a finance
charge if the policy is to continue servicing and assessing late fees from
time to time until paid.

In short, you may only use one late fee per account until the account is
paid in full. Service may then be resumed.

CREDIT CARD USE

Regulation Z imposes minimal compliance on those who merely honor a
credit card where no finance charge is imposed at the time of the
transaction.

CASH DISCOUNTS

This option is finding increasing favor by those who wish to encourage full
and immediate payment. The Truth-in-Lending Act continues to prohibit
a credit card issuer from prohibiting merchants from offering cash discounts, and thus the option is available provided that you can distinguish
your discount from a surcharge.[22]

For example, say the battery you are promoting goes for $50. You wish
to charge your credit card customers the going rate but offer a 10 percent
discount to those who pay cash.[23] You must present your discount in a
classic legal juxtaposition; your discount price must focus on the credit
card price and *not* the cash price. Also, all your customers must be aware of
your policy *before* they make their purchases.

You can do this by merely quoting the higher price verbally. If you print
or otherwise tag prices on your product, you should display only the credit

card price and *not* the cash price. Also, all your customers must be aware of your policy *before* they make their purchases.

You can do this by merely quoting the higher price verbally. If you print or otherwise tag prices on your product, you should display only the credit card price. By displaying both prices, you run the risk that someone will remove the credit card price. This can present a surcharge issue.

A surcharge can only result if the only price you feature is the price paid by your cash customers *after* the discount is given. In other words, if you post the price of the battery we discussed at $45 rather than $50, the $50 paid for the battery by your credit card purchasers is an *illegal* surcharge. Any credit card customer who pays the surcharge may sue you for damages for breach of the Truth-in-Lending Act.

This distinction between cash discounts and surcharges is important if you price the goods in a particular outlet as well as supervise the creative presentation of such price. This is another reason you should have your counsel work with you in designing all credit and discount promotion plans and copy.[24]

Note that we've been speaking only of cash discounts in lieu of credit cards. There is no surcharge problem if you are surcharging those who obtain credit from you without a credit card. For example, surcharges imposed on closed-end credit buyers who obtain credit without the use of a credit card are never illegal.

CONCLUSION

If your business practices are not within the realm of the areas covered in this chapter, the Truth-in-Lending Act does not directly affect you. If you are included or think you might be, consult your counsel. This is not an area where you can cross your fingers and "hope for the best"; most judges will demand literal compliance. Areas such as specific disclosures or even how such disclosures are placed on the copy become issues. For example, you may be required to use only one side of each piece of paper to avoid "hidden" disclosures on the back.[25]

Remember that with the Truth-in-Lending Act and all credit requirements discussed hereafter, more protective state statutes and regulations are usually permitted. In addition, the legislative and judicial dynamics at the federal and state levels are such that these laws constantly change through legislative amendment and court rulings.

REFERENCES

1 Pub. L. No. 90-321 as amended. 12 C.F.R. sec. 226; effective July 1, 1969, amended to April 1, 1981 (Regulation Z), 15 U.S.C. sec. 1601 *et seq.*

2 This area will be construed quite literally. *See* Anderson v. Rocky Mountain Fed. Sav. and Loan Ass'n, 651 P.2d 269 (1982).

3 12 C.F.R. sec. 226.2(a)(12).

4 12 C.F.R. sec. 226.4.

5 12 C.F.R. sec. 226.2(a).

6 12 C.F.R. sec. 226.5.

7 12 C.F.R. sec. 226.5(a)(2). The failure to so disclose renders a creditor liable to the customer for a penalty of twice the amount of the finance charge (no less than $100 or more than $1000). *See* 15 U.S.C.S. sec. 1631.

8 12 C.F.R. secs. 226.6–226.7.

9 Bustamente v. First Fed. Sav. and Loan Ass'n, 619 F.2d 360, 364 (1980). *See also* Ivey v. United States Dep't of Hous. and Urban Dev., 428 F. Supp. 1337 (1977), Davis v. FDIC, 620 F.2d 489 (1980), and Brown v. National Permanent Fed. Sav. and Loan Ass'n, 526 F. Supp. 815 (1981). *See also* Dixey v. Idaho First Nat'l Bank, 505 F. Supp. 846 (1981) ("technical errors" distinguished). Whether your customer can read or understand English is not relevant—the disclosure ritual is; *see* Zamarippa v. Cy's Car Sales, Inc., 674 F.2d 877 (1982).

10 12 C.F.R. sec. 226.7.

11 12 C.F.R. sec. 226.13.

12 12 C.F.R. sec. 226.11.

13 12 C.F.R. sec. 226.25.

14 Lawson v. Congers Chrysler, Plymouth & Dodge Trucks, Inc., 600 F.2d 465 (1979).

15 12 C.F.R. sec. 226.17(a)(1)–(2).

16 12 C.F.R. sec. 226.18(a).

17 12 C.F.R. sec. 226.18(b).

18 12 C.F.R. sec. 226.18(d). Footnote 41 states: "The finance charge shall be considered accurate if it is not more than $5.00 above or below the exact finance charge in a transaction involving an amount financed of $1,000 or less, or not more than $10.00 above or below the exact finance charge in a transaction involving an amount financed of more than $1,000."

19 12 C.F.R. sec. 226.18(e). For some very small transactions the regulation allows for some exceptions. Footnote 42 states "For any transaction involving a finance charge of $5 or less on an amount financed of $75 or less, or a finance charge of $7.50 or less on an amount financed of more than $75 the creditor need not disclose the annual percentage rate."

20 For assistance in this area, order *How to Advertise Consumer Credit*, which is an FTC Manual for Business. It contains a number of samples of disclosure wording you might find useful. Ask for Publication No. MO1-3, issued June 1982. You could call or write to any FTC office listed in Section 2 or write to the Federal Trade Commission, Division of Credit Practices, 6th & Pennsylvania Avenue, N.W., Washington, D.C., 20580.

[21] 12 C.F.R. sec. 226.4(c)(2). *See* comment 4(c)(2)-1. *See also* Vega v. First Fed. Sav. and Loan Ass'n of Detroit, 433 F. Supp. 624 (1977).

[22] 12 C.F.R. sec. 226.12(f)(1). When done properly, these discounts are excluded from finance disclosure requirements, 12 C.F.R. sec. 226.4(c)(8).

[23] Note that, prior to its recent amendment, the Truth-in-Lending Act required retailers to treat discounts greater than 5 percent of the credit card price as a finance charge and disclose it as such to their credit card customers. Under the law currently in effect, a lawful discount is not a finance charge no matter how large it is. However, you have the option to offer such discounts on *only* certain types of products or certain stores in a chain.

[24] Check with your counsel as to whether a surcharge problem still exists according to federal and/or state law. The federal prohibition should expire by March 1, 1984. However, it may be reenacted, or your state may have one, and such state law would *not* be "inconsistent" with the federal. You might also contact the FTC directly by calling (202) 724-1139 or writing Federal Trade Commission, Bureau of Consumer Protection, 6th & Pennsylvania Avenue, Washington, D.C., 20580.

[25] Chapman v. Miller, 575 S.W.2d 581 (1978) and Charles v. Krauss Co., 572 F.2d 544 (1978). For a pamphlet about what information the consumer may receive, contact the Director, Division of Consumer Affairs, Federal Reserve Systems, Washington, D.C., 20551, and ask for *How to File a Consumer Credit Complaint.*

CHAPTER

FIFTEEN

FAIR CREDIT BILLING ACT

Under early Roman law, creditors who could not obtain satisfaction from a debtor were allowed to cut up the debtor's body and divide the pieces. Recognizing that law always desires an alternative, the Romans also allowed creditors to leave the debtor alive and sell him into slavery. Now, however, debtors are better off and have more protections. One of these protections is the Fair Credit Billing Act.[1]

This act is an amendment to the Truth-in-Lending Act. This is the law each of your customers is familiar with, because it is restated periodically in their credit card bills. Your customer is on top of this one, so you'd better be too—both to protect yourself legally and to enhance customer relations.

The Fair Credit Billing Act was designed to protect your customers against unfair practices of issuers of *open-end* credit. The act requires credit grantors to inform debtors of their rights and responsibilities in a billing dispute which essentially involves five steps. It also requires creditors to resolve billing disputes within a specific time (activated by the customer's *written* correspondence) by making appropriate account adjustments or explaining why the original bill is believed to have been correct.

Many of you may have an electronic funds transfer (EFT) payment operation, or may otherwise fall within Regulation E's definition of "financial institution." The procedures for resolution of EFT billing errors are generally patterned after those found in the Fair Credit Billing Act, and we'll discuss where they differ.

MUST YOU COMPLY?

You'll want to review the definitions contained in the Truth-in-Lending Act, particularly that of open-end credit.[2]

Electronic fund transfer exemptions and nuances which might affect your firm's operations should be discussed with your counsel; we'll assume compliance to cover all bases. For our purposes we'll operate with a general definition that EFT means any transfer of funds:

1. Other than one originated by check, draft, or similar paper instrument
2. That is initiated through an electronic terminal, telephone, computer, or magnetic tape
3. Which orders or authorizes a financial institution to debit or credit an account

The term includes most transfers that take place at automated teller machines (ATMs) or point-of-sale (POS) terminals (including deposits), payment by telephone or transfer plans, direct deposit of payroll, government benefits, or annuities and automatic payments of bills, such as insurance premiums or mortgages.

The term *excludes* cash or check payments at ATMs, most direct payments made by composite check and check truncation systems. The Regulation E Commentary also excludes home banking terminals for purposes of the regulation's receipt requirement. Transfers initiated by means of home banking terminals, however, are subject to all of the regulation's other provisions.[3]

If your promotions do not fall within the definitions of open-end credit, you are not required to provide with your billing a statement informing the consumer of the right to dispute billing errors. However, if you honor credit cards in a consumer credit transaction, certain sections of the act should be reviewed with your counsel, specifically those which deal with open-end credit, credit card accounts,[4] and possible exceptions to the general rule.[5] As with all federal acts, all state laws on point should also be reviewed.[6]

Once you are satisfied that you are within the area covered by law, you may become involved with a billing error situation. A billing error can arise when:

1. The extension of credit is "not made to the consumer or to a person who has actual, implied, or apparent authority to use the consumer's credit card or open-end credit plan (this includes the question of a lost or stolen credit card).[7]

2. The consumer refuses to take delivery of goods because they were the wrong quantity, were delivered late, or otherwise did not comply with the contract.
3. The creditor failed to properly credit a payment or credit to the consumer's account.
4. There was a mathemetical error affecting the consumer's account.
5. Incorrect or unauthorized electronic fund transfers took place.[8]
6. There are any other legitimate grievances affecting an open-end credit plan. Remember that you're selling customer service and satisfaction as well as marketing a product, so don't try to be technical here. Follow the mandated procedure for billing dispute resolution.

KEEPING A CUSTOMER AND COMPLYING WITH THE LAW

If you and your counsel have determined that you must comply, you will be required to distribute a notice in the form prescribed informing all your customers of their rights under the act and the means to implement such rights.[9] You've probably received such notices in your own credit card bills every few months, so you are familiar with them.

You should acquaint yourself with the general and specific disclosure requirements of the Fair Credit Billing Act.[10] As a "covered" creditor, you are required to disclose to the consumer the following customer and creditor obligations under the act:

1. The notice must be given by the consumer personally. The creditor is not "notified" by discovering the error itself. The customer is required to put the complaint *in writing*. The written correspondence must include the name, description of the error, and any other pertinent information (such as type, date, and amount of error) and mailed to the company *within 60 days* of the alleged billing error. You have the right to require that it be received at the address designated for this purpose on the periodic statement. A telephone call will not preserve your customer's rights.[11]

EFT procedure: The notification may be oral or written. If the notice is oral, the institution may require a *written confirmation* to be received within 10 business days, if the consumer is advised of the requirement at the time of the call and given the appropriate mailing address.[12]

2. You, the creditor, must acknowledge the customer's written inquiry within 30 days of receipt. Then within two complete billing cycles after the end of the billing cycle in which the notification is received (and in no event more than 90 days), you must either correct the error or explain why you believe the bill was correct.[13]

EFT procedure: The institution has 10 business days to investigate, determine whether an error occurred, and transmit the results. It may extend this time up to 45 days, *if:*

a. It provisionally recredits within 10 business days of receipt of the error notice.

b. It recredits not only the disputed amount, but also interest, where applicable.

c. It promptly (within 2 business days) notifies the consumer of the amount and date of the credit and that he or she will have full use of the funds pending resolution.[14]

3. During this interval, neither you nor a collection agency may take any collection action concerning the amount in dispute. Action includes imposing a finance charge or any other such charge or compelling payment of a minimum periodic payment when only such minimum is involved. The consumer is, however, obliged to pay all undisputed debts during this interval unless the dispute is your failure to send a periodic statement. If this is the dispute, then it affects the entire balance owed, and your customer need pay none of the amount in question until he or she receives the statement. The customer then has the same amount of time to pay as he or she would have had if the statement had been received on time.

4. You must then investigate the dispute. To prove you are correct you must be able to provide written documentation of the purchase by the customer. If you are not correct, you must credit the account with the disputed amount and any related charges and must mail or deliver a correction notice to the customer.[15] If you are correct, you must inform the customer.

EFT procedure: The institution must promptly (within 1 business day) correct the account. The customer must be informed of the correction orally or in writing within 10 business days (or 45 calendar days, if applicable—see item 2) of receipt of the error notice. The amount of consumer liability for unauthorized use may be deducted from the amount to be recredited where appropriate.

5. Once you have explained the bill in the correct manner, you may then proceed to collect in the normal manner. After compliance you have no further responsibility under this section if the consumer "continues to make substantially the same allegation with respect to such error."[16]

EFT procedure: If it is determined that no error occurred or that an error occurred but in a different manner or amount than that alleged by the customer:

a. The institution will mail a written explanation mentioning the consumer's right to request documentation within 3 business days of the determination.

b. The institution may immediately debit the recredited amount, but concurrently it must give oral or written notice of the date and the amount debited and must disclose the fact that the institution will honor preauthorized transfers and checks payable to third persons for 5 business days after transmitting the notice.

c. If the consumer requests them, the institution must promptly mail or deliver the documents relied on.[17]

CONCLUSION

The Fair Credit Billing Act is primarily self-enforcing. The FTC has favored an education campaign to inform consumers of their ability to use and enforce the act. To comply with the act, you must set up a system internally to resolve open-end credit transaction billing disputes. Your specific practices should be reviewed with your counsel in light of this act and applicable state law, and possibly in light of the provisions of the Electronic Funds Transfer Act. If you are not strictly within the definitions set forth, this act's provisions provide a workable model that your customers understand from purchasing activity elsewhere and one that the FTC endorses.

REFERENCES

[1] 12 C.F.R. sec. 226.13, 15 U.S.C. sec. 1601. Since this is an amendment to the Truth-in-Lending Act, compliance is predicated on whether your practices come within the specifications of the definitions in that act governing open-end creditors (see discussion on point in previous chapter).

[2] 12 C.F.R. sec. 226.2(20). "Open-end credit" means consumer credit.

[3] Regulation E, 12 C.F.R. sec. 205.2(a).

[4] 12 C.F.R. sec. 226.2(15).

[5] 12 C.F.R. secs. 226.2(17)(i)–.2(17)(v), 226.12.

[6] For example, N.Y. Gen. Bus. Law secs. 701–707 (McKinney 1982).

[7] 12 C.F.R. sec. 226.13(a)(1).

[8] Regulation E, 12 C.F.R. sec. 205.11(a). As we discussed, if the extension of credit is incident to an electronic fund transfer, you must comply with these error resolution procedures rather than those of 12 C.F.R. sec. 226.13(i). *See* Robert J. Posch, Jr., "Credit Card and Electronic Fund Transfer Fraud," *Direct Marketing*, November 1983, pp. 97–101.

[9] 12 C.F.R. secs. 226.5, 226.6, 226.7, 226.8, and 226.9 should be reviewed.

[10] 12 C.F.R. sec. 226.13.

[11] 12 C.F.R. sec. 226.13(b)(1)–.13(b)(3).

[12] 12 C.F.R. sec. 205.11(b).

[13] 12 C.F.R. sec. 226.13(c).

[14] 12 C.F.R. sec. 205.11(c).

[15] 12 C.F.R. sec. 226.13(e).

[16] 12 C.F.R. sec. 226.13(b).

[17] 12 C.F.R. sec. 205.11(f).

CHAPTER

SIXTEEN

FAIR CREDIT
REPORTING ACT

A fact of life in this decade is that more and more information is being collected about individuals. Direct marketers do it for targeted marketing; credit bureaus and government bureaus collect other information about us. You can't escape it.

For many the constant computerization of credit and personal information raises the spectre of an Orwellian nightmare in which an individual's innermost thoughts and activities are collecting in someone's computer profile. This tension will increase; fingerprinting and social security numbers have created the ability to end all escape. Computerization has eliminated even the privacy afforded through the haphazard collection of files.

If you have a charge account, a mortgage on your home, a life insurance policy, or if you have applied for a personal loan or a job, it is almost certain that somewhere there is a file that shows how promptly you pay your bills, whether you have been sued or arrested, or if you have filed for bankruptcy. Such a file may include your neighbors' and friends' views of your character, general reputation, or manner of living. More insidiously, the information might be inaccurate or dated.

The Fair Credit Reporting Act (FCRA) was passed by Congress to protect consumers against the circulation of inaccurate or obsolete information and to ensure that consumer reporting agencies adopt fair and equitable procedures for obtaining, maintaining, and disseminating information about consumers.[1]

Because of its impact on customer lists and other information (as well as your personal credit history), we'll detail the FCRA as lucidly as possible to give you a basic understanding of its requirements.

Before proceeding, it should be understood that the credit industry had solid input into this act. It was a compromise between business's need for these reports and the Orwellian nightmare raised by some concerning the computerization of individual lives. The law is straightforward and sets forth due process protections for the subjects of credit reports. Some of these rights include:

1. Notification to the subject of denial of credit[2]
2. Disclosure of specific reasons for the denial
3. Right of the subject to dispute the information and compel possible reinvestigation[3]
4. Failing correction of the subject's file, the right of the subject to have an explanation included in the file.[4]

There are three key definitions essential to your understanding of the FCRA: the definitions of "consumer reporting agency,"[5] "consumer report,"[6] and what constitutes permissible purposes of these reports.[7] The full text of these definitions is included in the references, and I encourage you to review these at this time. If your activities fall within the wording of these definitions, you must comply with the provisions of the FCRA.

ENFORCEMENT OF THE ACT

Administrative enforcement to police credit-reporting agencies (but not lenders) rests primarily with the FTC. A violation of the FCRA subjects the offender only to an FTC cease and desist order; the FTC was not given civil penalty or redress powers.

A private enforcement action may, however, be maintained by an injured consumer in the form of a civil suit for willful noncompliance with the FCRA and for recovery of actual and punitive damages as well as attorney fees. There is no ceiling on the amount of punitive damages a consumer may recover, and a suit may be brought in any appropriate court in the United States without regard to the amount in controversy.

A 2-year statute of limitations from the date liability arises is provided for civil suits; however, where a defendant willfully misrepresented information required by the FCRA to be disclosed to a consumer, and the information is material to the establishment of the defendant's liability, the statute of limitations does not begin to run until discovery of the misrepresentation.

GETTING THE INFORMATION YOU WANT WHILE AVOIDING THE FTC

The term "consumer report" does not include any report composed entirely of information concerning transactions and experiences between the consumer and the person making the report which is based on trade experience. This trade experience will pass the FTC's permissible purpose test provided that it is limited to transactions and experiences between the person contacted for information and the consumer of the information and that the person contacted has first-hand knowledge of these experiences.[8] Congress exempted trade information reports for FCRA regulation, because a report based solely on a merchant's personal experience with a consumer is likely to be reliable.[9]

This test must be met for each name on the list. Essentially, that test requires that you demonstrate that you are contemplating the *immediate* extension of credit to (or otherwise have a permissible purpose for obtaining information on) *each* consumer on the list at the time you request or receive the list or information. This exception could apply to a list of applicants reviewed by a credit bureau or a sole individual call made by a merchant to a credit card issuer with respect to the current status of the purchaser's credit line. Similarly, in response to a request for credit information from a user, you cannot disseminate such a list unless you are satisfied that you have reason to believe that the user has received a request for credit from each consumer on the list.

For example, a firm may request, for its own use, information from another business concerning its dealings with a *particular* customer. As long as the original firm limits the use of the information received from the other business to its own application and does not disseminate it to third parties, it will not become a consumer reporting agency. The act of seeking credit information from other businesses might appear to be "assembling or evaluating" consumer credit information; however, as long as the information is strictly for the firm's own use, such assembling or evaluating cannot be said to be for the purpose of furnishing consumer reports to third parties.

COMMERICAL FREE SPEECH

The right to commercial free speech is expanding, although, when the FCRA was enacted, commercial free speech enjoyed few if any First Amendment protections. The FCRA has a chilling effect on the collection of certain data; shouldn't the collection of such commercial information now be constitutionally protected?

The U.S. Supreme Court held that the free flow of information in the commercial sector is as much a part of First Amendment values as the robust and open debate of political issues.[10] In fact, the Court went so far as to state that the "particular consumer's interest in the free flow of commercial information . . . may be as keen if not keener by far, than his interest in the day's most urgent political debate."[11] This statement, while criticized by some, is patently obvious. A lot more people may remember a beer commercial than a news brief or even the name of their local assemblyperson. An even more obvious example is the fact that a lot more people actively shopped in the December Christmas season than voted in the November election.

However, the strongest endorsement from the Court came in the following quote:

> *Advertising, however tasteless and excessive it sometimes may seem, is nonetheless dissemination of information as to who is producing and selling what product, for what reason, and at what price. So long as we preserve a predominantly free enterprise economy, the allocation of our resources in large measure will be made through numerous private economic decisions.* It is a matter of public interest that those decisions, in the aggregrate, be intelligent and well-informed. To this end, the free flow of commercial information is indispensable. . . . *And if it is indispensable to the proper allocation of resources in a free enterprise system, it is also indispensable to the formation of intelligent opinion as to how that system ought to be regulated or altered.* [Emphasis my own.][12]

The U.S. Supreme Court has held that the flow of commercial information is vital to a free enterprise economy and is as much a part of First Amendment values as the robust and open debate of political issues. Obviously, it could be argued that list information is therefore protected. This information is built in your data base, and restrictions on the creation of your data base might constitute a prior restraint on the content of your message and a general restraint on the free flow of ideas in the commercial marketplace.

The first state court to take up the constitutionality of the FCRA is in Maine.[13] The court invalidated provisions of the *state* statute that:

1. Require users of investigative consumer reports to obtain the consumer's written authorization before obtaining a report

2. Prohibit reporting of information about the consumer's race, religion, color, sexual preference or orientation, or political affiliation
3. Prohibit the reporting of specific categories of obsolete information

Obviously this is not the last word. The Supreme Court ruled on advertising, not on the free speech of consumer reporting agencies. However, it should be noted that the Supreme Court had the opportunity to review the decision on certiorari and did not.[14] Obviously, this matter is in flux, and you should anticipate future litigation to clarify certain areas. Stay abreast of the area with your counsel. In the interim, there are certain contractual points you should consider.

CLEAR CONTRACTUAL PROTECTION

You will probably need the assistance of a credit bureau. Outside of your own in-house collection file, the bureau is your primary source of information about deadbeats or delinquent payers. However, a firm in your industry or product line (especially a competitor) might be preferable, because that firm is more likely to possess the bad file histories of consumers you wish to avoid. Set up a formal arrangement to exchange the information.

Whether you employ the services of a credit bureau or exchange information with another firm, have your attorney draw up a basic contract to protect your interests. Your contract should state that all parties to the contract agree not to homogenize their lists. Otherwise you will no longer be relating your respective individual experiences but the total experiences accumulated from your own lists and the lists of the other contract parties.

If you are dealing with credit bureaus, your contract should also have an air-tight indemnification clause. The credit bureau should protect you with the following warranties:

1. The credit bureau should warrant to you that it is not guilty of negligence (for example, in correcting its list, recording judgments, and removing stale names from its list). These issues are important. In a recent decision the court noted that a credit-reporting agency is not automatically liable each time it reports inaccurate information, but it must do something reasonable to verify its information, *especially after a consumer has refuted it.*[15] An inaccurate list wastes your money on useless names.

a. The time for retaining adverse credit records may vary. The FTC's current position is 7 years, but New York State's is 5.[16] Therefore, you don't want New York State names a day older than 5 years (bank-ruptcies may be reported for 14 years).

b. The time for the removal of stale names varies. New York State requires every consumer reporting agency to clarify their records within 60 days of a proper or partial satisfaction piece.[17]

2. Your indemnification clause and related insurance coverage should specify protection against private actions, e.g., libel protection. Although administrative enforcement of the FCRA rests primarily with the FTC, a private right of enforcement may be maintained by a consumer in the form of a civil suit for willful noncompliance with the FCRA. One such area of noncompliance you might be exposed to is libel.[18]

In general, a credit report sent by a commercial credit agency to an interested subscriber is privileged and immune to attack for libel. However, the report must have been furnished in good faith and not be the result of malice or a gross and reckless disregard of known facts.[19] However, although there is no strict liability for inaccuracies in a credit report, the credit agency must follow reasonable procedures to ensure the maximum possible accuracy of information concerning the individual about whom a credit report relates.[20] A consumer may also recover damages from a credit bureau for negligently releasing a report on a consumer to someone who has no right to it.[21] In one case, a court judged that a credit-reporting agency had properly refused to provide a credit report in response to a grand jury subpoena.[22]

The onus of any negative performance will probably be directed against your agency from the first instance, and you are well advised to clarify this in your contract with your agency.

3. The credit bureau must warrant to you that it is in compliance with all relevant federal, state, and local laws and regulations and that it routinely monitors and updates its system as ongoing legislative dynamics impose changes. This warranty not only enhances the integrity of the names acquired but also follows the FTC's mandate that any firm acquiring credit information must use its best efforts to obtain only accurate information about delinquent debtors.

COMPLIANCE WITH FCRA

There are two ways to get yourself involved in consumer reports: volun-tarily and involuntarily. We'll discuss the latter first, because, without due caution, you can easily become involved in reporting consumer credit.

For example, a firm furnished merchants (by subscription) with "alert lists" of consumers who allegedly had passed bad checks.[23] The lists did not pertain to a particular customer a firm was preparing to do business with, but rather contained 30 to 500 names provided at random.

The firm did not have an adequate system either to check the allegations on its list or to delete the names of those incorrectly placed on the list. Further, the subscribers did not have a *legitimate business need* for the data, and the firm did not obtain certifications from its subcribers that such subscribers would only use the lists for permissible purposes.

The FTC held that such lists are not "consumer reports" because the information was not collected for consumer reporting purposes and because it could not be reasonably anticipated that they would be used in connection with a legitimate business transaction with persons reported on. It is not sufficient that the consumer report be distributed in *anticipation* that a permissible purpose will subsequently arise.

The primary purpose of the alert lists was to warn potential victims of the habits, practices, and descriptions of alleged check forgers, swindlers, and others. If such bulletins remain devoid of information collected or reasonably expected to be used for the purpose of establishing the subjects' eligibility for consumer credit, insurance, employment, or other purposes, they cannot be afforded the protections of the FCRA.

You should note that you might be able to overcome this problem of indiscriminate alert lists by designing a proper coding system.[24] The system you review with your counsel should consist of (at a minimum) a unique identifier, other than a name, through which the subscriber may identify the consumer and decode the information in connection with a business transaction. Thus the decoded information will become available to the subscriber only when a legitimate business need for the information arises in connection with a business transaction involving the consumer.[25]

The FTC has stated that *credit guides* ("alert lists"), which are alphabetical listings of random consumers assembled and sold to users, violate the FCRA. No recipient could conceivably have a transaction with every individual in the guides.[26]

If you are unsure whether your firm may be dealing in consumer reports, it would be a good idea to review a few other FTC decisions on this topic and, of course, to consult counsel.

VOLUNTARY COMPLIANCE

As a consumer reporting agency you must do whatever is reasonable under the circumstances to minimize the chances that an alleged debtor will be harmed by inaccurate reporting.[27] Your alleged debtor has the right to the following services.

1. When a consumer (alleged debtor) is adversely affected by information contained in the report, the user of the report must, without awaiting any request by the consumer, notify the consumer of the adverse action and provide him or her with the name and address of the consumer reporting agency making the report.[28]

2. The consumer may then contact you and when given proper indentification, you must disclose the "nature and substance of all information in your files on the consumer" at the time the request is made, including the sources of such information. The procedures of correcting disputed information extend to *all* the information in a consumer's file, not just to information included in a consumer report. The term "file," when used in connection with information on any consumer, means all the information on that consumer recorded and retained by a consumer reporting agency regardless of how the information is stored.[29]

3. You must furnish the names of any persons who have received a report on the consumer within the last 6 months.

4. When giving consumers access to their files, you must provide trained personnel competent to explain their contents or use or to decode any data.

5. Consumers may have obsolete, inaccurate, or unverifiable information deleted from their files.

6. You must reinvestigate the information in the file if its accuracy is disputed by the consumer.

7. If the information remains in dispute, the consumer may file a brief explanatory statement (not more than 100 words) concerning the disputed items. The consumer's statement *must* be included in the file and furnished to users of the consumer report.

8. If an error was made, you must notify creditors who received the file during the past 6 months that an error was made.

9. All adverse information must be deleted from the consumer's file after 7 years except in certain situations. State laws may require deletions in a shorter period of time.[30]

Further, compliance includes proper encoding to ensure anonymity and to avoid involvement with the publication of overbroad "protective bulletins" or alert lists. Every name reported on must be an ascertainable *individual* person. "Address hits" if so used (and many firms do) must produce specific information which concerns only the person who is the subject of an inquiry. Address hits which report on others at the same address are prohibited by the FTC.[31] This is in keeping with the trend in the law to maintain credit histories on individuals and not family units (discussed in detail in Chapter 17).

CONCLUSION

As discussed, compliance in the area of fair credit reporting will be altered by litigation and possibly narrower state statutes; however, in the interim, compliance with this law makes good business as well as legal sense. As we'll discuss in Section 7, in-house creditors were exempted, because these collectors generally want to do business with the alleged debtor again.

Likewise, in this instance accurate information is needed to avoid doing business with a deadbeat. But what is more important, you need accurate information so that you do not lose a business opportunity with a good payer classified incorrectly by obsolete information.

Finally, an unpleasant experience in this area will turn off a potential buyer who wants to do business with you. If the buyer is good, you want him or her. Demanding accurate information from your credit bureau is in the best interest of you and your customer.

REFERENCES

[1] 15 U.S.C. sec. 1681 (1974). The FTC has an excellent report on point entitled "Compliance With the Fair Credit Reporting Act." You should order one from: Bureau of Consumer Protection, Federal Trade Commission, Washington, D.C., 20580. *See also* Robert J. Posch, Jr., "Fair Credit Reporting Act—Another List Issue," *Direct Marketing*, August 1983, pp. 130–143.

[2] 15 U.S.C. sec. 1681(m). Note that there is a tighter law in California for certain notification (Civil Code sec. 1785.10–.20) relating to such agency's *automatically* advising a consumer of the agency's obligation to make a written disclosure to the consumer. This disclosure should be made each time the agency gives information to a client. The law further increases consumers' access to their files, although I have privacy reservations about this section, since it permits a consumer to contact by phone—a potentially improper way to access confidential information about another.

[3] 15 U.S.C. sec. 1681(i).

[4] 15 U.S.C. sec. 1681(c).

[5] The term "consumer reporting agency" [15 U.S.C. sec. 1681(a)(a)] means:

> . . . any person which, for monetary fees, dues *or on a cooperative nonprofit basis regularly engages in whole or in part* in the practice of assembling or evaluating consumer credit information or other information on consumers for the purpose of *furnishing consumer reports to third parties,* and which uses any means or facility of interstate commerce for the purpose of preparing or furnishing consumer reports. [Emphasis my own.] [Whether or not your firm operates for profit and whether this reporting constitutes a major part

of your business has no bearing on determining whether you may be considered a consumer reporting agency.]

6 At the heart of the FCRA is the definition of the term "consumer report" [15 U.S.C. sec. 1681(a)–1681(d).

> . . . any written, oral or other communication of any information by a consumer reporting agency bearing *on a consumer's credit worthiness, credit standing, credit capacity, character, general reputation, personal characteristics, or mode of living* which is used or expected *to be used or collected in whole or in part* for the purpose of serving as a *factor* in establishing the consumer's eligibility for (1) credit or insurance to be used primarily for personal, family, or household purposes, or (2) employment purposes, or (3) other purposes authorized under section 604 (15 U.S.C. 1681(b). *The term does not include any report containing information solely as to transactions or experiences between the consumer and the person making the report.* [Emphasis my own.]

7 Permissible purposes of reports [15 U.S.C. sec. 1681(b)]. A consumer reporting agency may furnish a consumer report under the following circumstances *and no other:*

> To a person which it has reason to believe:
> a. intends to use the information in connection with a credit transaction involving the consumer on whom the information is to be furnished and involving the extension of credit to, or review of collection of an account of that consumer's; or
> b. intends to use the information for employment purposes; or
> c. intends to use the information in connection with the underwriting of insurance involving the consumer; or
> d. intends to use the information in connection with a determination of the consumer's eligibility for a license or other benefit granted by a governmental instrumentality required by law to consider an applicant's financial responsibility or status; or
> e. *otherwise has a legitimate business need for the information in connection with a business transaction involving the consumer.*

8 *See* FTC Informal Staff Opinion Letters, April 1, 1971, April 15, 1971, and July 1971. 15 U.S.C. sec. 1681(a)(d)(A).

9 *Hearings on S. 823 Before the Subcomm. on Financial Institutions of the Senate Banking and Currency Comm.*, 91st Cong. 1st Sess. 62 (1969).

10 Virginia State Board of Pharmacy v. Virginia Citizens Consumer Council, 425 U.S. 748 (1976). *See also* Robert J. Posch, Jr., "Commercial Free Speech—The Argument for Our Side," *Direct Marketing*, February 1983, pp. 92–94.

11 Virginia State Board of Pharmacy v. Virginia Citizens Consumer Council, 425 U.S. 763 (1976).

12 *Id.* at 764.

13 Equifax Serv. v. Cohen, 420 A.2d 189 (1980), *cert. denied*, 450 U.S. 916 (1981).

14 This is an appellate proceeding for the reexamination of an inferior court's record to enable the higher court to review the questions of law.

15 *In re* Equifax, 96 F.T.C. 844 (1980).

16 N.Y. Gen. Bus. Law sec. 380(j)(1)(f)(ii) from Assembly Bill 6051-A, effective January 1, 1980.

17 N.Y. Gen. Bus. Law sec. 380(z) from Assembly Bill 5619, effective September 1, 1981.

18 Thornton v. Equifax, 619 F.2d 700 (1980).

19 Oberman v. Dun & Bradstreet, Inc., 586 F.2d 1173 (1978) and Peller v. Retail Credit Co., 359 F. Supp. 1235 (1974). *See also* 15 U.S.C.S. sec. 1681(n), 1681(o). When there is no allegation of malice or willful intent, there can be no action for libel or invasion of privacy under the FCRA.

20 Millstone v. O'Hanlon Reports, Inc., 383 F. Supp. 269 (1974), 15 U.S.C. sec. 1681(e)(b), 1681(m), and 1681(o). *See also* Hauser v. Equifax, Inc., 602 F.2d 811 (1979). *See also* Colletti v. Credit Bureau Serv., 644 F.2d 1148 (5th Cir. 1981).

21 Credit Bureau of Pulaski Co., Inc. v. LaVoie, 627 S.W.2d 49 (1982), *but see* Freeman v. Southern Nat'l Bank, 531 F. Supp. 94 (1982).

22 United States v. TRW, 633 F.2d 825 (9th Cir. 1980).

23 *In re* Howard Enterprises, Inc., No. 9096 (June 12, 1979) [overturning a January 16, 1978, decision by FTC Administrative Judge Parker, 93 F.T.C. 901 (1979)].

24 *Id.*

25 16 C.F.R. sec. 600.1(c), .1(d). Depending on circumstances, you should consult 16 C.F.R. sec. 600.1–.8 (1982).

26 *In re* Hooper Holmes, Inc., No. C-3020, 45 *Fed. Reg.* 44260 (1980) (respondent furnished information concerning individuals other than those inquired about— an allegation which if true is a clear violation of the Fair Credit Reporting Act) and *In re* Equifax, No. 8954 (1981).

27 15 U.S.C.S. sec. 1681(f).

28 15 U.S.C.S. sec. 1681(m)(a). *See also* Carroll v. Exxon Co., USA, 434 F. Supp. 557 (1977). You are not responsible for a mechanical, electronic, or clerical error made in good faith [15 U.S.C. sec. 1691(d)(3)]. *See also* Bryant v. TRW, 48 F. Supp. 1234 (1980).

29 15 U.S.C. sec. 1681(a)(c).

30 For example, New York State mandates 5 years.

31 See Ref. 26.

CHAPTER

SEVENTEEN

EQUAL CREDIT OPPORTUNITY ACT_____

The Equal Credit Opportunity Act (ECOA) was appended to the Consumer Credit Protection Act in 1974 to prohibit credit discrimination or other credit partiality based on sex and marital status.[1] The ECOA does not create a legal right to credit for anyone, just equal *access* to credit for everyone. You should further note that the Equal Credit Opportunity Act governs commercial as well as consumer credit.

The heart of the ECOA is a prohibition against credit discrimination in *any aspect* of a credit transaction. Examples include:

1. Discouraging applicants who are members of a protected category. Such protective categories now include race, color, religion, national origin, sex, marital status, age (provided the applicant has the capacity to enter into a binding contract), applicants whose income derives entirely or in part from any public assistance program, or applicants who have, in good faith, exercised any right under the Consumer Credit Protection Act.
2. Use of discriminatory criteria in the credit evaluation decision.
3. Imposition of one or more onerous terms on a prohibited basis.
4. Requiring cosigners on a prohibited basis (although cosigning may also be permissible depending on your policy and the facts of the individual case).
5. Failure to furnish adverse action notices to a rejected credit applicant.
6. Failure to retain and report separate credit histories for married persons.

The ECOA provides that an aggrieved applicant may sue for actual damages. This means more than merely proving a creditor's violation of the ECOA. The applicant must actually prove that he or she was damaged and at least approximate the extent of such actual damages quantitatively. The aggrieved applicant may also seek punitive damages (not limited to willful violations) and equitable and declaratory relief.[2] A successful litigant is also entitled to recover costs and a reasonable attorney's fee.[3]

THE EFFECTS TEST

The following is one of the most significant footnotes in the ECOA: "The legislative history of the Act indicates that the Congress intended an 'effects test' concept, as outlined in the employment field by the Supreme Court in the cases of *Griggs* v. *Duke Power Co.* . . . and *Albemarle Paper Co.* v. *Moody* . . . to be applicable to a creditor's determination of creditworthiness."[4] The "effects test" deals with the information which may be requested in connection with an application for credit. If you fall into the category of creditor, you should be aware that the test for discrimination is the *use* of information. The coverage provided by the ECOA includes not only discriminatory motivation but also the discriminatory effects of facially neutral actions. Thus there is no requirement that the creditor *intends* to discriminate, and applicants do not have to prove any motive to do so. The effects test, developed in employment discrimination law (although a slightly more lenient standard as we shall discuss)[5] is incorporated into this act; the use of an otherwise neutral criterion may be illegal if it has a discriminatory impact and is not justified by business necessity.

The test requires that the plaintiff show that your credit policy criterion under attack hurts protected applicants (e.g., blacks, married couples) in disproportionately greater numbers than other applicants (e.g., whites, singles). The disproportionate numbers are "proof" of the "effect" of your intent to discriminate, and the burden is now on you to prove that the criteria were neutral as to the protected categories and that the effect is accidental.

The ECOA, unlike some other consumer protection laws such as the Truth-in-Lending Act, requires more than just that the creditor follow the black letter rules. The ECOA proscribes not only overt discrimination but also practices that are fair in form but discriminatory in operation.

The best way to understand the effects test is to review the cases cited in Ref. 5 as well as the following case.

THE EFFECT OF ZIP CODES

In most credit allocation systems, creditors take into account a number of elements; some are general standardized screening devices, but most are based on the creditors' own experience with others with whom an applicant shares certain key characteristics. Each criterion is weighed in accordance with the individual creditor's view of its importance to the credit-scoring decision.

One popular criterion today is a person's zip code. An individual's zip code is considered to be a solid predictor of creditworthiness. With the advent of the 9-digit zip code, census tracts will provide even more useful credit applicant segmentation.

Although neutral on their face, use of zip codes in credit reporting *may* have a tendency to lead to negative effects on a protected class. An obvious situation is the reality that races can be segmented or at least estimated by their address falling within certain zip codes due to the prevailing housing patterns in the United States. An interesting twist to this involved a case with Amoco Oil Company.[6] Amoco used a complex system to evaluate applications. It took into account 38 predictive and objective factors, including the level of income, occupation, and prior credit experience in the U.S. Postal Service zip code area where the applicant resided.

They received an application for credit from a white female typesetter living in a predominantly nonwhite residential area of Atlanta. The applicant was denied a credit card in part because of Amoco's previous credit experience in her immediate geographical area, based on its use of zip code criteria.

The woman argued that she was denied a credit card because of her residence. She alleged that the use of such zip code criteria was the equivalent of racial discrimination due to the segregated pattern of housing in the Atlanta area. Thus, her individual right to be evaluated on the basis of her own merit was denied.

The applicant argued that a disproportionate impact of this credit policy fell on a protected class. Amoco then proved a direct and positive business purpose for the criterion (one of 38 criteria used). The ECOA states that a statistically sound system must separate creditworthy from noncreditworthy applicants at a statistically significant rate.[7] Amoco did this admirably. Amoco demonstrated that its zip code ratings did not tend to adversely affect black applicants disproportionately. Further, this geographic factor was more difficult to falsify than information about job or income, and since the ECOA prevented them from asking the race of the applicant, the company had no conscious idea or ability to create de facto discrimination by race in its rejections. Therefore, Amoco proved that there was no adverse intent or effect accomplished by its credit scoring system for new applicants.

A lesson to learn is that, although your in-house system evidences no intent to discriminate, you must also carefully monitor (*at least annually*) the quantitative impact or effect on the various prohibited basis categories set forth in Regulation B. Here you'd want the advice of your counsel and a statistician (preferably experienced in demographics) who could assist you in interpreting your numbers.

Finally, if you think all this sounds complex, you're right. The positive aspect of this complexity is that it will discourage private individuals from suing, since they are unlikely to possess the type of statistical analysis that is required to bring an effects test case.

MUST YOU COMPLY?

The ECOA sought to balance the often very real conflict between the rights of an applicant and the creditor's need to have discretion in making a credit decision. As a result of the balancing of interests and civil rights aspects of this law, the definitions and other key phrases may vary. Please read through carefully.

The ECOA requires *full* compliance from all creditors covered by the Truth-in-Lending Act (reread the discussion in the beginning of this section to determine if you must comply with Truth-in-Lending Act).

Specialized treatment is afforded credit grantors who extend incidental credit to consumers and/or business credit for commercial purposes falling within any of the five categories.[8] This area has been amended from time to time, and you should update internal compliance with counsel. Creditors who fall within the limitations of this section should review carefully the extent to which Regulation B affects them. The five categories are[9]:

1. Public utility credit[10]
2. Securities credit transactions[11]
3. Credit transactions primarily for business or commercial purposes, including agricultural purposes[12]
4. Extensions of credit to governments or government agencies[13]
5. Incidental consumer credit transactions not involving credit card accounts or finance charges and not payable in more than four installments[14]

The fifth category comprising incidental consumer credit is the one most likely to affect you if you are not covered by Truth-In-Lending. If it might, Section 202.3's definitions should be reviewed, specifically "consumer credit,"[15] "credit,"[16] "creditor,"[17] and "extend credit."[18]

The above sections read with Section 210(a) and 210(b) would define your inclusion as an incidental creditor under this act. It is important to note that the definition of "creditor" in this act may be broader than that of the Truth-in-Lending Act.[19] It excludes a person who merely honors a credit card but nothing more. Check this out before you exempt yourself from compliance.

If your operations do exclude you from compliance, you're home free. If not, you are either an "incidental creditor" or a full creditor under the act (both areas are discussed later). Either way, you should be aware of the prohibited areas to avoid and qualified areas to watch out for.

PROHIBITED AREAS

The determination of creditworthiness is singularly the most significant aspect of the credit extension process. You cannot permit any of the following criteria to influence your process.

1. You may not ask questions (oral or in your written forms) concerning anything to do with your applicant's
   a. Race
   b. Color
   c. Religion
   d. National origin
   e. Sex
2. You may not ask questions referencing sex such as titles of respect (e.g., Mr., Mrs., Miss, or Ms.). You are safest if you just ask for initials and a last name. If you must for one reason or another place such titles on your application form, you *must* state that such terms are optional. Otherwise your application forms may only include sex-neutral terms.[20] Courts have indicated that where a violation is proven that the creditor failed to disclose the "optional" on the application, punitive damages and costs may be recovered even where an applicant cannot prove actual damages.[21] You are extremely foolish if you don't have each and every credit form you use reviewed by your counsel.
3. You must furnish separate credit histories for a husband and wife. Such histories must stand separate and apart from each other. Therefore, avoid credit criteria based on street address where the bad credit history of a spouse could deny credit to another spouse with either no credit history or a good credit rating.

4. You may not discount an applicant's income on the basis of any of the protected classes.
5. You may not inquire into birth control practices or family plans of an applicant or use any similar criteria in your credit evaluation or credit-scoring system.[22]
6. You may not take the existence of a telephone listing in the applicant's name as a valid criterion for evaluation in your credit-scoring system.[23]

QUALIFIED AREAS

These areas can be used in credit evaluation, but review all of them with counsel.

1. The presence of a telephone in the applicant's home may be considered in your credit-scoring system.[24]
2. You may make limited inquiries into the applicant's marital status, age, and receipt of public assistance benefits.

AGE. Age can be a prohibited basis except when used to determine whether the applicant is of the age of majority (that is, old enough to sign binding, *not* voidable contracts). Usually this age is 18 or over, but the law of each specific state should be reviewed. Preference to those 62 (defined as "elderly") or over is usually OK. Otherwise age is a prohibited basis for various reasons. Many of those over 62 were the solid citizens who paid as they went and never accepted credit. Now, ironically, their having no debts hurts their credit history.[25] When they apply for credit, many are on fixed incomes traceable to public sources, unemployed, and prone to changing their residence after retirement (having been "stable" homeowners, they become "transient" renters when they sell their homes).

Thus you may not make an *arbitrary* credit decision based on age. You may use relevant statistical characteristics of a given age group provided that the age of an older applicant is not assigned a negative value.[26]

PUBLIC ASSISTANCE INCOME. This means any federal, state, or local government assistance program, including but *not limited to* Aid to Families with Dependent Children, food stamps, rent and mortgage supplemental programs, Social Security, and unemployment compensation.[27] Unlike age, the applicant's receipt of public assistance income may not be used in any empirically derived credit system.

MARITAL STATUS. You must be particularly sensitive to what you do and don't ask about marital status, especially in a community property state. Even "innocent" things such as signature lines can get you into trouble. You must grant individual credit to a creditworthy applicant who wants individual credit. It is a violation of the law to request that the spouse cosign the agreement, although it's not a violation to question how many dependents an applicant has.[28] Further, to avoid problems with the marital status category, you must apply the same criteria to engaged couples (and possibly those merely living together) who apply for credit jointly (e.g., aggregate income) as you would married couples.[29]

NOTICE OF REJECTION

In general, a creditor must notify the applicant within 30 days after receiving a completed application for credit.[30]

> Any notification given to an applicant against whom adverse action is taken shall be in writing and shall contain: a statement of the action taken; a statement of the provisions of section 701(a) of the Act; the name and address of the Federal agency that administers compliance concerning the creditor giving the notification; and
> i. a statement of specific reasons for the action taken; or
> ii. a disclosure of the applicant's right to a statement of reasons within 30 days after receipt by the creditor of a request made within 60 days of such notification, the disclosure to include the name, address, and telephone number of the person or office from which the statement of reasons can be obtained. If the creditor chooses to provide the statement of reasons orally, the notification shall also include a disclosure of the applicant's right to have any oral statement or reasons confirmed in writing within 30 days after a written request for confirmation is received by the creditor.[31]

The statement of reasons for adverse action shall be sufficient if it is specific and indicates the principal reason for the adverse action.[32] This is strictly enforced by the FTC.

One firm established a credit-scoring system based on various factors.[33] When denied credit (including the right to defer payment), the customer would receive notice that credit was denied. The customer could then inquire into the specifics of the denial. Often the reasons given in response were incorrect. Certain specific reasons for denial, such as the geographic area in which the applicant lived, determined by zip code (a principal reason for taking adverse action against an applicant), were *never* disclosed. The FTC alleged that the firm violated the Equal Credit Opportunity Act. The civil penalty payment provided for by the resulting consent order was the largest to that date to involve either the Equal Credit Opportunity Act or an FTC trade regulation rule.

INCIDENTAL OR FULL COMPLIANCE?

Earlier we discussed whether you crossed the threshold of compliance. Now let's examine what the ECOA requires of an incidental or full creditor.

INCIDENTAL CREDITOR. If you fall into this category, you are effectively excluded from the more onerous sections of the ECOA we've discussed.[34] Essentially all that is left is the general rule prohibiting discrimination, which states that "a creditor shall not discriminate against an applicant on a prohibited basis regarding any aspect of a credit transaction" (i.e., race, color, religion, or any category mentioned).[35] However, one area not protected is that of the noncitizenship (alienage) of an applicant.[36] Here the court made a point of noting that no showing was made that Vietnamese noncitizen aliens were less favorably treated than other groups of aliens. If such disparity existed, an argument for natural-origin discrimination *might* have existed.

You should watch legislative developments in this area. There have been various efforts in Congress to amend this act's prohibited basis criteria to include residence and geographic location. If this takes place and you engage in address hits or zip code qualification criteria, a problem may result

Further, you may not make the existence of a telephone listing in your applicant's name or a specific telephone number a prerequisite for doing business.[37] Any question about a telephone listing or number is a red flag for a consumer agency. However, such a question may be labeled as "optional." (The number may be desired as intelligence for follow-up telephone marketing.) You may *ask* whether a telephone exists at the applicant's residence.[38] (Creditors are leery of people with so few roots that they don't even have a telephone.)

Finally, watch the laws of your state. Congress was solicitous not to invade the state's traditional dominion in the area of property law and relations. The ECOA preempts only inconsistent state laws and only to the extent of the inconsistency. A state law is not inconsistent if it is more protective of the applicant.[39]

FULL COMPLIANCE. If you're covered by the ECOA, but not as an incidental creditor, then you must undertake full compliance.[40] Tight compliance is enforced both through the civil rights aspects discussed and through the authorization which the FTC has to enforce this act as if it were an FTC trade regulation rule.[41] Enforcement to date has resulted in stiff fines and penalties for alleged violations of the act.[42] The Justice Department also has been very active in this area.[43] In addition to the fines (which are *not* deductible business expenses), the paperwork burden is considerable for all violators. In general, all fines are the result of alleged violations of the use of prohibited basis criteria.

CONSUMER REMEDIES

Since the FTC is charged with the ECOA's overall enforcement, a violation of the ECOA is a violation of the FTC Act.[44] An applicant may also seek private enforcement (actual and punitive damages up to $10,000 per aggrieved individual) or a class action. Similar to the Fair Debt Collection Practices Act (reviewed in Section 7), the aggrieved applicant may sue in any federal or state court of competent jurisdiction regardless of the amount in question.[45] Certain equitable relief is also available. It is even possible for the turned down applicant to recover for embarrassment, humiliation, and mental distress, plus damages to reputation and credit-worthiness.[46] In any of these legal actions, the applicant is entitled to a trial by jury.[47] Last but not least, the resulting bad publicity may have an adverse impact on your bottom line and to current and possibly future marketing efforts.

To prepare for any legal eventuality, the creditor must maintain certain records of each transaction: application forms, copy of notification of action taken and reasons for it, as well as any written statements disputing the decision filed by the applicant.[48]

SOME FINAL THOUGHTS

The Equal Credit Opportunity Act is more understandable than others because it is based on "newspaper law," that is, the obvious, straightforward, nonesoteric legal debate you've witnessed unfolding and accelerating since the late 1950s.

Each person is uniquely different and must be considered for and granted credit solely on the basis of individual merit. You may not base your decisions concerning a particular applicant on your general experiences with a race or sex.

Although many managers will fall into the category of incidental creditors, be careful to understand the prohibited bases for discrimination as well as to refrain from requesting telephone numbers on ad copy unless the ad copy request specifically states "optional" and the answer, if given, does not impact the decision to extend credit.

The manager should remain vigilant at the state and federal levels to prevent the enactment of zip code and residence restrictions which would adversely affect lists in general and compiled lists in particular. (See discussions of how to systematically monitor such legislation in Section 2.) You might order the FTC's eady-to-read outline on point.[49]

Even the best-intentioned firm may blow it if its application for credit is worded in such a way (even innocently) that a particular group is merely *discouraged* from applying. Again, counsel should read all documents interfacing with the public as well as all internal credit-granting criteria. The test of equal credit opportunity—at every stage of the process from application through final notification to the applicant—revolves around the question: Have the avenues of acceptance been opened equally to all?

REFERENCES

[1] 15 U.S.C. sec. 1691 *et seq.*, 12 C.F.R. Sec. 202 *et seq.* Also known as "Regulation B," this was an amendment to the Truth-in-Lending Act. If you want a solid book in this area, investigate the *Equal Credit Opportunity Manual*, Warren, Gorham & Lamont, Inc., 210 South Street, Boston, Massachusetts, 02111. This manual also has a periodic supplement service to keep it current.

[2] 15 U.S.C. sec. 1691(e)(a)–1691(e)(c).

[3] 15 U.S.C. sec. 1691(d). The Federal Reserve Board is empowered with the responsibility for providing further sanctions if necessary. 15 U.S.C. sec. 1691(b).

[4] 12 C.F.R. sec. 2029.6(a) n.7.

[5] The so-called effects test is derived from the decision of the U.S. Supreme Court rendered in Griggs v. Duke Power Co., 401 U.S. 424 (1971). Here a high-school diploma was required for employment—the effect being to exclude a significantly greater percentage of black applicants. The Supreme Court stated that tit. VII (42 U.S.C. sec. 2000) not only proscribes intentionally discriminatory conduct but also looks to the consequences of conduct, whether or not the intent to

discriminate is present. If the *effect* is also discriminatory, it became the employer's burden to show that the job requirement was related to job performance.

Note that, of all the credit statutes enforced by the FTC, the Equal Credit Opportunity Act is taken the most seriously and enforced the most vigorously precisely because of its civil rights background.

[6] Claire Cherry v. Amoco Oil Co., 490 F. Supp. 1026 (N.D. Ga. 1980). Eventually Amoco agreed to settle by discontinuing the use of a zip code or any other geographic unit smaller than the individual's state in determining creditworthiness. They also had to pay an unjustified civil fine of $200,000 as part of the consent agreement. *See also* Noel Capon, "Credit Scoring Systems: A Critical Analysis," *Journal of Marketing*, Spring 1982, p. 41.

[7] 12 C.F.R. sec. 202.2(p)(2).

[8] 12 C.F.R. sec. 202.3(d). This shall be read with 12 C.F.R. Sec. 202.3(a)(3).

[9] 12 C.F.R. sec. 202.3.

[10] 12 C.F.R. sec. 202.3(a)(1), .3(b).

[11] 12 C.F.R. sec. 202.3(a)(2), .3(c).

[12] 12 C.F.R. sec. 202.3(a)(4), .3(e).

[13] 12 C.F.R. sec. 202.3(a)(5), .3(f).

[14] 12 C.F.R. sec. 202.3(a)(3), .3(d).

[15] 12 C.F.R. sec. 202.3(h).

[16] 12 C.F.R. sec. 202.3(j).

[17] 12 C.F.R. sec. 202.3(e).

[18] 12 C.F.R. sec. 202.3(q).

[19] 12 C.F.R. sec. 226.2(17).

[20] 12 C.F.R. sec. 202.5(d)(3).

[21] Smith v. Lakeside Foods, Inc., 449 F. Supp. 171 (1978).

[22] 12 C.F.R. sec. 202.5(d)(4).

[23] 12 C.F.R. sec. 202.6(b)(4).

[24] *Id.*

[25] Certain evidence suggests that older applicants are more likely to repay than similarly situated younger ones. 12 C.F.R. sec. 202.6(b)(2)(iv).

[26] 12 C.F.R. sec. 202.6(b)(2)(ii).

[27] 12 C.F.R. sec. 202.2(aa).

[28] *But see* Cragin v. First Fed. Sav. and Loan Ass'n, 498 F. Supp. 379 (1980).

[29] This area may be getting too far-fetched (as bureaucrats tend to do). See "Credit without Benefit of Clergy," *Consumer Credit and Truth-in-Lending Compliance Report*, vol. 10, no. 3, 1979, p. 1. The article discusses an unofficial FRB ECOA staff interpretation possibly indicating credit card issuers should give equal dignity to marriage and living-together arrangements. *See also* Markham v. Colonial Mortgage Serv. Co. Assoc., 605 F.2d 566 (1979).

30 12 C.F.R. sec. 202.9(a)(1)(i)–.9(a)(1)(iii), *but see* 202.9(a)(1)(iv) for 90-day exception.

31 12 C.F.R. sec. 202.9(a)(2)(i), .9(a)(2)(ii).

32 12 C.F.R. sec. 202(b)(2).

33 United States v. Montgomery Ward & Co., No. 79–140 (D.D.C. 1979). Although not admitting guilt, Montgomery Ward agreed to:
a. Pay $175,000 in civil damages;
b. Contact every applicant who had been denied credit since March 23, 1977, and had inquired as to the rejection. Such applicants would be informed that Montgomery Ward may have failed to comply with the Equal Credit Opportunity Act, provided with an FTC pamphlet informing them of their rights under the act, and invited to resubmit an application for credit.
c. Provide all applicants denied credit in the future with *specific* reasons for credit denial (e.g., age, number of dependents, rent).
d. Make available to the FTC *all* credit-scoring records for the next 10 years; and
e. *Not* consider zip codes or any other geographic unit in evaluating future credit applications. *See also* Carroll v. Exxon Co., USA, 434 F. Supp. 557 (1977).

34 12 C.F.R. sec. 202.3(d)(1)–.3(d)(8) after amendments.

35 12 C.F.R. sec. 202.4.

36 Nguyen v. Montgomery Ward & Co., 513 F. Supp. 1039 (1981).

37 12 C.F.R. sec. 202.6(b)(4).

38 *Id.*

39 12 C.F.R. sec. 202.11(a).

40 Two good articles on point are: Noel Capon, "Discrimination in Screening Credit Applicants," *Harvard Business Review,* May–June 1978, p. 76, and Noel Capon, "Credit Ratings and Rights," *Washington Post,* December 17, 1977.

41 15 U.S.C. sec. 1671(d), 12 C.F.R. sec. 704(c).

42 *See e.g., In re* Aldens, Inc., 92 F.T.C. 901 (1978) and 12 C.F.R. sec. 202(b)(2).

43 United States v. Federated Dep't. Stores, No. 79–1412 (D.D.C. 1978) (failure to consider alimony, child support, and separate maintenance payments as income).

44 15 U.S.C. sec. 1691c(c).

45 15 U.S.C. sec. 1691e(a), 1691e(c), 1691e(f).

46 Schuman v. Standard Oil Co. of Cal., 453 F. Supp. 1150 (N.D. Ca. 1978) and Sayers v. General Motors Acceptance Corp., 522 F. Supp. 835 (1981).

47 *Vander Missen v. Kellogg-Citizens National Bank of Green Bay,* 83 F.R.D. 206 (1979).

48 12 C.F.R. sec. 202.12.

49 Equal Credit Opportunity Act, Federal Trade Commission, Equal Opportunity, Washington, D.C., 20580.

SECTION

SEVEN

YOUR COMPLETE GUIDE TO DUNNING COMPLIANCE

The United States is now a credit-oriented consumer society. Credit often is the life's blood necessary to sustain your customers' ability to purchase. Not all such customers prove honest, although more often than not adverse personal circumstances account for customers' inability to pay on time. They and you have a bad-debt problem.

You can't control interest rates, but you can control how much credit you extend and to whom. Obviously, you must have a strategy for being repaid. Collection may influence your market, the advertising medium you use, segments of the medium, and possibly even the decision of product selection. Certain states do not even permit a recovery of the sales tax paid on your bad debts, although efforts are being made in some of them to correct this injustice.[1]

In this section we'll discuss your legal exposure in collecting your debts. We'll highlight the Fair Debt Collecton Practices Act, although it may not apply directly to you and your firm.[2] If the act doesn't apply to your case, you still must contend with the FTC's enforcement powers under the FTC Act's Section 5.

221

GENERAL GUIDES FOR ALL COLLECTORS

All debt collectors are governed by Section 5 of the Federal Trade Commission Act, which authorizes the FTC to penalize collectors whose harassment or misrepresentations constitute unfair methods of competition or deceptive trade practices.[3] The best case on point for you to review is the cease and desist order issued against Capax.[4] Reviewing this case will give you a working understanding of the concepts as well as the exact points the FTC looks for in your delinquent communication. *Capax* is useful for two reasons:

1. It helps you understand the Fair Debt Collection Practices Act, which codified prior FTC case law defining unfair and deceptive collection acts.
2. It outlines what the FTC will do in the future. Remember, too, that courts generally defer to the FTC's judgment as to what constitutes deceptive and unfair collection practices.

Capax established the following principles.

Layout. If your layout is a violation (e.g., a simulated telegram), then you're in violation no matter how innocuous your dunning wording is.

Legal action. Even the inference of legal or similar action is not permitted unless there is a "realistic possibility" that suit (or other threatened action) will be undertaken where it is threatened.[5] The FTC doesn't want a lottery (i.e., many entrants but few selected) when it comes to your suing. Likewise, if a legal action is undertaken in certain states but never in others, you may not use legal threats in the states in which you know you will never act.

Other threats. The standard is truth; you can only state that you will do what you actually will do. If you threaten adverse impact on the debtor's credit rating, then you must be prepared to back up the validity of your claim.

Imminence of action. You may not threaten action with a false sense of urgency; unless you are prepared to carry out the threatened action if payment is not received by the stated deadline, you may not imply that immediate action is needed. Remember that wording such as "urgent," "imperative," "reply immediately," "reply within 48 hours," or "action will be taken if not paid within 1 week" may not be used unless such statements are true and the threatened action will occur if payment is not received by the stated deadline. If a debtor's failure to meet such a "deadline" or to act "immediately" results in no more than the receipt of the next form letter in the series, there is no urgency to reply.

Internal organization. You may not use fictitious job titles or department designations (e.g., fictitious in-house legal department) in collection material, although you can use a "desk name" or alias for individual collectors (to protect them from retaliation) provided that all other descriptions are accurate.

Test. The test is the *capacity* to deceive. The intent to deceive or actual deception is not necessary.

Attorney letterheads. Attorney letterheads should be reviewed with counsel. In general, it is a misrepresentation for a debt collector to send out a collection letter under an attorney's letterhead, even if the attorney has approved the form you are using.[6]

If you read just one decision, read the *Capax* decision. With the exhaustive analysis presented in *Capax* and the enforcement powers granted by the Fair Debt Collection Practices Act, the FTC clearly sets forth in one decision most of your legal obligations in collection.

If the compliance problems seem complicated, then explore other options. One option is to buy "insurance" by using standard credit card payment options. Then American Express, Visa, etc. absorb your bad debts after they approve the order. Offsetting this advantage, however, are certain disadvantages inherent in employing the credit card payment option, primarily the costly fees (5 to 7 percent). Although this figure is fixed (unlike the variable market bad-debt figure), it is a cost which must be built into the cost of your product and/or taken off the bottom line.

FAIR DEBT COLLECTION PRACTICES ACT

Federal law became necessary in the area of debt collection because of widespread public complaints and the states' inability to control interstate (WATS calls and mail) debt collection. Responsible debt collectors also recognized a need for some form of uniform legislation.

The few bad apples were not amenable to self-regulation, and a national effort to require a license for each debt collector would have presented a bureaucratic nightmare. Many responsible groups, such as the American Collectors Association and the Associated Credit Bureaus, encouraged legislation on point. What evolved was a controversial but workable law on point.

WHO AND WHAT IS GOVERNED BY THIS LAW

The act was controversial, since it applied only to *third-party* collectors and excluded the actual entity that extended the credit in the first place. Specifically, the act applies to:

1. Debts defined as "any obligation or alleged obligation of a consumer to pay money arising out of a transaction in which money, property, insurance or services which are the subject of the transaction are primarily for personal, family or household purposes, whether or not such obligation has been reduced to judgment."[7]
2. Such debts must be consumer debts, that is the purchase of goods or services for primarily personal, family, or household services. Commercial debts were not covered, because it was thought that a commercial entity had more savvy to protect itself in the marketplace.

If you have these debts, must you comply with the act? A debt collector is defined as: "any person who uses any instrumentality of interstate commerce or the mails in any business the principal purpose of which is the collection of any debts or who regularly collects or attempts to collect, directly or indirectly, debts owed or due or asserted to be owed or due another."[8]

Banks, credit unions, loan companies, and retailers are excluded, because their primary business purpose is the extension of credit rather than the collection of debts. Further excluded is "any officer or employee of a creditor while, in the name of the creditor, collecting debts for such collector."[9] This provision expressly ensures that in-house collectors are not covered by this act.

Three questions might come to your mind about now:

1. *Why were they all excluded?* Congress made a judgment that in-house and other collectors do not act abusively in attempting to collect debts because their primary business is to do more business with the debtor once the account is paid.

2. *Who's left?* The third-party creditor who does collection for a living is left. The act regulates communications by the debt collector with the debtor, prohibits a number of debt-collecting practices, requires certain disclosures to be made to the debtor, and addresses legal actions available to the parties. We'll examine each of these areas in detail.

3. *I'm not covered—why read on?* A few good reasons:

    a. Many provisions apply to in-house collectors as well (both as to common sense and because they're found in law and consent agreements).

b. The FTC and certain members of Congress have indicated a desire to incorporate all collectors. Elsewhere, a few bills have been introduced into Congress to narrow this exclusion, and certain cities (e.g., New York City) already have.[10] In certain states (e.g., Pennsylvania) the law is tighter than in most states but is not as all-inclusive as New York City's.[11] Further, there is an increasing legislative trend to make firms more responsible for their outside collection efforts. You should also be aware that although the act does not govern cash sales, it does govern efforts by a collection agency you hire to collect personal checks.[12]

c. The outside collector your firm retains reflects on your firm's goodwill. You should screen all dunning letters and scripts employed before you pay a retainer and sign a contract. Although they are independent contractors, you certainly have a right to insist that they obey the law. The public will view the outside collector as an extension of your company's judgment. Any adverse actions will reflect badly on you. You will not upset a worthwhile relationship with an independent contractor by protecting the good name of your firm.

Although it's a good idea for anyone to read further, if you're a third-party collector, you *must* master the following concepts.

COMMUNICATION REQUIREMENTS

The initial task of a debt collector is to discover the debtor's address and possibly a telephone number where he or she can be reached. This "location information" is the most valuable data a collector can possess.[13] Our society is mobile, and, to get the job done, the collector must keep up with the debtor. Therefore, for this and other reasons, both the profession and the law put a premium on knowing the individual circumstances of the debtor.

THIRD-PARTY COMMUNICATION

Although a debt collector is permitted to contact third parties (e.g., employers) to locate the debtor, the act provides certain guidelines which must be followed.[14]

1. Debt collectors must identify themselves (not necessarily by true name, provided that no deception is used) and state that they are looking for certain location information about an individual.[15] If you are contacting an employer, you must be very careful to do nothing which would interfere with the debtor's employee-employer relationship.

2. Collectors may *not* tell the third party that the person whose whereabouts are being sought owes a debt. Also, collectors should identify their employer (i.e., the debt collection agency) only if specifically requested by the third party.

3. Collectors may not contact the third party more than once unless such contact is absolutely necessary to obtain more complete or correct information (or unless the third party can now supply complete information) or unless requested to do so by the debtor.

4. Collectors may not place an indication, mark, symbol, or any other language on the outside envelope of the letter or telegram which identifies the sender as a debt collector. An innocuous firm name or simple return address is all that is permitted. Obviously you are prohibited from using postcards.

5. Collectors may not contact third parties for any reason once the collector knows that the debtor is represented by an attorney *with regard to the debt*[16] and can contact the attorney (that is, the collector knows or can readily obtain the attorney's name, address, and/or phone number) *unless* the attorney fails to respond to the debt collector's communication within a reasonable period of time.[17] I consider 14 days to be reasonable, but whatever your policy, it should be consistent. Once contact with the attorney is made, you must direct all communication to the attorney *unless* the attorney consents to your communicating directly with the consumer. If this happens, get such consent in writing or confirm the conversation in a *certified* letter to the attorney and client debtor.[18]

DIRECT COMMUNICATION WITH DEBTOR

The debt collector may not contact the debtor in regard to the collection of the debt at a place or time inconvenient to the debtor or at the debtor's place of employment if the employer does not allow such calls. A convenient time is assumed to be between 8:00 a.m. and 9:00 p.m. at the debtor's location (taking into account the different time zones). Avoid any calls on Sunday. If the debtor has indicated (or the collector discovers this) that such hours are not convenient (if, for example, the debtor works at night and sleeps in the morning), he or she has the right to be contacted at more convenient times.[19]

If the debtor is a minor, you may contact the debtor's parents.[20]

After the initial oral communication, you must follow up in a writing (or in your first letter if you write directly) within 5 days and notify the debtor that if such debtor disputes the validity of all or any portion (e.g., finance charges are a portion) of the debt, he or she *must* notify you within 30 days of receipt of this notice, or it will be assumed that the debt is valid. If the debtor notifies you in writing within 30 days of the receipt of notice, you will obtain verification from the creditor or, if a judgment exists, a copy of same and mail the debtor a copy of the verification or judgment. If the debtor does not identify the current creditor and writes to you to that effect, you must provide the name and address of the original creditor if different from that listed.[21]

If the debtor does dispute your bill or asks for the identity of the original creditor in writing within 30 days of receiving the notice, the debt collector must stop all collection of the debt or any disputed portion of the debt. However, collection efforts may be resumed when the information requested by the debtor is *mailed* to the debtor.

It should be noted that even if a consumer does *not* dispute the debt within the 30-day period, that in itself is not an admission of guilt or any other waiver of rights on the consumer's part.

Debtors may inform the debt collector *in writing* that they refuse to pay the debt or desire that further communication from the debt collector cease. In this event, the debt collector may not contact the debtor except to advise the debtor that all collection efforts are being terminated and/or to inform the debtor that a certain *specific* action will be taken. This action must then actually happen. This section is strictly enforced; if even an innocent additional message is sent, the sender may be liable for breach of the law[22] as well as intentional infliction of emotional distress.[23]

This law puts the debtor in control of the collection process in another way: If a debtor owes more than one debt and makes a payment, the debt collector may not apply the payment toward the disputed debt and must, where applicable, apply the payment according to the debtor's instructions.

PROHIBITED PRACTICES

The act precludes the collector from engaging in any conduct "the natural consequence of which is to harass, oppress, or abuse any person in the collection of a debt."[24] The law presents a nonexclusive list of examples of such conduct which include:

1. Threats of violence, physical harm, extortion, blackmail, or criminal prosecution
2. Use of obscene or abusive language (the latter includes abusive statements such as "You shouldn't have children if you can't afford them")[25]
3. Publication of deadbeat lists, except publication for consumer reporting agencies (see discussion in Section 6 under the "Fair Credit Reporting Act")[26]
4. Placement of anonymous or harassing telephone calls[27]
5. *Soliciting* postdated checks and depositing or threatening to deposit a postdated check before the designated date[28]

Note that what is misleading or deceptive generally relates to the total effect your message might have on a reasonable debtor. However, some courts will look less at the reasonable person standard and more at the reading comprehension and mental ability of the actual recipient of your message.[29] The multitude of subsections cover a whole gamut of violations; if you have any doubt about whether you or your collection agency may be in violation here, review this section with your counsel.

A classic case of what *not* to do under the law is found in *Housh* v. *Peth*[30]:

> The record shows that the defendant deliberately planned a systematic campaign of harassment of the plaintiff, not only in numerous telephone calls to the plaintiff herself *every day* for a period of three weeks, some of which were *late at night,* but also calls to her superiors over the telephone, informing them of the debt, that she was called out of the classroom *three times within 15 minutes;* that she lost a roomer at her rooming house because of the repeated calls, and was threatened with loss of employment unless the telephone calls ceased. The calls to the employer, and the rooming house, were all part of the pattern to harass and humiliate the plaintiff and cause her mental pain and anguish and cause her emotional disturbance for the purpose of coercing her to pay the debt. [Emphasis my own.]

We've gone over the don'ts. One positive area to investigate is a national and regional nonprofit service, Consumer Credit Counseling Services.[31] The service charges a percentage fee but is often successful in working out a payment schedule with a debtor. This is a useful social function in times of economic vaguery, when even the best-intentioned individual may suddenly face credit problems due to an unexpected loss of job or reduction in overtime. If the debt is large and/or the debtor acts in good faith in notifying you of her or his plight, recommending this service will assist the debtor to get back on his or her feet. It may also preserve a good customer who will make purchases again when a paycheck begins arriving. Finally, it will serve *you* well if you are having personal problems in this area.

PENALTIES

The original House-passed version of the act contained a criminal law enforcement provision. This was dropped in favor of just civil enforcement by private individuals (both individually and as a class)[32] with the FTC as the major enforcement agency.[33]

Individual debtors may bring suit within 1 year of a violation in any appropriate U.S. district court without regard to the amount in controversy.[34] The consumer may collect actual damages caused by a collector's violation of the act, statutory damages up to $1000,[35] reasonable attorneys' fees, and court costs.[36] In assessing damages, the court must take into account the nature of the violation, the frequency and persistence of noncompliance, and the extent to which the debt collector's noncompliance was *intentional*[37] Debt collectors are in the clear if they can show that violations were not intentional *and* resulted from a bona fide error.[38] If the court finds that any action was brought by a consumer in bad faith and for harassment purposes, the court may award the debt collector reasonable attorneys' fees and costs.[39] It is hoped that this will dissuade some nuisance suits by debtors.

Don't forget state laws—the act provides an exemption for state regulations and laws that are substantially similar to the act (which means that the laws of the state in which you are collecting may be narrower than the federal act).[40] Discuss with your counsel the laws of the states in which you do business.

TELEPHONE DUNNING

Because of the allegedly more intrusive aspects of telephone dunning (than mail, for instance) and for other reasons, telephone dunning has aroused a lot of legal action in the last few years. There are certain public policy issues as to telephone intrusion—3 to 10 days may be the norm, but I'd recommend no call interval shorter than 1 week (for the same debt). There is no prohibition of dunning if you place your dunning call the same day or the day after the arrival of your dunning letter. Likewise, you are permitted to follow up on any "promises to pay" with a letter confirming the conversation and amount and date of promised payment. A coordinated policy such as this, carried out with reasonable restraint, is not intrusion.

All dunning calls should be manually dialed unless you have carefully examined the law of the state you are calling (see the discussion of "Telephone Marketing" in Section 4, Chapter 9).

No harassing or abusive calls are permitted. Immediately calling the debtor after the debtor has hung up the phone is an example of harassment. All calls should be made in a businesslike manner with a subdued tone.

Finally, you are expected to use well-trained professionals in your debt contact. Courts like to see "a program of constant on-the-job training, coupled with telephone monitoring, supervision, and reference to a standardized manual as a procedure reasonably adopted to avoiding violations of the Act."[41] However, if you are thinking of taping or otherwise listening to employee calls for employment training purposes, first review the following discussion.

MONITORING EMPLOYEE CALLS

Congress passed a comprehensive electronic surveillance law in Title III of the Omnibus Crime Control and Safe Streets Act of 1968.[42] This act was intended to deal with increasing threats to privacy resulting from the growing use of sophisticated electronic monitoring devices, which threatened an average citizen's reasonable expectation of privacy.

Unlike many pieces of legislative overkill, this act was worded to strike a fair balance between privacy rights and legitimate business practices. For your business needs, an understanding of certain definitions in 18 U.S.C. sec. 2510 is important. To violate the act, you must intercept an oral or wire communication. A telephone conversation is a wire communication. However, an interception does not occur unless an "electronic, mechanical or other device" is employed. The definition of these devices specifically excludes a telephone used in the regular course of the subscriber's business. Specifically, the law grants an exception to

a. any telephone or telegraph instrument, equipment or facility or any component thereof, . . .

i. furnished to the subscriber or user by a communications common carrier in the ordinary course of its business and being used by the subscriber or user in the ordinary course of its business.[43]

If you request that the telephone company install a monitoring device which will permit you to listen to telephone conversations between employees and customers in the ordinary course of business only, there will be no interception. This is predicated on the fact that duties in the ordinary course of business include only lawful and proper activities.

LAWFUL AND PROPER ACTIVITIES

The courts that have reviewed the issue do not want to see evidence of surreptitious monitoring or monitoring for personal gain or gossip. At all times you should be able to demonstrate that the monitoring was undertaken from the sole interest of the company's business operations. At no time do you wish to appear to have monitored a strictly "private" call.

For example, the Bell system installed monitoring equipment on telephones in those departments of a newspaper organization that had direct contact with the public. The business purpose of this monitoring was to assist the employee training program as well as to protect employees from abusive calls. The monitoring was not surreptitious; on the contrary, it was performed with the prior knowledge of management and all affected employees (who were informed in writing). The court held that there was no interception, since the equipment was used in the ordinary course of the employer's business.[44]

One sobering case involved monitoring performed over a simple extension phone. A supervisor was invited to listen to a call—the employee had been visibly upset by a previous call from this person, and the supervisor's curiousity had been aroused.[45] The caller issued a death threat to the employee, a threat he proved only too capable of following through on. The trial court convicted the murderer in part based on the supervisor's testimony.

This decision was reversed by the appellate court, but the Florida Supreme Court upheld the trial court's conclusion that there was no interception, despite the issue of the supervisor's "curiousity." The supervisor was acting in her official capacity, concerned with the employee's emotional state affecting her job. The employee gave prior consent. The business purpose performed during business hours satisfied the test for ordinary course of business, establishing that there was no interception.

Is monitoring permitted without an employee's prior consent or notification? Yes, in limited circumstances. A manager had justifiable suspicion to believe an employee was acting in concert with an agent of a competitor to the possible detriment of the manager's corporation. The manager warned the employee not to disclose confidential information to this outside party. The manager believed that something still was not right.

When the manager was subsequently informed that the parties were on the phone with each other, he decided to validate his suspicions. He listened to and recorded a part of a telephone conversation by means of an extension phone without the prior knowledge of the employee or the third party. The act of listening in was limited in purpose and time—just enough time to confirm his suspicions. The U.S. District Court held that there was no interception, because the manager was acting in what he legitimately believed was the company's best interest.[46] While in no way condoning the manager's actions, the court held that his use of the telephone satisfied the ordinary-course-of-business test.

Finally, note that the use of an extension telephone to intercept a phone call by someone who is not authorized to use the telephone (e.g., non-management employees, if phones are restricted to management) cannot be considered conduct "in the ordinary course of business" under any circumstances.[47]

PROTECTING YOUR MONITORING

If you can demonstrate that your procedures for monitoring employee telephones are lawful and proper and used in the ordinary course of business, you are in fairly good shape. However, your worries are not over, and the following precautions are in order.

1. State and local legislative and regulatory activity should be routinely audited. The laws in place should be reviewed with counsel. The federal law we have discussed permits more stringent state standards, and some states do have more stringent laws on point.[48]

2. Neither the surreptitious use of a telephone extension to record a private telephone conversation nor a general practice of surreptitious monitoring would qualify as a legal exception. You should never tape a call as "evidence" that a customer agreed to do something.

3. Do not attempt to monitor personal calls to "prove" a violation of a legitimate business policy against such calls without extending prior warnings to an individual concerning such violation.

4. To meet the ordinary-course-of-business test:

    a. State this purpose when you procure the equipment from the common carrier.

    b. Give advance written notice to all managers and employees involved, stating the business purpose of the monitoring.

c. Obtain a written release from each employee involved, stating that they are aware of the fact that their supervisor will listen in unannounced and that they agree to this policy. (See further discussion under "Contractual Protection.")

5. With the increased growth of international business in general and marketing in particular, one final comment is useful. The provisions of the Wire Interception and Interception of Oral Communications Act apply only within the territorial jurisdiction of the United States. The law of the nation where the monitoring takes place (situs) governs the validity of such monitoring, even if a United States citizen is involved and/or the intercepted telephone conversation traveled in part over the U.S. communications system. Therefore, a firm physically located in the U.S. may monitor calls to Canadian customers subject to U.S. law. Likewise a Canadian-based firm monitoring calls to U.S. customers is bound by Canadian law on this point.

WRAPPING UP TELEPHONE MONITORING

In monitoring any aspect of employee calls (e.g., training) managers must be careful not to monitor in a manner which would "intercept" calls. There is no interception under federal law if the acquisition of the contents of the communication is accomplished through telephone equipment used in the ordinary course of business.

CONTRACTUAL PROTECTION

Despite a few agencies' problems with the FTC, hiring an outside agency for collection expertise may be a wise investment, depending on the size of the debts and volume of calls you wish to make or the amount of letters you wish to mail.

Obviously your contract is going to be reviewed by counsel, but before you begin negotiations with an agency, you might first check with the FTC, the state attorney general's office, the better business bureau, and the consumer affairs department. There might have been complaints against the agency, but were they satisfactorily resolved? If not, it doesn't pay to get involved with a disreputable agency. If so, make sure your agency is bonded and insured to your satisfaction. A good agency has a professional liability insurance (libel, slander, and other errors and omissions) policy. Obtain a copy and review it with counsel in light of your particular needs.

Also, is your agency licensed? If not, have counsel review the applicable state law. The states have the power to require licensing of debt collectors under the Fair Debt Collection Practices Act. Maryland requires licensing of all agencies collecting in that state.[49] Connecticut prohibits employing unlicensed agencies.[50] California makes it a misdemeanor to engage an unlicensed collection agency.[51] You'll probably want to see a license.

Now to the text of the contract. You'll wish to state a clear relationship between the parties, that is, separating yourself from the independent agency and narrowly drafting its duties and authority. Reserve the right to an overview, however. Examine all letters and scripts in advance, and have your agency *warrant* that it will only use those that you have approved in advance. For the protection of all concerned, such approval should be in writing.

The agency must warrant that it is aware of all the complex laws and regulations on point, that it monitors and stays atop all compliance developments, and that it will abide by the law and professional ethics (including, at a minimum, that all statements made in communication with a debtor are true). Be sure you are indemnified against the breach of this and all other warranties. I personally recommend that you have your agency warrant that it will comply with the Fair Debt Collection Practices Act literally and that it will require the same standard from each secondary agency it might employ.

Provisions specifying the duration of the relationship, compensation, termination, assignability, state of interpretation, and integration clause should be included in the contract.

If you are supplying a list of names, you should get a warranty specifying the confidentiality of such names and that such names are at all times your sole property. Your lawyer will write it in such a way that you'll obtain consequential damages. Of course, as a prudent businessperson, you'll "seed" the names if you have the capacity. (Seeding includes the sending of a few "dummy" names you can trace and monitor.)

CREDIT BALANCE

We shall now go from the problem of bad debts to the possible problem of overpayment. Can overpayment be a problem? Maybe! Review your policy as to credit balances; credit balances apply not just to credit card balances but to in-house charges as well, even if no finance charge, late fees, etc. are involved.

A credit balance is created when the creditor receives or holds funds in an account in excess of the total balance due from the customer on the account. Obviously, you credit your customer's account.

Then the FTC requires that you provide charge or other credit account customers having credit balances with periodic statements setting forth credit balances no less than three times in a 6-month period following the creation of the balance. Each statement must notify customers with credit balances of their right to an immediate cash refund of the balance. If your customer sends a written request for the money, you must refund it as soon as possible.

If you hear nothing from your customer, then, after the lapse of 7 months all credit balances over $1 must be refunded to the customer. Credit balances under $1 may be written off. However, you must be prepared to refund within 30 days any credit balance requested within 5 to 6 years of its creation.

What do you do after repeated good-faith efforts to refund the balance and the check is returned "addressee unknown" or "no forwarding address"? Here the respective state escheat laws must be examined in light of your firm's specific business practices. You need not have all the checks pile up. However, to protect yourself you should keep a record of your effort. Both the check and the envelope showing attempted delivery should be microfilmed. Then retain it for the applicable period (5 to 6 years). After that, if still unclaimed, it will probably be escheated to the respective state of the "owner." Your consolation is that you had the "float" value of the funds during this interval.

The respective state and federal laws should be reviewed with counsel as to when and how such balances must be refunded.

YOUR DUNNING CHECKLIST

As part of an overall systematic and professional management of your bad-debt problem, you'll want to create a checklist of legal compliance. You should do this whether or not you must comply with the act. Your checklist will include the following:

1. Are we retaining an independent agency to collect for us? If so, have we confirmed in writing that the agency is licensed, bonded, and insured? Have we thoroughly reviewed the agency contract with our counsel?
2. How are we handling person-to-person communications?
   a. Are we careful not to tell third parties that the person we're looking for owes a debt?
   b. Are we avoiding contacting third parties more than once in our

      location efforts unless absolutely necessary to get correct and complete information?

   c. Do we refrain from contacting the debtors directly when we know they are represented by an attorney with regard to the debt?

3. How are we handling our written communications (e.g., dunning letters)?

   a. Have we carefully examined all envelopes to make sure there is no reference of a collection effort visible on them (careful as to name used in return address)? Obviously only envelopes are considered, since all forms of postcards are prohibited.

   b. Do any of our communication pieces misrepresent the nature and urgency of the communication, that is, no simulated telegrams, mailgrams, court process documents, or any wording such as "urgent," "immediate," or "10 days to reply" (unless such wording has legal significance)? Do we threaten *immediate* action? Even if such actions are eventually pursued, no likelihood of immediate action can be indicated if no immediate action will take place (e.g., the phrase "it must be settled immediately" is not acceptable if such is *not* the case).

   c. Does the wording of any communication misrepresent in any way, directly or by implication, the purpose, intent, and procedure of our collection efforts with the debtor?

   d. Do any communications threaten any consequence we do not *routinely* follow through on? For example:

     (1) Reporting the debtor to a consumer reporting agency

     (2) Taking legal action

     (3) Arranging for attachment or garnishment

   e. Does our use of an attorney's letterhead imply directly or by implication that legal action will result? If so, will we act accordingly? Have we confirmed in-house or with the outside agency that such attorney is a real living member of the bar and not some fictitious or deceased individual? Have we reviewed with counsel whether this form of letter in these circumstances is permissible at all?

   f. Are we sending the debtor a notice within 5 days of the first communication that includes all the following items?

     (1) Name of the creditor owed

     (2) Identification of the debt by amount and account number

     (3) Nature of default and how it can be cured

     (4) Name, mailing address, and (where applicable) telephone number to contact for verification of the debt

     (5) The right to obtain verification of the debt

     (6) The procedure for verification

     (7) The right (and consequences resulting from the exercise of

     such right) of the debtor to have the collector cease communication

4. How are we handling internal procedures?

   a. If the debtor disputes the debt or requests the name of the creditor, are we stopping our collection efforts until we have mailed the verification of the debt or the creditor's name? If the debtor disputes the debt, claiming unordered merchandise was sent, do we carefully confirm that this is not the case? (See discussion of laws on direct marketing of unordered merchandise in Section 4, Chapter 9.) It is against the law to send collection letters demanding payment *or* return of merchandise which was never requested in the first place. If selling on approval or through negative option plans, you must carefully review the wording in your coupons or order forms with your counsel.

   b. Is every statement made in each follow-up letter or call true and in compliance?[52]

   c. If we receive a check from the debtor, do we have a written screening policy for the following?

     (1) What to do when a postdated check arrives.

     (2) What to do when a check arrives which is insufficient payment but has "paid in full" on the back. Merely crossing out such endorsement often is not enough; sometimes the best policy is to send back the check if it is for an unacceptable amount. Here you'll have to balance this with your own business judgment as well as your counsel's input.

     (3) How to apply payment if the debtor owes multiple debts and makes a single payment with specific directions concerning how the payment should be applied.

  Remember that, unless you are careful to document your employee training, these procedures may be of little assistance in a legal action.

  When involved in telephone dunning, add the following items to your checklist.

1. Have counsel screened all our telephone scripts as to their legal compliance? Have we screened them for their readability to our callers and for comprehension by our debtors?

2. Have all our employees been informed in writing of our policy (and the penalties of same) for obscene or profane language, use of threats, etc.? Are all calls made in a professional manner in a subdued tone?

3. Do all our callers properly ask for and obtain the proper and specific person desired?

4. Do our callers properly identify themselves and the nature of the call?

Within 5 days of the first call, are we sending the debtor a follow-up *written notice* of the right to verification of the debt, the right to dispute the debt, and the right to end communication?

5. Are all calls reasonably spaced and at a proper hour (time zones verified) to avoid harassment?
6. Are our employee-testing procedures lawful?
7. Finally, have we established written systems, procedures, and checklists to demonstrate to an investigating body that any error was accidental and not a matter of policy or negligence?

Remember that the FTC takes a very literal view of the wording of laws on point. That "other firms are doing it" is no defense for noncompliance—they just haven't been caught yet!

REFERENCES

[1] These include Alabama, Arkansas, Connecticut, Massachusetts, Michigan, Nevada, Ohio, Oklahoma, Pennsylvania, South Carolina, and West Virginia.

[2] 15 U.S.C. sec. 1692. This law codifies prior FTC case law defining unfair deceptive collection acts.

[3] 15 U.S.C. sec. 45.

[4] *In re* Capax, No. 9058, (1978). A dunning letter series in compliance with *Capax* would more than pass muster with the FTC's fair debt collection practices enforcement. See also a prior consent order agreed to in United Compucred Collections Inc., 87 F.T.C. 541, 542 (1976) (speedgrams were prohibited "which form by its color and appearance, styling, printing and format simulates a telegraphic message and which, by virtue of said simulation, misleads the recipient as to its nature, import, purpose and urgency").

[5] Trans World Accounts, Inc. v. F.T.C., 90 F.T.C. 350 (1977), 594 F. 2d. 212 (1979) (discussion of immediacy and urgency in communications; here the standard is one of a "realistic possibility" that the legal action will be pursued).

[6] Encyclopedia Britannica, Inc., 87 F.T.C. 421, 539–50 (1976); Compact Electra Corp., 83 F.T.C. 547 (1973); New Process Co., 87 F.T.C. 1359 (1976) and Pay 'N Save Corp., 86 F.T.C. 688 (1975).

[7] 15 U.S.C. sec. 1692(a)(5). *See also* Robert J. Posch, Jr., "Consumer Credit, Debt Collection and You," *Direct Marketing*, March 1983, pp. 154–157

[8] 15 U.S.C. sec. 1692(a)(6).

[9] 15 U.S.C. sec 1692(a)(6)(A).

10 Regulation 10.1(4) of the New York City Consumer Protection Law provides for certain exclusions but *not* the exclusion of in-house collectors (effective February 27, 1979). It applies to creditors located *within* the five boroughs.

11 Debt Collection Practices, 37 Pa. Code Ch. 303, adopted July 27, 1979. This regulation requires your outside agency to include the name, mailing address, and telephone number of the debt collector *and* the creditor.

12 *In re* Scrimpsher, 17 Barb. 999 (N.D.N.Y. 1982).

13 15 U.S.C. sec. 1692(a)(7).

14 15 U.S.C. sec. 1692(b).

15 The only exception is that individual collectors may use an "alias" (in writing and calls) to protect themselves from disgruntled debtors who might approach them personally. Section 806(6) requires that some identifiable name be given. The caller *must* correctly identify the collection agency as well as the fact that the call concerns the attempt to collect a debt. *See* Wright v. Credit Bureau of Ga., Inc., 548 F. Supp. 591 (1982).

16 A debtor's divorce or estate attorney, even if known to you, is not the debtor's attorney with regard to the debt unless such attorney informs you accordingly.

17 The original bill in Congress stated "seven calendar days" but this was amended to "a reasonable time."

18 Use certified mail in all legal matters; your receipt is proof that the party who signed for it received the letter. A secretary's signing for the letter will be acknowledgment for the attorney.

19 Again, watch for narrower state versions of this law.

20 Harvey v. United Adjusters, 509 F. Supp. 1218 (1981).

21 15 U.S.C. sec. 1692(g)(a).

22 Binghorn v. Collection Bureau, Inc., 505 F. Supp. 864 (1981).

23 Carrigan v. Central Adjustment Bureau, Inc., 494 F. Supp. 824 (1980). The court also fined the firm for a violation of the state licensing law.

24 15 U.S.C. sec. 1692(d).

25 Blackwell v. Professional Business Servs. of Ga., Inc., 526 F. Supp. 535 (1981).

26 Binghorn v. Collection Bureau, Inc., 505 F. Supp. 864, 874 (1981).

27 15 U.S.C. sec. 1692(d)(1)–1692(d)(6).

28 15 U.S.C. sec. 1692(f)(2)(1)–1692(f)(2)(4) ·

29 See *supra*, Ref. 25.

30 165 Ohio St. 35, 133 N.E.2d 340 (1956).

31 Consumer Credit Counseling Services, National Foundation for Consumer Credit, 1819 H Street N.W., Washington, D.C., 20006.

32 15 U.S.C. sec. 1692(k)(a).

33 You might want to get on the FTC's mailing list to stay abreast of current activities: FTC News Summary, Federal Trade Commission, Washington, D.C.,

20580. You can call the general information number (202–523–3598) to order any cease and desist order from the FTC which is discussed in the FTC News Summary; you'll need to indicate the name of the firm and its assigned docket number.

34 15 U.S.C.A. sec. 1692(k)(d).

35 15 U.S.C.A. sec. 1692(k)(a)(1)–1692(k)(a)(2).

36 15 U.S.C.A. sec. 1692(k)(a).

37 15 U.S.C. sec. 1692(k)(b)(1).

38 15 U.S.C. sec. 1692(c). In addition to proving the existence of an unintentional clerical error, the debt collector must show that there existed systems and procedures reasonably adapted to avoid such error.

39 15 U.S.C. sec. 1692(k)(a)(3).

40 15 U.S.C. sec. 1692(o).

41 Binghorn v. Collection Bureau, Inc., 505 F. Supp. 864, 871 (1981).

42 18 U.S.C. secs. 2510–2520. *See also* Robert J. Posch, Jr., "Can You Monitor Employee Phone Performance?" *Direct Marketing,* November 1981, pp. 108–109.

43 18 U.S.C. sec. 2510(5)(a)(i). Note that a "beep tone" is no longer required when recording *interstate* calls. However, it is necessary to get the other party's *consent.* You should review any narrower laws affecting local or *intrastate* calls with your counsel. Also review with your counsel any particular taping your firm considers. Privacy cases turn on the "reasonable expectation of privacy" of the person whose conversation is being recorded. Taping is rarely worth the exposure—monitor, don't tape. *See* Moore v. Telfon Communications Corp., 589 F.2d 959 (1978).

44 James v. Newspaper Agency Corp., 591 F.2d 579 (10th Cir. 1979). *See also* Stimmons v. Southwestern Bell Tel. Co., 452 F. Supp. 392 (1978).

45 State v. Nova, 361 So. 2d 411 (1978) (Florida).

46 Briggs v. American Air Filter Co., 630 F.2d 414 (1980).

47 State v. Harpel, 493 F.2d 346 (10th Cir. 1974).

48 For example, Ga. Code Ann. art. 26-3001–26-3010. (Harrison Co. 1982).

49 Md. Ann. Code sec. 329B, 329C (Michie Co. 1982).

50 Conn. Pub. Act 78–226, sec. 2(b) (from S. 186, 1978). *See also* Ariz. Rev. Stat. secs. 32-1001-2(b), -1021-22 (West Pub. Co. 1982).

51 Cal. Civ. Code sec. 1788.13, .16, Cal. Bus. & Prof. Code secs. 6871, 6886, 6915.4, 6902.5, 6927 (from S. 1463, West Pub. Co. 1980).

52 One good reason to routinely read and review FTC complaints and consent orders on point is that all problem letters at issue are attached as exhibits. Therefore, you can review the exact letters and use them as a guide to avoiding these problems.

SECTION
EIGHT
THE LAW AFFECTING YOUR PROMOTIONAL POLICY

As you know, a successful promotion must communicate in a persuasive manner, blending creativity and timing with thorough product analysis. However, the promotion manager must realize that advertising is the most regulated communications tool and that all compliance procedures must be monitored and updated regularly. Legal compliance issues affect all the traditional promotional questions.

Before undertaking any promotion campaign, you must conduct a thorough product analysis. Your product (i.e., whatever is to be marketed) must be understood as to its use and performance. Is it seasonal? What conditions surround its manufacture? What is the competetive environment? To best understand the product, analysis (and reanalysis) is necessary. The product must b examined, tested, criticized, evaluated, and put to the various uses for which it was designed. (See Section 3 for specific legal issues on point.)

This analysis must be done regularly, since the product must change as demand changes, and each such change will require reexamining your legal compliance requirements. A major aim of research is to know demand intimately, to adapt accordingly to show the targeted audience that it needs the product (through benefits offered), and to create a preference for this product over others in its class.

This section addresses the three major areas of promotional policy: traditional advertising, personal selling, and nonpersonal sales promotion. Traditional advertising is by far the biggest aspect, and we discuss it in detail in Chapter 18. The FTC gets heavily involved, so we'll take a look at what the FTC wants from you and how best to deal with this ubiquitous agency. Topics such as visual demonstrations, endorsements and testimonials, comparative and corrective advertising, as well as several others are reviewed in detail.

Personal selling is the process of assisting and persuading a prospect to buy a product or to act on an idea through the use of person-to-person communication. Chapter 19 addresses the issues of door-to-door sales, customer referrals, and telephone sales and arms you with the knowledge you need to avoid "bait-and-switch" tactics.

Nonpersonal sales promotions include those marketing activities other than personal selling, advertising, and publicity that stimulate consumer purchasing and dealer effectiveness, such as displays, shows and exhibitions, demonstrations, and various nonrecurrent selling efforts not in the ordinary routine (e.g., a sweepstakes promotion). Chapter 20 takes a close look at this form of promotion.

The easiest way to stay in compliance is to draft with your counsel a compliance checklist for promotion policy which updates all relevant legal and regulatory compliance (e.g., legislative enactments, court decisions, consent orders) affecting your particular promotional strategy. Consult this checklist routinely and each time you embark on a new promotion.

To assist your drafting such a checklist many of the following topical areas include questions you should ask. These questions are broad, and you should consult your counsel as to the particulars of your own promotional strategy. After all, it's counterproductive to spend valuable time and dollars convincing people to buy your product or service only to have a big chunk of your profits taken off the bottom line because of fines, legal fees, and damages paid, not to mention your valuable time and that of other members of your business staff diverted from their usual duties.

CHAPTER

EIGHTEEN

TRADITIONAL ADVERTISING

Marketing and advertising . . . can you conceive of one without the other? Indeed, advertising is such an integral part of the marketing process that it warrants a rather lengthy discussion, particularly since it's a pet target for the FTC and the courts.

INTERACTION WITH THE FTC AND THE FDA

There are many regulatory hurdles involved with regulatory agencies, particularly the FTC. Why not clear your promotion in advance with the FTC? Obviously, you'll have to review the trade-offs with your counsel—one drawback may be that you don't wish to heighten your general exposure to the FTC. However, if you do want an opinion from the FTC, a review of a few current requirements follows.[1]

In 1979 the FTC substantially changed its advisory opinion procedures. The FTC will issue formal opinions on written applications by specified parties (*unnamed parties may not receive a response*) in the following areas.

1. Where the matter involves a substantial or novel question of law and there is no clear precedent
2. Where a proposed merger or acquisition is involved
3. Where the subject matter is of significant public interest

Requests for advice and the FTC's response are placed on the public record immediately after the requesting party has received the advisory opinion.

Any advice received does not preclude the FTC's right to reconsider, rescind, or revoke. However, the original requesting party will be notified in advance. The FTC will not proceed against you if you rely in good faith on its advice, provided that you gave them all relevant facts, completely and accurately, and that your promotion is promptly discontinued if you're notified that the FTC has rescinded its approval. If you are concerned whether an advisory opinion is still valid, call the FTC at (202) 523-3598.[2]

FTC NATIONAL STANDARDS AND REGULATION OF ADVERTISING

Understanding government regulation affecting your promotional policy is facilitated by an understanding of the FTC's general principles governing advertising regulations.[3] In general, the FTC, under Section 5, has a broad mandate to root out "unfair methods of competition in or affecting commerce, and unfair or deceptive acts or practices in or affecting commerce."[4] It may act against materially deceptive speech (i.e., that speech which may influence the consumer's purchasing decision) when the injury is either to the consumer or to the advertiser's competitor.[5] The FTC has jurisdiction over violations "in or affecting commerce."[6]

Throughout its history, the FTC has attempted to follow the ideal that its regulation would serve two objectives: to provide truthful data and to maintain effective competition. Some standards which the FTC generally follows for all types of advertisements include:

1. The proof of a lack of good faith or of the intention to deceive is *not* a requirement for a finding that you violated the FTC act, since the purpose of the statute is not to punish a wrongdoer but to protect the public (including other businesspersons). The cardinal factor is the probable effect which the advertiser's handiwork will have on the eye and mind of the reader.

2. Advertisements will be considered in their entirety—the advertisement's total net impression governs.

3. Literal or technical truth will not save an advertisement if it is misleading when read in the context of the entire advertisement. One example of this is when the advertisement as a whole may be completely mislead-

ing even though every sentence separately considered is literally true.[7]

4. The advertisement is deceptive if any one of two possible meanings is deceptive or false or where it fails to reveal a material fact.[8]

5. Expressions of subjective opinion (puffery) are not actionable (that is, the FTC won't come after you!), unless they convey the impression of factual representations or relate to material terms. Words such as "easy," "perfect," "amazing," "wonderful," and "excellent" will generally be regarded in law as mere puffing, on which no charge of misrepresentation can be based.[9]

6. An advertisement is generally tested by the net impression it is likely to have on the general populace, ordinary purchaser, or an appreciable segment of the public (although advertisements directed at special audience groups, for example, children, will be interpreted on the basis of their meaning to that group). In general, the general public standard will mean that the advertisement will be judged on the basis of the meaning conveyed to the average or unsophisticated person, that is, those more likely to be influenced by an impression gleaned from a first glance and not tempered by mature reflection.

If your promotion doesn't live up to the FTC's standards, you must return to the drawing board. If it does, you are now ready to review the specific compliance factors necessary for your particular promotion and/or its wording.

LABEL OR ADVERTISEMENT?

Any firm governed by the Food and Drug Administration (FDA) or covered by a broad interpretation of its authority (e.g., if you're marketing any form of diet aids, even if only 100 percent "natural" ingredients are used[10]), must consult its counsel as to the FDA's separate (and sometimes overlapping) jurisdiction with the FTC.

The FDA is charged with enforcing advertising claims appearing on the label or package of food, drug, and cosmetic items. (For prescription drugs the FDA controls *all* advertised claims, including *premarketing* approval of such claims.) It may even seize shipments of goods on receipt of evidence that its regulations have been violated. Labeling or packaging includes written, printed, or graphic material accompanying the article as well as certain point-of-purchase materials.[11]

The FDA does the testing of the product efficacy in the areas of its mission. The results of these experiments may then by used by the FTC as it enforces its mission of misrepresentation or fraud in marketplace advertising.

At first glance there appears to be significant overlapping jurisdiction between the FTC and FDA. However, there is a functional difference between advertising and labeling. The former affects all product or service promotion the consumer will see in the mass media. However, once consumers purchase a product within the jurisdiction of the FDA, they are concerned with the instructions on the label. Often labeling instructions are more narrowly drawn by the FDA than they are by the broader mission of the FTC. For example, a drug is considered misbranded unless its labeling bears adequate directions for use *and* adequate warnings against unsafe use.[12]

Managers who review label copy and who promote a product governed by the FDA must consult counsel on areas which are not discussed in this chapter. The FDA's influence is increasing in the marketplace because the food, drug, and cosmetic industries are among the largest purchasers of advertising time and space. Further, misfortunes such as the events surrounding the Tylenol poisonings in 1982 will encourage greater consumer demand for accountability. If you are at all in doubt, consult your counsel on FDA compliance, FTC compliance, and general product liability and warranty principles.

COPY HEADLINER COMPLIANCE

All copy wording must be truthful (within the realm of "puffing") and able to be substantiated where necessary. Certain words catch your customers' eye and make them want to read on. One such word is "warranty." Another might be your logo or trademark (see Section 3 for both warranty and trademark legal issues). There are certain other words which always capture your viewer's eye and interest, including "sale," "discount," "new," and "free."

Last year my wife and I received a circular from a local store addressed to its "preferred" customers. The circular aroused our interest for four reasons: it advertised the store's semiannual *sale*, it offered a 20 percent *discount* to preferred customers during the 2-day promotion, it stated that all the items on sale were *new*, and it promised a *free* bottle of wine just for responding to the ad. Judging by the thriving business they did the evening we went, the promotion was obviously successful.

Yours will be too. As an added bonus, the knowledge you pick up (here as elsewhere in this book) will assist you in your personal life as well. Once you leave the office you're a consumer, too, and will want to know these areas for your own protection.

SALE

The term "sale" will always catch your customer's eye. The FTC knows this and has enacted guides on point.[13] Most states, the District of Columbia, Guam, Puerto Rico, and the U.S. Virgin Islands have enacted so-called little FTC acts to prevent deceptive and unfair trade practices. Your customers are familiar with the general terms and you should be, too. Long-term goodwill as well as legal compliance is at stake.

WHAT IS A SALE?[14]   One of the most frequently used forms of bargain advertising is to offer a reduction from the advertiser's own former price for an article. If the former price was the actual, bona fide price at which the article was offered and *sold* to the public on a regular basis for a substantial period, it provides a legitimate basis of price comparison. I emphasize "sold," since this sales test is a necessary hurdle which must be overcome and demonstrated with objective evidence.

A former price is not necessarily fictitious merely because no sales at the advertised price were made. However, you must be able to objectively prove that your price was openly and actively offered for sale, for a reasonable period of time, in the recent, regular course of your business, honestly, and in good faith.

In any sale you must confirm that the amount of your reduction is not so insignificant as to be meaningless. Because it is a material term (i.e., influences the decision of whether to purchase the item) it must be objectively truthful as well as avoid the tendency or capacity to mislead the consumer. It is particularly important that you consider the nature of your audience. A sale involving computer equipment to professionals will receive much less scrutiny than a sale directed to a particularly vulnerable group such as children. A nominal reduction of your price (for example, less than 5 percent) may be such an omission. Depending on your targeted audience, ticket price, and trade practices, 10 percent or more from the most recent actual going price would be a safe *starting* point, although this may vary in certain state laws or municipal codes. Review these with your counsel.

MUST EVERY ITEM IN A SALE PROMOTION BE REDUCED?

Segregate your catalog pages—if only certain items are on sale, only those items may be so identified. If you call your catalog a "sale catalog" or a similar name, then *every* item advertised in the "sale catalog," or every item included in the "annual sale," "Fall sale," or other such term must represent a reduction from a recent former price that was openly and actively offered for sale for a reasonable period of time in the regular course of business. Also, if you state "at our lowest price ever," *all* merchandise included in this description must actually be at its lowest price ever.

The manufacturer, distributor, or retailer must in *every* case act honestly and in good faith when advertising in any local or trade area (a trade area is one where you do business). Likewise, retailers should not advertise a retail price as a wholesale price. They should not represent that they are selling at "factory" prices when they are not selling at prices paid by those purchasing directly from the manufacturer. When it comes to price reductions, objective verification is the rule, and puffery is not permitted.

Use the following checklist to monitor your sale to ensure that you don't "donate" your profits from the sale to some local, state, or federal agency.

1. If quantities are in some way limited, you must disclose any limitation up front. Otherwise you might encounter time requirements. For example, at least one state requires that if your ad does not state a specific time during which your merchandise will be available, you must maintain a sufficient quantity to meet reasonable anticipated demand during 3 consecutive business days beginning with the effective date of the ad. This does not apply to exclusively in-store ads.[15]
2. Your sale price must be a reasonable and honest statement of a valid and recent actual former market price which is now reduced on a temporary basis. Sales which are permanent or continue for a long time are always suspect.
3. All items advertised as on sale in a sales promotion should represent an honest bona fide reduction from your previous benchmark price.
4. You should be prepared to substantiate your claim that every item in a sale was *sold* previously in the relevant marketplace (and was not merely offered).
5. The duration of the sale offer and items not on sale in a sales promotion must be distinctively identified and distinguished.

NEW MERCHANDISE

Merchandise may not be offered as "new" if it has been used or refurbished. This means returned merchandise may not be cleaned or "improved" in any way and then returned to inventory. It is a deceptive price if you offer seconds or imperfect or irregular merchandise at a reduced price without disclosing this fact. Unless stated otherwise, merchandise offered as new may not have been used during a trial period or otherwise. (See the discussion of trial versus examination later in this chapter).

If customers come to your place of business, they are not obligated to inquire whether articles for sale are new, used, or refurbished. There is an implied warranty in all your promotions to the customer that the article is new (that is, not previously sold or used) unless you specifically and clearly disclose otherwise.[16]

The word "new" is also used to promote a product which has either not yet been introduced into the marketplace or has been "improved," enabling the marketer to advertise the item as "new and improved." Also a new product should constitute the latest model in a particular product line which has not been offered for more than 6 months.[17] However, in a bona fide test marketing of a new product which does not cover more than 15 percent of the population and does not exceed 6 months in duration, the 6-month rule does not apply until the test period has ended.

Certain states have very exact disclosure requirements; therefore, as stressed throughout, ask counsel to review all state laws impacting your operations and routinely monitor their legislatures.[18]

FREE RULE

The cardinal rule of any promotion is that your ad must immediately hold your customer's attention. One way to do this is to open with your highest card, namely, whatever is of most significant benefit to the consumer, especially if that benefit appeals to the self-interest of your reader or listener. Not many people wouldn't like to receive something for nothing; the beauty of the simple word "free," therefore, is that it inspires self-interest.

However, it is often subject to abuse by certain firms. For example, have you followed up on a "free checking" sign only to find out that there is a host of strings attached? Representative Frank Annunzia stated in a news release concerning proposed legislation that "the legislation will put an end to abuses regarding so-called 'free' checking. To me 'free' checking means just that—no minimum balances, no limit on the number of checks, no required purchase of other services."[19] The lack of clear and conspicuous disclosure of the costs and conditions of services such as consumer-banking services is no defense to you in promotions (although as a consumer of banking services you are free to complain). Your test is that the word "free" is prohibited unless the item is truly without cost or un-disclosed obligation.

WHAT IS A FREE ITEM?   The public understands that, except in the case of introductory offers in connection with the sale of a product or service, an offer of free merchandise or service is based on a regular price for the merchandise or service which must be purchased by consumers in order to avail themselves of that which is represented as free. In other words, when purchasers are told that an article is free to them if another article is purchased, the word "free" indicates that they are paying nothing for the article and no more than the regular price for the other. Thus, a purchaser has a right to believe that the merchant will not directly or immediately recover, in whole or in part, the cost of the free merchandise or service by marking up the price of the article which must be purchased, by the substitution of inferior merchandise or service, or otherwise.[20]

If you are a direct marketer, such immediate recovery includes shipping and handling charges. Shipping and handling charges cannot be built into or added to a free item. For example, if a package is sent to a customer for a "free 15-day examination," the cost of returning the article must not be borne by the customer. A prepaid mailing label must be provided *or* some other device must be used to guarantee no postage costs, such as refunding the cost of the postage or crediting the customer's account for the expense incurred. The use of an item during a trial or examination period is not considered free if recipients must pay the cost of returning the item, should they so desire. This area is often overlooked but is enforced, so review your copy clearly to make sure shipping and handling charges are included in a free order.

DISCLOSURE OF CONDITIONS.   When making free or similar offers, all the terms, conditions, and obligations on which receipt and retention of the free item are contingent (these include credit limitation, prepayments,[21] etc.) should be set forth clearly and conspicuously at the outset of the offer to leave no reasonable probability that the terms of the offer might be misunderstood. Thus all the terms, conditions, and obligations should appear in close conjunction with the offer of free merchandise or service. For example, disclosure of the terms of the offer set forth in a footnote of an advertisement to which reference is made by an asterisk or other symbol placed next to the offer is not regarded as disclosure at the outset. However, mere notice of the existence of a free offer on the main display panel of a label or package is not precluded, provided that:

- The notice does not constitute an offer or identify the item being offered as free.
- The notice informs the customer of the location, elsewhere on the package or label, where the disclosures required by this section may be found.
- No purchase or other such material affirmative act is required to discover the terms and conditions of the offer.
- The notice and the offer are not otherwise deceptive.

The following checklist summarizes the free rule.

1. Any and all terms, conditions, and obligations you are imposing should appear in close conjunction (physically adjacent) so that the elements are naturally read together without undue difficulty with the offer of free merchandise. If you don't set forth your limitations, the item is free to all, even to those individuals who have a definite history of credit delinquency.
2. The type size must be at least half as large as the largest type size of the word "free" in the introductory offer copy, exclusive of numerals. (This is the rule in New York City and may be in your state as well.)[22] I recommend a minimum type size of 6 to 8 points where possible.
3. The qualification terms must be stated together in the same location of the ad, not separated by copy or graphics.
4. Disclosure of the terms of the offer set forth in a footnote of an advertisement to which reference is made by an asterisk or similar symbol does *not* constitute disclosure at the outset and will result in noncompliance.
5. If you are a supplier of goods who knows, or should know, that a free offer which you are promoting is not being passed on by a reseller or otherwise is being used by a reseller as an instrumentality for deception, it is improper for you to continue to offer the product as promoted to such reseller. You should take appropriate steps to bring an end to the deception, including the withdrawal of the free offer from your commercial customer. This policing of your resellers is good business as well as legal compliance.
6. Any wording having the practical effect of a free offer is governed by the free rule. Words of similar connotation such as "gift," "no cost or obligation," "at no extra cost," "given without charge," or "bonus" "which tend to convey the impression to the consuming pubic that an article of merchandise is Free" are governed by the free rule.[23]
7. In the timing of your free promotion you should be aware of the following:

a. A single size of a product should not be advertised with a free offer for more than 6 months in any 12-month period, and at least 30 days should elapse before another such offer is promoted.
b. No more than three such offers should be made in any 12-month period.
c. During this period, your sale of the product in the size promoted should not exceed 50 percent of the total volume of your sales in the same size of the product.

COST, WHOLESALE, AT A LOSS, AND SIMILAR TERMS

The standard for these terms is simple truth. However, one of the narrowest regulations on point is New York City's, and, if you comply with it, you'll be fairly safe—but check with your counsel about specific municipal and state regulations.

In New York City you may use terms such as "manufacturer's wholesale" or "factory price" only where your offering prices are compared to the prices currently and generally paid for such merchandise by retailers in the New York City trading area who buy that category of merchandise directly from the manufacturer. Also, in New York City, terms such as "below manufacturer's wholesale cost," "manufacturer's cost," and "our list price" are prohibited as inherently misleading terms.[24]

If you are running a "going-out-of-business sale," you must really be going out of business; the sale must be of limited duration and must not involve an early reopening under the same auspices. Again, check with your counsel as to whether a license is required—some states and cities require them.[25]

TRIAL VERSUS EXAMINATION

The distinction between "trial" and "examination" is one of my favorite subtleties in regulatory law. The words "trial" and "examination" are important and distinguishable, but if you review various advertisements you see each day, you'll observe that your uninformed competitors use them interchangeably. These are not words of similar import. Use of the term "trial" may cost you dollars and/or regulatory harassment and fines. Correct use of these terms will prevent legal problems without a loss of sales, since legal compliance means using the words in their logical context.

As discussed earlier, you may not substitute a used product for a new one without disclosing this fact. Merchandise which has been previously used on a "trial" basis (for example, "15-day home trial") and then returned may not be offered for resale as anything but a used product. In an investigation, the FTC will review your inventory records and may study the disposition of all your returned merchandise.

The FTC distinguishes between the practice of "trial" (implying a sustained use) and that of "inspection" or "examination" (indicating a mere looking at but not use). If you plan to refurbish and resell your returned merchandise, use the term "free examination." If your firm enters a joint promotion with another firm, it is coequally liable for the deceptive practice penalties incurred for disseminating used merchandise as new. Therefore it is important that you review your contracts with your vendors to make sure you have solid protection in your indemnification clause.

Finally, don't try to replace visual inspection with words. Use of the word "examination" will not insulate you from a deceptive practice charge if it is apparent from a visual inspection that the products have been used or otherwise significantly handled. Likewise, the legal result of the use of the word "trial" is never mitigated by a policy of visual inspection which eliminates obviously used products. *All* products are presumed tried and therefore used. In short, you must combine correct use of terminology with an adequate visual sampling of your returns.

TO SUM UP

Major compliance issues arise when certain wording is used either orally or in print to capture the reader's interest or to break down buyer resistance. A premium is placed on clear and conspicuous accuracy—ambiguity is no asset. A thorough knowledge of the subtleties of the words "sale," "free," "new," "at cost," "trial," "examination," and words conveying similar meanings will greatly assist your goal of maximizing reader interest while minimizing negative allegations of unfair and deceptive advertising.

WHEN AND HOW TO USE ENDORSEMENTS AND TESTIMONIALS

In days of yore, commercial transactions involved face-to-face communication. Buyer and seller often knew each other personally, which heightened credibility. As we entered the world of impersonal sales, credible trademarks and brand names somewhat replaced this personal touch, although such marketing was still product-oriented. Endorsements by experts, celebrities, and the person on the street, however, can personalize a product as well as attract attention, and the endorser's credibility enhances your product's image. In a promotional campaign you must carefully research the endorser's value to your target market, paying attention to age, sex, regionalism, and other unique audience acceptance factors.

Do endorsements work? Statistically, over 30 percent of advertising contains some form of endorsement. However, statistics aside, perhaps the best-run consumer-oriented company in the United States is Procter and Gamble. Two of their best-known products were given a decisive edge by endorsements, neither of which were the traditional celebrity type you normally think of.

Back in 1882 few people were aware of the benefits of an "absolutely" pure soap—that is, Ivory Soap. How could this asset best be conveyed? By getting an expert to say so. A chemical consultant performed tests on the soap. The analysis of B. Silliman, a professor of chemistry, was extensively advertised; along with his testimonial was born one of the most famous advertising slogans in history—Ivory Soap is "99 and $^{44}/_{100}$% pure."

Then Procter and Gamble added flouride to a toothpaste. Sales were initially disappointing because the benefit was not immediately observable. Since their potential customers couldn't see the benefit of flouride, they needed to hear of the benefit from an expert. Procter and Gamble submitted their product to the American Dental Association—a group which had never endorsed a toothpaste before. After 6 years of testing and efforts to seek its approval, on August 1, 1960, the *Journal of the American Dental Association* reported the now familiar (though then landmark) "Crest has been shown to be an effective anticaries decay preventive that can be of significant value when used in a conscientiously applied program of oral hygiene and regular professional care."[26]

We've seen that endorsements work. However, not all firms do the leg work to make sure they work right.[27] Therefore, there are some regulations and quotes on point, because the FTC staff has consistently taken the position that when an advertisement contains a reference to a source of authority, consumers are particularly likely to believe the claims asserted, especially when such claims are directed to or involve the central attributes of your product.

The FTC has issued guides on this point.[28] We will review these guides with particular emphasis on changes (and there were quite a few) from the previous guides. These changes are especially important if you haven't reviewed and rewritten your in-house compliance policies since 1980. First, however, let's briefly look at endorsements in general.

ENDORSEMENTS AND TESTIMONIALS AS EFFECTIVE PROMOTIONAL DEVICES

What does the use of a person's (particularly a celebrity's) status contribute to an advertisement? It attracts attention. Any name—or more particularly—any picture of a person attracts attention to an advertising message or, if used at the point of purchase, to a product or service. Attracting the potential customer's attention to a product is the first step in selling the product, and to the extent that the use of a likeness attracts attention to a product, that use benefits an advertiser.

Names and pictures do more than merely attract attention to an advertisement or product. They may suggest endorsement and otherwise influence decisions to purchase. They give the advertisement or product appeal that the advertiser's own statement about the product or organization may lack by itself.

The testimonial of a satisfied customer capitalizes on human nature's tendency for people to believe the words of "one of their own," who had nothing to gain, rather than the words of the seller, who has a pecuniary interest in the product. Of course such testimonials must be true *and* must reflect the typical results which the average user of the product could expect to obtain.

When using endorsements and/or testimonials, remember the following points:

1. Don't relate the comments out of context or distort the opinion expressed.
2. Don't attribute any particular experience, competence, or expertise to a person's comments unless it is warranted.
3. Don't use endorsements from anyone indicating approval of your product unless such a person is a bona fide user of your product.
4. Don't use endorsements from persons no longer using your product or service (especially experts).
5. Do get a signed release and contractual arrangement permitting the use of the endorser's name, comments, photographs, and illustrations (this can't be emphasized enough). This should include a specimen or a precise description of the advertisement and its authorized use (print advertising, direct mail, TV broadcast, etc.) as well as a detailed description of the product or service to be advertised.

Points 1 to 4 are required by the FTC.[29] The fifth point protects you from marketplace realities as well as legal problems.

THE FTC SPEAKS

First, let's review the key definitions—is there any difference between an endorsement and a testimonial? No. For your compliance purposes and its enforcement purposes, the FTC makes no distinction between the two.[30]

How does a slice-of-life advertisement differ from an endorsement? The former is an "obvious fictional dramatization of a real life situation."[31] By contrast, an endorsement (emphasis my own) "means *any* advertising message . . . which message consumers are likely to believe reflects the opinions, beliefs, findings or experience of a party *other than the sponsoring advertiser.*" Such endorsement can be made without any verbal statement but merely by association or the net impression conveyed through the context of the setting.[32]

Who is a spokesperson and how does such person differ from an endorser? As stated, the endorser is directly relating a personal opinion based on personal experience. A spokesperson does not do this. The spokesperson merely speaks in the place of or on behalf of the advertiser rather than on the basis of personal opinion. Such a person is usually not recognized by the public and makes no claims of special expertise. The FTC exempts spokespersons from the scrutiny through which endorsers must pass under the guides.[33]

How does an expert endorsement differ from that of an ordinary consumer? The expert must possess training or expertise greater than ordinary individuals. Such expertise must be relevant and on point to the particular product or service endorsed.

For example, a leading case on point concerned certain toy products aimed at children (a vulnerable target audience enjoying great FTC protection).[34] In this specific area of endorsements, the FTC prohibits endorsements of the worth, value, or desirability of a particular toy to a child by famous celebrities unless they also have the experience, special competence, or expertise to form the judgment expressed in the endorsement.

For your compliance purposes, much depends on whether you are using an expert or ordinary consumer, since significant guides distinguish the two, many of them new to the 1980 guides.

CONSUMER ENDORSEMENTS

You probably have one type of consumer endorsement available in your mailroom each day. Unsolicited letters from your satisfied customers, quoted in context, help sell others. Such letters capitalize on the human tendency to believe the statements of one's peers. One note of caution here—obtain a detailed written irrevocable release and agreement (for valid consideration) for any use of another's name in endorsement promotions, including the use of your customer's address. This release and agreement should include a full description of the advertised product or service and nature of the intended use.

Any endorsement by an individual consumer should typify what consumers in general will experience, that is, a "significant proportion." This area was discussed at length in *In the Matter of Porter & Dietsch, Inc.,* which concerned the promotion of a diet aid.[35] Several of the advertisements included testimonials reciting weight reduction and/or figure improvement purportedly attained by lay users of the preparation X-11. As indicated on the ad copy, the testimonials of ordinary consumers were presented and accompanied by statements such as "from Georgia to Nebraska to California." The net impression implied the general nationwide success of the users of X-11. Such results (as to amount of weight lost) were not an accurate reflection of the typical or ordinary experience of consumers who used X-11 under circumstances similar to those depicted in the advertisements. The advertisements did not disclose or identify this difference.

Thus a material fact (that is, a fact likely to affect the purchase decision) was not disclosed in the advertisements. The ads were found to be false and misleading. The decision not only held the firm liable but maintained that any retailer who runs an ad prepared by a supplier is legally liable for the truthfulness of everything in it.

Another variation of the "typical and ordinary" theme was found in a case concerning the Ford Motor Company.[36] The company advertised mileage test results for five small cars; there was an implied "you" in the mileage claims for driving performance—that is, "you" the purchaser would have a similar result if you drove the company's cars.

Here it was found that evidence of actual deception is not necessarily essential to a finding that an advertisement is unfair and deceptive. The capacity to deceive is important. Even if people submitting a testimonial honestly believe they obtained the results or that "you" will obtain similar results, consumers as a group are subject to too many variables that affect gas mileage, such as how fast they start and stop and actual driving conditions. Ford ceased advertising mileage claims which could be construed, with reference to the EPA mileage standards, as implying the success of a typical driver. Such problems have been alleviated by the federal EPA mileage standards.

A final case on point involved the National Dynamics Corporation.[37] Here endorsements were published which stated the history of select and highly successful performance incomes of users of this particular service. Although all statements were true, many were no longer current, and few releases had been obtained in writing. In the future, the firm's endorsements must be current, and each endorser must have given permission in a signed document.

The commission's experiences in these cases suggest that the more specific the endorsed experience is, the more likely that the representation will be considered a claim that the average consumer can expect similar results.

One of the current changes to the 1980 guides concerns consumer endorsements. A disclaimer to product performance is now permitted, although not encouraged, when an advertiser is not sure it can expect equivalent performance by other consumers using the product.[38] A simple statement that "not all consumers will get this result" or a similar vague disclaimer will *not* be considered adequate. The overall net impression governs, and the FTC will expect to see such a disclaimer as to product performance prominently displayed and integrated with the endorsement. Furthermore, the burden of proof as to prominence and integration is on you, the advertiser, and not on the FTC.

Formerly the advertiser was required to check at reasonable intervals to determine whether *all* endorsers continued to use the endorsed product. The 1980 guides were changed to *exempt consumer endorsements* from ongoing verification as to whether the endorsers are still bona fide users.[39] This reflects the marketplace reality that most consumer endorsements are one-time encounters, and the expert or celebrity is more traceable as a public person or more likely to have signed a contract with the advertiser.

Another important change concerns compensation:

> When the endorser is neither represented in the advertisement as an expert nor is known to a significant portion of the viewing public, then the advertiser should clearly and conspicuously disclose either the payment or promise of compensation prior to and in exchange for the endorsement or the fact that the endorser knew or had reasons to know or to believe that if the endorsement favors the advertised product *some benefit, such as an appearance on TV,* would be extended to the endorser.[40] [Emphasis my own.]

This change is significant. An expert or celebrity need only disclose an unusual connection to the endorsement, for example, one that "is not reasonably expected by the audience." Therefore, so long as such an expert or celebrity does not represent that an endorsement was given without compensation, no payment need be disclosed. However, this is not so for a consumer. The 1980 guides mark the first time that the FTC has required an *unpaid* consumer endorser to disclose any information in the endorsement. Intangible benefits, such as the opportunity to appear on television, are considered disclosable compensation.

The key here is prior knowledge, whether the consumer knows beforehand that an advertisement is being made (for example, personal notification, or a sign in a window). Such is prior compensation, which must be disclosed. However, if consumers are filmed by a hidden camera or in some other way so that they "had no reason to know or believe that their response was being recorded for use in an advertisement," then no issue as to compensation need be disclosed.[41]

Two other points need to be mentioned. If actors are used to represent "ordinary consumers," the 1980 guides do not require that you state that they are actors, just that the persons depicted are not "actual consumers." Also, payment to these actors need not be disclosed. Finally, the new guides now *permit* consumer endorsements of "any drug or device," if the *advertiser* has adequate scientific substantiation for the endorsement and such endorsement is not contrary to FDA determinations.[42]

Why the increasing regulatory attention? Quite simply, this form of promotion really works well. For an excellent article on the utility of unprompted consumer responses providing more credibility than many script writers could hope to produce, consult Ref. 43.

EXPERT ENDORSEMENTS

Under the guides, two distinct types of expert endorsements are recognized: organizational and individual. A good example of the former is the endorsement by the American Dental Association we discussed earlier. Such an endorsement is not given lightly. An organization's endorsement is perceived as less subjective because it embodies the varied opinions of many people. Specifically, the guides state that the organization's "collective experience exceeds that of any individual member and whose judgments are generally free of the sort of subjective factors which vary from individual to individual. Therefore, an organization's endorsement must be reached by a process sufficient to ensure that the endorsement fairly reflects the collective judgment of the organization."[44] Thus, it is improper to represent a minority opinion of an organization as the organization's official opinion.

The guides further require that when an organization is represented as being expert, it must use "an expert or experts recognized as such by the organization and suitable for judging the relative merits of such products."[45] The individual expert must actually possess the training and expertise he or she is purported to have, and such expertise must be relevant to the actual product endorsed (unless discussing taste or price). For example, the guides indicate that an "engineer" endorsing an automobile must be an expert in automobile engineering and not, say, chemical engineering.[46] Further, only unusual material connections between the advertiser and expert need be disclosed; routine compensation is presumed.

The advertiser must remain alert as to whether the celebrity or expert endorser continues to subscribe to the views presented. Once the endorser ceases to be a bona fide user of the product, the advertisement must cease. Depending on the nature of the promotion, you should formally contact your endorsers in writing as to their use of the product every 6 months, but never delay longer than 1 year—you might consider contractually obligating the endorser to contact you on cessation of use. Supplying the endorser with your product will help.

Finally, endorsers must make objective inquiry into the truthfulness of their claims. This is particularly true in the case of an expert's endorsement, because the total impression created on the targeted audience is one of the expert's endorsing a product both from experience as an expert in the field *and* as a personal user.

The pitfalls of ignoring or haphazardly approaching such inquiry are illustrated in the *Coogo Moogo* decision.[47] *Coogo Moogo* was the first time in the history of the FTC that an endorser of a product agreed to be personally accountable for representations made in an advertisement. Pat Boone was prominently featured in a television and magazine advertising campaign to promote an acne remedy. The remedy failed to live up to the claims made for it. Boone agreed to personally pay a percentage of any restitution ordered against the manufacturer. He also agreed to make reasonable inquiry into the truthfulness of any products he would endorse in the future.

This decision stands for the principle that an endorser must verify the claims made for the advertised product before the first commercial goes on the air or appears in print, or risk FTC action. As to the means of verification, if endorsers are not experts, they must look to independent and reliable sources to check out claims, tests, or studies supplied by the advertiser.

CONCLUSION

The guides we've just reviewed, while not carrying the force of substantive law such as a trade rule, nevertheless should be studied with caution. Read the guides with sections 5 and 12 of the FTC act. Together they prohibit any unsubstantiated or deceptive representation made by an endorser in any form of advertisement or media.

Be aware of the other related regulations on point, such as those promulgated by the Bureau of Alcohol, Tobacco and Firearms, which forbid an active athlete to endorse alcoholic beverages (that's why all the light-beer endorsements feature only retired athletes). There are also self-regulatory codes such as those advertising guidelines issued by the National Association of Broadcasters (check with your counsel as to their current status). Here, for example, endorsements by celebrities and "real-life authority figures" are not permitted in children's advertising.

The endorsement is an excellent vehicle for all media, especially commercial and cable TV and mail. To best use this promotional device, carefully monitor FTC and other regulatory activity affecting these promotions. There were significant changes in the revised 1980 guidelines, and marketplace dynamics will undoubtedly dictate further interpretations. Not staying on top of these areas could be costly to you. Ask yourself the following questions before beginning your endorsement promotion:

1. Have you reviewed with your counsel whether this situation involves an endorser or a spokesperson? All promotions must be reviewed individually and specifically with counsel.
2. How was the endorser selected, and how was the contract prepared?
3. Was the endorser a user of the product or service prior to this promotion? Is he or she still a satisfied user?
4. Has this person ever been employed by the promoting firm, or has this person in any other way possessed a pecuniary interest in the success of the firm or product?
5. Is this person a professional performer? An "average" customer? Or is the person merely a fictional personality of a pen name? If the person is the latter, a specific clause should be placed in the contract whereby a real and accountable person stands behind the fictional name.
6. If performance claims are made, what competency or expertise (or lack of same) does the endorser have in evaluating this particular product?
7. Is the total impression that this promotion creates on the targeted audience one of an endorser endorsing a product from his or her experience (as an expert?) in the field and/or as a user?
8. Has an adequate written legal release been obtained for any and all names, photographs, and the like that are to be used?
9. Has an affidavit been obtained, signed by the endorser and attesting to the truthfulness of the endorsement? Such affidavit should relate the full text of your endorser's comments to prevent any ambiguity.

Endorsements will be carefully scrutinized by the FTC in the 1980s. All such promotions should be reviewed with counsel, particularly the drafting of the necessary releases or the overall context of the contract itself if you are employing an outside firm or agency to manage your promotion.

DEMONSTRATING YOUR PRODUCT VISUALLY

Demonstrating your product visually is in effect an "endorsement by sight" of your intended audience. Television is the ideal vehicle for this type of advertising. Unless otherwise indicated, we're speaking of commercial as well as pay television (e.g., cable, direct broadcast satellite).

The product or service demonstration on television has the advantage of emotional involvement and the combination of sight, sound, and motion. Because of its costs, there is little incentive to inform the target audience as to the detailed merits of the product. The advertiser is buying time, not advertising, and desires to fill such time with selling hooks.

The advertiser must balance this desire to sell rapidly to a mass or semitargeted audience with the possibility that a premium on speech might result in a *material* omission which may incur the wrath of the FTC.

The FTC is the major federal agency keeping an eye on deceptive advertisements. Any advertisement disseminating a deceptive commercial over broadcast or cable television is subject to the FTC's jurisdiction. An important concept to the FTC in its evaluation of ads is the element of materiality—does the error, omission, or deception affect the decision to buy? If it does, it is material.

Four other issues you should consider in demonstrating your product visually include:

1. Your demonstration must actually prove something relating to the quality of the product.
2. Your demonstration must accurately reflect the honest experience a user would have.
3. Consumers are entitled to see what they are told they are seeing.
4. Your message should be presented in good taste. Further, there should be no visual misrepresentations of any premium, merchandise, or gifts which would distort or enlarge their value in the minds of your audience.

We'll highlight each of these points. To best appreciate these issues in their overall legal context, read the text on endorsements reviewed at length earlier in this chapter.

DOES MY DEMONSTRATION ACTUALLY PROVE SOMETHING?

In print advertising the FTC considers the entire advertisement as a whole.[48] The FTC construes ambiguous statements against the advertiser and gears its review to the low audience standard of the ignorant, credulous, and unthinking.[49] However, so long as the advertisement is true when read in the context of its entirety (qualified where necessary) the advertisement will pass muster.[50]

This is not true on television. When you seek to promote by sight, sound, and motion, your demonstration *must* be relevant to your product's major attribute—in other words, you can't beg the issue.

For example, a leading consumer products company marketed a product called "Baggies," designed to prevent food from spoiling. On television the demonstration focused on the more visually dramatic ability of Baggies' capacity to keep water off the enclosed food. The FTC obtained a consent order stating that the demonstration of Baggies' capacity to keep water out (though true) was irrelevant to its ability to prevent food spoilage. Here, an irrelevant demonstration, although true and accurate in its own right, might influence the purchase of an item not being sold for its primary purpose.[51]

DOES MY DEMONSTRATION REFLECT THE HONEST EXPERIENCE OF THE TYPICAL USER?

A toy company demonstrated its robot commando, representing that this toy would perform acts as directed by the user's vocal command.[52] In reality, each act was governed by a manual setting of a control on the toy; the toy would perform only the specific act set on the control. If you wished a different act, you could use your "vocal command" until you were blue in the face—the robot would only ignore you. Only when you manually changed the setting would the robot follow your command.

The FTC did not like this. It was a milder agency in those days and merely required the firm to cease and desist from "stating, implying or otherwise representing by words, pictures, depictions, demonstrations or any combination thereof, or otherwise, that any toy performs in any manner not in accordance with fact."[53]

It is important not to exaggerate or mislead in any demonstration. During the early 1970s, there were many gasoline additives on the market in an attempt to capitalize on the post-1973 oil embargo and the ensuing gas price hikes as well as to cultivate the environmentally conscious market. In one advertisement, an oil company showed a car pulling two boxcars and a caboose—over 100 tons![54] How could your car do this too (if you really desired to pull a train)? By using their 260 blended gasoline.

After you heard the pitch, you saw a repeat of the demonstration with the statement "you're seeing Sunoco premium deliver in this car."[55] However, the consumer would find in typical driving that the gasoline did not have qualities unavailable in competitive brands. The blend did not consistently provide more engine power than a gasoline of a comparable octane rating.

There was no intent to deceive. The firm sought to capture customer attention by its demonstration. However, its demonstration misrepresented realistic consumer experience and was at best a gross exaggeration. The firm sought to enhance a product with a vivid visual perception which would remain with the viewer. However, no such demonstration is permitted if it states or implies a material untruth.

DOES THE DEMONSTRATION ACCURATELY PORTRAY WHAT THE VIEWER IS SEEING?

Prior to the recent advancements in lighting and photography which television put into place in the mid-1960s, "mock-ups" or "props" were widely used. These were used to compensate for the technical deficiencies of the day and to make products appear on television as they do in real life.[56] This form of substantiation in demonstration advertising came to a head in a landmark Supreme Court decision in 1965.[57] Involved was a television demonstration in which Palmolive Rapid Shave cream was applied to a substance that the viewer was told was sandpaper. The thrust of the commercial was to give the viewer visual "proof" that Rapid Shave could soften the sandpaper. However, the shaving cream the viewer saw on TV did not actually come into contact with sandpaper but rather a simulated prop or mock-up made of Plexiglas to which the sand had been applied.

The Court stated that the emphasis of a legal review should be on the impression the demonstration will have on the viewing public. Here the FTC has broad discretion due to its presumed expertise in this area.

> In commercials where the emphasis is on the seller's word, and not on the viewer's own perception, the respondents need not fear that an undisclosed use of props is prohibited by the present order. On the other hand, *when the commercial not only makes a claim, but also invites the viewer to rely on his own perception for demonstrative proof of the claim,* the respondents will be aware that the use of undisclosed props in strategic places might be a material deception.[58]

In the final analysis, it was decided that consumers are entitled to see what they are told they are seeing. The FTC need not prove actual deception or that the advertising actually influences consumer decisions.

To measure deceptiveness, the FTC looks at the total impression and will reject "literal truth" as a defense if the overall impression is false or deceptive.

Although this was a tough, drawn-out case, in other cases, the issues are less complicated. For example, an advertiser for a soup company placed marbles at the bottom of the bowl of soup to force the solids up.[59] The visual effect achieved by this demonstration was to show a cup or bowl of piping hot soup jammed with vegetables. This technique was found to be deceptive since viewers were not seeing an accurate portrayal of what they would actually consume. Seeing is believing when it comes to a legal evaluation of your product demonstration.

ARE MY DEMONSTRATIONS IN GOOD TASTE? The question of good taste involves trade practice and goodwill more than the law. You don't want to turn people off by producing an ad with negative racial, sexual, or other overtones.

Two good groups to keep an eye on are the National Advertising Board and the National Advertising Review Board (two self-regulatory groups sponsored by the Council of Better Business Bureaus in 1971). You can keep track of these organizations' findings by reading trade magazines and by getting on their mailing lists.

WHAT SHOULD YOU DO?

Tighten (or set up) internal and advertising agency procedures so that you can assure any regulatory or consumer group questioners that what is seen in your TV commercials is an authentic depiction of what actually occurred. To accomplish this, require that an affidavit be provided for each television commercial produced for your company. The affidavit (which should be signed by two responsible people present during the filming) must outline the actual production steps, materials, and techniques which are relevant to the truth and accuracy of your commercial. No commercial should be used on the air unless an adequate affidavit has been provided in advance.

Finally, go through the checklist concerning visual demonstrations (at the end of this chapter) from time to time as a refresher on general points in this area.

NEW TECHNOLOGIES—NEW LAWS?[60]

Computer data bases tied to interactive cable marketing, informercials, home computers, videotext, etc. will personalize the ability to gear a demonstration to a much more targeted audience. Comparative pricing, demonstrations of utility, and in-depth warranty information will all enhance the knowledge of the consumer. The new technologies will present commercials your customers will want and possibly will pay extra for!

This personalized marketing may make current laws on point obsolete. If a consumer can insert a personal shopping profile into a home computer and have it print out advice based on ad input, then what is "material" information to a purchase decision may be radically altered.

Increasingly, the legal environment you must comply with will be based on the advertising channel you use and the audience you reach through it. For example, the municipality granting your cable franchise agreement might contract for specific regulations governing product demonstrations. Your franchise agreement should be carefully reviewed with counsel as to regulations narrower than current federal and state laws on point.

It is obvious that the nonselectivity of product demonstration to a mass audience is in eclipse. Therefore, as you advertise through varied media in the next few years (e.g., videotext), it is imperative that you review your various contracts and ads with counsel. Don't merely carry over what worked and was in legal compliance with your commercial television marketing strategy.

The following are questions to consider for your visual demonstration.

1. If this is a simulation, will these words appear across the screen to inform our viewers?
2. Will the demonstration disclose all relevant information necessary so that my purchaser can make an informed decision?
3. Will the demonstration prove something which is material to the product's utility to the viewer?
4. Did we carefully review the demonstration to eliminate any express or implied exaggerations or excessive puffery? If the demonstration asserts a scientific argument, have objective and well-controlled tests been performed and documented to verify *all* statements made and/or visually demonstrated?[61]
5. Are we demonstrating a product requiring legal disclosures? For example, if the commercial involves the printing of "free" across the screen, are any qualifications in acceptable print size to pass a Flesch readability test? If the presentation is oral but requires disclosures, have your demonstration reviewed by one of the agencies which do audio recall tests as well as with your counsel.

6. Is our demonstration in compliance with any FTC orders issued against our firm? If you subsequently violate such orders *each* broadcast of your commercial may be a separate violation.
7. Are we well versed on the endorsement issues when we're using a personality or spokesperson in the advertisement? The preceding chapter should be mastered so as to refine your questions for review with your counsel.

Don't forget that there are still consumer groups and individuals engaging in private verification of demonstrations. (They are usually looking for accuracy, not legal compliance.) *Consumer Reports* magazine is one example of a large testing group, and individuals such as David Horowitz, whose show tests the tests of the advertisers, are also involved. One article quoted Horowitz as stating that one out of four ads flunk their own performance tests.[62] As we briefly mentioned in the Colgate discussion—in all these areas more than dollar damages and nuisance penalties are involved. You may have the problem of the emerging issue of *corrective advertising*.

Finally, review with your counsel the current status of the self-regulatory code of the National Association of Broadcasters (NAB). Since 1952 this trade association has sponsored a television code which provides broadcasters with guidelines in various areas. In 1982 a federal district court designated one of the NAB's advertising standards as a violation of the antitrust laws.[63] Although the NAB has suspended enforcement of its code until the area of self-regulation is clarified, by the time you read this the issue might have been resolved, so consult your counsel.

LINGERING FALSE BELIEFS— THE CORRECTIVE ADVERTISING REMEDY

Those who have followed the hamburger advertisement disputes have probably noticed that the debate has focused on many issues relevant to managers.[64] First of all, the companies involved adopted the politicians' tactic of turning their commercials into media events. McDonald's and Wendy's charges against Burger King created a lot of free media coverage and increased public attention to their respective commercials.

Burger King initiated the debate in September 1982, with an assertive comparative ad campaign. McDonald's sought an injunction, and Wendy's sought damages and corrective advertising as well as an injunction.

McDonald's also countered with a wave of interview-format *customer testimonials*.[65] The debate involves three areas of interest: the limits of permissible comparative advertising (see the next topic in this chapter), commercial free speech, and the much threatened but rarely invoked remedy of corrective advertising.[66] Let's review just how this remedy has come about and your exposure to it (which will arise primarily if not exclusively from a regulatory body, since the remedy is rarely sought by a competitor).

FTC REMEDIES AGAINST DECEPTION

The FTC is charged with the regulation of unfair and deceptive trade practices, including false advertising. The usual remedy in deceptive advertising cases has been the conventional cease and desist order, which defines, in fairly broad terms, those categories of claims which the FTC has found to be deceptive or unfair and proscribes similar conduct in the future. The FTC can move against all products sold by a party even if false advertising has been found in only one product or group of products, unless the party terminated the alleged practice before the consent order was issued or the party did not act in blatant disregard of the law. The consequence of failure to comply with such an order can be a penalty of up to $10,000 per day per violation.[67]

Traditional false advertising has been grouped into three areas: advertisements possessing misleading implications, advertisements which are deceptive by omission, and advertisements whose lingering effects require some form of correction. Each of these areas requires that an advertisement have the tendency or capacity to mislead an appreciable or measurable segment of the consuming public. As we've discussed, advertisements directed to a particularly vulnerable group such as children will be subject to special scrutiny.[68] The deception must be material, that is, one which may influence the consumer's purchasing decision. It need not deal with the substantive qualities of the product; any extrinsic fact that may influence the purchasing decision may be material.[69]

For those of you in advertising, be aware that your agency may be held liable for your client's deceptive advertising, depending on the extent of your knowledge of and participation in the deception.[70] The only significant exception is that advertising agencies are exempt from certain criminal penalties imposed on deceptive claims (see discussion at the end of this chapter).[71]

DECEPTION BY MISLEADING IMPLICATIONS. This area concerns advertisements which deceive through half-truths rather than outright lies, that is, through claims not literally true but which give a false impression. The advertisement may contain affirmations which are themselves true but which necessitate disclosure of further facts to avoid creating a misrepresentation in the minds of the consuming public.

The FTC's general approach has been to attempt to cure this type of deception through disclosures.[72] In a recent case which received much publicity, the FTC brought suit in the Seventh Circuit against an association making certain nutritional claims about eggs.[73] The association had argued to the effect that no scientific evidence existed that eating eggs increased the risk of heart and circulatory disease. The FTC obtained an injunction against the ad as worded on the grounds that the company presented a one-sided opinion as fact (rather than opinion) and that such presentation was misleading due to the controversy between the company's position and that of many, if not a majority of, experts in the field.

DECEPTION BY OMISSION. An advertisement may be deceptive if it fails to disclose material facts necessary to correct a disparity between consumers' normal expectations about a product and its actual performance, for example, advertisements that do not disclose that clothing is made of flammable fabrics.[74] Similarly, deception by omission can stem from your customer's basic assumption about the condition of your product. For instance, the mere advertising of a product wihtout qualification can raise the assumption in the minds of your customers that your product is new (see discussion earlier in this section about copy headliners).[75]

This theory was codified in 1938 by the Wheeler-Lea amendments to the FTC act, which defined false food and drug advertisements to include the failure to reveal material facts regarding the consequences of using a product in either the customary manner or under the conditions prescribed in the particular advertisement.[76]

EVOLUTION OF THE CORRECTIVE ADVERTISEMENT REMEDY. Many of you are familiar with the celebrated Listerine case. However, this was not the beginning of the FTC's employment of the corrective advertising remedy; rather, the principles of this case had a solid foundation in legal precedent, although the Listerine case was the first corrective advertisement order to be approved by the courts.

In general, the FTC follows the following procedure. When it has reason to believe a product has been advertised deceptively, it issues and serves a complaint. The complaint usually calls for a cease and desist order to force the advertiser to halt any alleged deception and to refrain from such deception in the future, and the commission has wide discretion as to the order's nature and terms. Many, if not most, respondents will agree to a cease and desist order.

The respondent has the option to be heard before an administrative law judge who is the fact finder for the commission proceedings. Such judge's findings become the decision of the FTC unless a petition for review is filed. The respondent or the commission may then appeal, in which case the commission reviews the judge's decision. This decision is then subject to review on appeal to the United States Court of Appeals and then by the Supreme Court.

Prior to the Listerine case, the FTC had built precedents through affirmative disclosure cases, advertising announcing penalties imposed, and consent orders specifically requiring corrective advertising. One of the affirmative disclosure cases involved a baking powder company, which for 60 years had widely advertised that its product was superior because it contained cream of tartar rather than phosphate.[77] Eventually the firm changed its ingredients to include phosphate. Although it could no longer claim that its product contained cream of tartar, its labels retained their original name, lettering, coloration, and design—they appeared exactly as they always had.

The FTC required and the court upheld an extension series of disclosures including the mandatory use of the word "phosphate" as part of the name of the product. The court recognized that it was an unfair trade practice to make sales of an inferior product "on the strength of the reputation attained through 60 years of its manufacture and sale and wide advertising" as a superior powder.[78]

In a more recent but similar case, an established (150 years) Massachusetts clock company transferred its trade name, trademark, and goodwill to a successor corporation, which began to import clocks from Europe for resale in the United States.[79] The imported clocks were widely advertised as the "product of Waltham Watch Co., a famous 150 year old company." To correct this false impression, the FTC ordered disclosures to correct the lingering belief that the clocks sold under the trade name were the same Massachusetts clocks. The court upheld the FTC's order relying on "the well-established general principle that the Commission may require affirmative disclosures for the purpose of preventing future deception."[80]

In both these cases, the courts clearly recognized the latent affect of prior advertising on the purchasing habits of consumers. At the time of the Listerine case, the FTC established another form of corrective advertisement for lingering effects of prior advertising by requiring a manufacturer to pay for advertisements announcing the imposition of substantial civil penalties for making claims that the FTC alleged were not substantiated.[81]

The FTC first discussed its authority to impose corrective advertising in a 1970 consent order.[82] A soup manufacturer allegedly advertised soup in a deceptive manner by placing marbles at the bottom of the bowl, forcing the vegetable upward to make the soup appear richer for a visual demonstration on camera. The FTC did not impose corrective advertising but did assert its right to do so in the future if the situation merited a stronger remedy than the traditional cease and desist or affirmative disclosure order.

The FTC's first corrective advertising consent order was obtained in 1971 from ITT Continental Baking Company.[83] The order required that at least 25 percent of the company's advertising for Profile Bread during the next year contain corrective advertising disclosures. Ten other consent orders followed from 1971, ranging from sugar's not being a unique source of strength, energy, and stamina[84] to cranberry juice's not containing more vitamins and minerals than tomato or orange juice.[85]

In 1971, the Federal Trade Commission issued a complaint against Warner-Lambert Company, a pharmaceuticals manufacturer, alleging misrepresentation in the company's advertising of Listerine mouthwash.[86] At the factfinding hearing, the administrative law judge found that the advertisements were deceptive. Further, many years of promotion for Listerine mouthwash had fostered a lasting but erroneous impression in the minds of consumers that Listerine was effective in preventing or treating colds. The court upheld the FTC's requirement that the company not only cease making the false claim but also add a disclaimer in future advertising.

Initially, Warner-Lambert was required to state the following: "Contrary to prior advertising, Listerine will not help prevent colds or sore throats or lessen their severity." This statement would be added to all Listerine commercials until $10 million had been expended. The case was appealed.[87] The FTC's decision was affirmed except that "contrary to prior advertising" was stricken from the required disclosure. In affirming the FTC's power to impose corrective advertising, the appeals court suggested that if advertisements did not have a long-lasting effect, then "companies everywhere may be wasting their massive advertising budgets."[88]

The criteria for "lingering beliefs" will probably be developed on a case-by-case basis. This remedy is one all managers, especially those employing visual demonstrations (discussed earlier) or comparisons (discussed next), must reckon with in the future.

Corrective ads are imposed because of past deceptive claims which have resulted in present lingering beliefs by consumers. If such a lingering effect is found, the remedy is imposed for a period necessary to reduce the incorrect or false beliefs to an "acceptable level."

Whether this remedy will be used often or selectively by the FTC and private parties remains to be seen. In the interim, consider this potential penalty as you design your own advertisements.

COMPARATIVE ADVERTISING

Many agree that the Avis "We Try Harder" campaign inaugurated the modern era of comparative advertising.[89] However, without the subsequent prodding by the FTC, the consumer would probably still be witnessing comparisons with "brand X." As was the case with professional advertising, comparative advertising was at one time held back by self-imposed industry regulations as well as public restraints, for example, the CBS and ABC networks systematically rejected commercials that named competitors, leaving advertisers little incentive to produce a comparative campaign that could run only on NBC or in the print media.[90]

In 1972, the FTC directly intervened with a series of informal visits and correspondence by staff personnel, and the two recalcitrant networks agreed to allow specific comparative advertisements on the air.[91] NBC and ABC have subsequently issued guidelines which seek to ensure that comparative ads are both fair to competitors and of value to consumers. The American Association of Advertising Agencies has adopted a similar approach.[92] By 1978, most restrictions were eliminated with the exception that comparative advertising must not be "disparaging." Further, all comparisons must be material, and must relate to specified product characteristics or properties, and any differences highlighted or compared must be significant.

ADVANTAGES OF COMPARATIVE ADVERTISING

The FTC has taken an aggressive stance in promoting the use of non-deceptive comparative advertising because it has the potential to:

1. Make the marketplace of commercial ideas self-correcting
2. Provide consumers with valuable information
3. Facilitate competition

First Amendment theory has traditionally encouraged "free and robust debate" so that all ideas can potentially generate counter ideas. Comparative advertising, by providing a medium for commercial speakers to counter the false claims of competitors, could result in an analogous self-correcting marketplace of ideas. Further, it would reduce the general social cost of FTC policing and the specific cost to a firm of an FTC investigation. As one commentator succinctly put it: "Fears of legal problems will most likely impel advertisers to use greater caution in making sure their advertisements are based on clear, honest and substantiable facts, which is of course a major benefit the FTC hopes will come from greater use of comparison advertising."[93]

Such self-policing might have saved STP and Wonder Bread producers (to name a few) much time, litigation, fines, and bad publicity. The self-correcting marketplace remains a theoretical goal at present, but it provides a firm philosophical basis for encouraging the development of comparative advertising in the future.

VALUABLE SOURCE OF INFORMATION

By contrasting the attributes of competing products in a single format, comparative advertising can provide a useful frame of reference for evaluating a seller's claims and can significantly reduce the cost to consumers of obtaining information.

The mere listing of product attributes is not enough. These attributes will be seen as significant by the consumer only when they are shown to meet the demands of the consumer's evaluative criteria for that specific decision. Comparative advertising can contribute to the total information environment in which individual consumers make purchase decisions.

The sequence of events which leads up to a decision to purchase a product may be summarized in the following steps:

1. **Problem recognition.** Realization that a problem needs to be solved
2. **Diagnosis.** Determining the cause of the problem
3. **Examination of the alternatives.** Searching out possible solutions
4. **Product selection.** Termination of purchase decision when the consumer chooses one product from the alternatives examined

Information from a wide variety of sources can be used by consumers at each step.[94] Consumers generally acquire information for decision making through a combination of two basic types of search: (1) internal, through which the consumer retrieves previously acquired information from memory and (2) external, by which the consumer actively seeks information from a number of different sources.

FTC SUPPORT

In general, the FTC's position is as follows:

> *The Commission has supported the use of brand comparisons where the bases of comparison are clearly identified. Comparative advertising, when truthful and non-deceptive, is a source of important information to consumers and assists them in making rational purchase decisions. Comparative advertising encourages product improvement and innovation, and can lead to lower prices in the marketplace. For these reasons, the Commission will continue to scrutinize, carefully, restraints upon its use.*
>
> 1. Disparagement—*Some industry codes which prohibit practices such as "disparagement," "disparagement of competitors," "improper disparagement," "unfairly attacking," "discrediting," may operate as a restriction on comparative advertising.* The Commission has previously held that disparaging advertising is permissible so long as it is truthful and not deceptive.
>
> 2. Substantiation—*On occasion, a higher standard of substantiation by advertisers using comparative advertising has been required by self-regulation entities.* The Commission evaluates comparative advertising in the same manner as it evaluates all other advertising techniques. The ultimate question is whether or not the advertising has a tendency or capacity to be false or deceptive. *This is a factual issue to be determined on a case-by-case basis. However, industry codes and interpretations that impose a higher standard of substantiation for comparative claims are inappropriate and should be revised.*[95] [Emphasis my own.]

It is quite apparent that the FTC favors comparative advertisements and is loathe to encourage narrower self-regulation by the industry.

QUALITY COMPARISONS

In quality comparisons, there is latitude for puffery; i.e., "our products are better than our competitors'."[96] However, puffery claims become subject to substantiation when they make verifiable representations of fact. For example, "our products are best" or "our car gets the most gas mileage" implies *overall* superiority and must be substantiated against all competitive products. Therefore, it goes without saying that the quality base against which a comparison is made must be identified clearly and conspicuously.

When you make a quality comparison, you have the problem of standards: If you assert a claim against all your competitors, you must have objective evidence that you really tested against *all* of them. If you did, fine; if you didn't, don't even imply that you did.

What about independent findings? You may quote them in a manner that is both meaningful to your audience and truthful. This means that you may not edit "in such a way as to create an entirely false and misleading impression."[97] Literal statements may not be truthful when they are taken out of context, when they contain deceptive omission, or when they are measured against your targeted audience.

A specific example of this deceit by omission was the Lite Bread case.[98] In this case, the FTC found an implied comparison to white bread in the representation by Lite diet bread that it could help control weight in that it contained only 45 calories per 17-gram slice. In fact, the only reason that a slice of Lite Diet contained fewer calories than ordinary bread was that the bread was sliced thinner. The omission obviously was material and therefore was deceptive.

The FTC has considered comparative advertising misleading when it emphasizes immaterial differences between products. An immaterial claim is one that involves a distinction between the products that is so insignificant that it does not affect product performance. An irrelevant comparison (although true and accurate in its own right) might influence the purchase of an item not being sold for its primary purpose.

Finally, if you are comparing "brand X" against your product (and "brand X" can be quite specific when there are relatively few competitors in your market), the appearance and the size or shape of "brand X" in your copy or commercial must not be distorted. The impression conveyed must be similar to what your viewer would encounter upon actual inspection and purchase.

WRAPPING UP COMPARATIVE ADVERTISING

The attributes that you stress in comparing products must actually benefit the purchaser. An advertising campaign employing misleading statements or outright deception is as illegal today as ever. If a quantitative case can be made by your victimized competitor for its proportionately slipping sales, you may suffer damages as well as an injunction.[99]

Setting forth a full and accurate comparison is a problem on commercial TV, but the longer informercials and print advertising are effective media for presenting comparative advertising.

Finally, almost all other advertising law comes into play. If it is capable of being read in a misleading way by the viewer, it is misleading in the eyes of the FTC.[100]

ADVERTISING SUBSTANTIATION

Before 1981, advertising substantiation was becoming more and more regulated in the areas of prior testing and substantiation of the accuracy of any claims made. Now matters are in flux, and you must consult with your counsel routinely and update and revise your checklist accordingly.

However, false advertising (including innuendo, indirect intimations, and ambiguous suggestions) is illegal. Further, no performance claims about your product can be made unless you have a reasonable basis (you should document all tests in writing) for making them. The FTC is particularly strict when a false advertising campaign is geared to infrequently purchased items or one-time sales (e.g., dishwashers), where there is little self-correction in the marketplace.[101]

AGENCY LIABILITY FOR FALSE ADVERTISING

Since we're discussing advertising, we shouldn't forget the advertising agency (used here as a generic term for media-buying services, creative boutiques, etc., although their liability may differ depending on circumstances). No longer may the agency send out its account executive to work on ideas and services alone. The agency will probably be responsible with the advertiser for false, deceptive, or unfair advertisements concerning the product of the agency's client. Remember, your buying public is not under any duty to make reasonable inquiry into the truth of the advertising.

This liability is a factor both sides must consider in drafting their contracts—particularly as the trend to "a la carte" services develops. For example, you and your counsel must get in writing exactly what you and the agency are doing together and what documentation and testing are available to substantiate claims made.

You must be able to substantiate each objective claim (performance, mileage, and other tangible attributes which are measurable and verifiable). If a claim needs qualification, then such qualification must be made in language understandable to the vast multitude of people, which includes the ignorant, the unthinking, and the credulous.[102]

Those who've been in advertising for a while will remember that at one time there was great latitude for puffery. This is changing; puffery is permissible but narrowly construed. Clearly subjective statements and hyperbole which are opinions which are not provable are permissible. However, an opinion statement cannot be used as a subterfuge to transform an objective, verifiable claim into puffery. Superlatives, too, contain substantiation problems. If you claim to have the "most," "best," or "fastest" in comparison to the competition, you must exceed all competitors in the category to which your superlative statement makes reference.

Clear claim substantiation protection from the agency's client is necessary because the advertising agency liability policy may not protect the agency from an incorrect description of the article or commodity featured. (It may not protect the agency as to trademark infringement or a mistake in the advertised price either.) A particular area of possible exposure nowadays are claims arising from comparative advertising.

The agency has a fairly complicated legal posture in presenting its client's message. How has this come about?

EVOLUTION OF AGENCY LIABILITY

It was not always this way. Back in 1949 agencies were not held responsible. At one time, the FTC dismissed complaints against agencies despite their clients' false and misleading advertising if it was determined that the agencies at all times acted on the direction and under the control of their client. It was held that the agency acted as an agent for media purchasing. At most, the agency only disseminated the advertising, and this was not enough to constitute deception. The client was held to have the *final* authority and responsibility for the advertising.[103]

The position was in keeping with the traditional view of the agency relationship. Such relationship is a legal and fiduciary one whereby one person is authorized to act for another in business transactions (usually in the area of some expertise) with third parties. Such agent must measure up to the standards of skill possessed by other agents engaged in the same business.

WHERE WE ARE TODAY

In 1963 we arrived at what is basically the legal standard today, when a court finally addressed the salient issue: "Is one carrying out the will of another to be held responsible for the results of his actions?"[104] The court believed the proper criterion should be the extent to which the advertising agency actually participated in the deception. Here, the agency was liable since it had worked with its client for years, had developed the idea to emphasize a deceptive claim, and had written the storyboards and assisted in other preparation for promoting the product.

An agency will also be held liable when the deception stems not from the false information but from the use of correct information by the agency. This can include a false impression made by words and sentences which are literally and technically true but which are framed in such a way to mislead or deceive. In taking exception to the repeated use of unqualified medical claims, the court wrote:

> The skillful advertiser can mislead the consumer without misstating a single fact. The shrewd use of exaggeration, innuendo, ambiguity and half-truth is more efficacious from the advertiser's standpoint than factual assertions. . . .

> To the contrary, the agency knew that the products were recommended only for the relief of minor sore throat pain, mouth and throat irritations. Despite this knowledge, it developed advertising, which by the use of "exaggeration, innuendo, ambiguity and half-truth" conveyed the false impression that the products would cure or help cure existing throat infections and would be effective in relieving severe pain of sore throat. . . .

> The agency, more so than its principal, should have known whether the advertisements had the capacity to mislead or deceive the public. This is an area in which the agency has expertise. Its responsibility for creating deceptive advertising cannot be shifted to the principal who is liable in any event.[105]

This is where we are today. The standard of care to be exercised by an advertising agency in determining what express and implied representations are contained in an ad and in assessing the truth or falsity of those representations increase in *direct relation* to the advertising agency's participation in the commercial project. The degree of its participation is measured by a number of factors, including the agency's role in writing and editing the text of the ad, its work in creating and designing the graphic or audiovisual material, its research and analysis of public opinions and attitudes, and its selection of the appropriate audience for the advertising message. As to the knowledge it does possess, an advertising agency has an affirmative duty to ensure the truthfulness of claims made in the promotion they produce.

In fashioning a remedy, both the courts and the FTC have wide discretion in structuring an appropriate remedy and will impose a penalty which has a reasonable relation to the unlawful practices found in the specific circumstances of each individual case. This underscores an agency's need for a uniform procedure of verification, editing, and other in-house standards to check and recheck the veracity of both its own claims and those of its clients for each promotion.

LOOKING TO THE FUTURE

The advertising agency is now a partner in legal liability when it lacks substantiation for any objective claims dealing with performance, efficacy, preference, mileage, taste, and other tangible attributes which are objectively measurable and verifiable. Any superlatives such as "best" must be exactly that or must be qualified.

In proceedings against advertisers, it is now an acknowledged FTC staff procedure to include the advertising agency. Examples can vary from being able to substantiate the nutritional value of the products intended as a central selling message[106] to being responsible for verifying that test results not only are accurate but also do not convey a misleading impression.[107] The FTC has stated that unless advertising agencies are under this duty to make independent checks of information relied on in their advertising claims, the law would be placing a premium on ignorance.

The practical effect of a court decision or FTC order against your agency, aside from its adverse effects on getting new clients, can include fines, being barred for a period of time from engaging in certain categories of product promotions, or even being barred from certain promotions themselves (e.g. sweepstakes, endorsements, or visual demonstrations).

It's good business for both the agency and its client to comply with the applicable legal rules affecting the particular promotion. It's also good business to investigate your legal exposure further. For example, unless you've protected yourself contractually, the agency is liable to pay the media even if the advertiser fails to pay the agency. Written contractual protection with all parties is a must in the 1980s.

CONCLUSION

These topics concern themselves with areas generally familiar to all advertising in the media. However there are areas you should also be familiar with when dealing with personal and nonpersonal promotions, which we discuss in the next two chapters. Don't forget to bring to these chapters ideas we've just reviewed. For example, the legal principles concerning copy headliners don't change whether they are in print, on TV, or delivered in a sweepstakes promotion.

REFERENCES

[1] 16 C.F.R. sec. 1.1–1.4

[2] We discussed monitoring the FTC in Section 2. Again, I recommend that you obtain the *FTC News* and the *FTC News Summary*. You should also investigate a subscription to the *BNA Antitrust and Trade Regulation Reporter* as well as the CCH's *Trade Regulation Report*.

[3] Again, state and local laws may be narrower. We'll cite some instances as we go along, but you should review such impact with your counsel when designing your promotion.

[4] 15 U.S.C. sec. 45(a)(1) (1976). *See generally* Millstein, *The Federal Trade Commission and False Advertising*, appearing in *Symposium: The Fiftieth Anniversary of the FTC*, 67 Colum. L. Rev. 385, 439 (1964); *Symposium: Federal Trade Commission Regulation of Deceptive Advertising*, 17 U. Kan. L. Rev. 551 (1969); Comment, *False Advertising: The Expanding Presence of the FTC*, 25 Baylor L. Rev. 650 (1973). *But see* Thompson, *Government Regulation of Deceptive Advertising: Killing the Consumer in Order to "Save" Him*, 8 Antitrust L. & Econ. Rev. 81 (1976).

[5] *In re* Pfizer, 81 F.T.C. 23 (1972). Note that the deception need not deal with the substantive qualities of the product; any extrinsic fact that may influence the purchasing decision may be material. *See* F.T.C. v. Colgate Palmolive Co., 380 U.S. 344, 386 (1965).

[6] Magnuson-Moss Warranty—FTC Improvement Act, 15 U.S.C. sec. 45(a)(1) (1976). This effectively eliminated the uncertainty created by F.T.C. v. Bunte Bros., Inc., 312 U.S. 349 (1941) ("in commerce" language of the Wheeler-Lea Amendment was held to preclude FTC jurisdiction over completely intrastate activities).

[7] F.T.C. v. Sterling Drug, Inc., 317 F.2d 669 (2d Cir. 1963).

[8.] 15 U.S.C.S. sec. 55(a). A "material fact" is one which will influence your purchaser's decision whether to buy or not.

[9] Carlay Co. v. F.T.C. 153 F.2d 493 (7th Cir. 1946).

[10] For a good example of the marketplace confusion and debate that can occur, see Nancy Giges, "Diet Aids Face FDA Block," *Advertising Age*, June 21, 1982, p. 3.

The FDA serves a useful role in enhancing consumer confidence. For example, if you buy peanut butter, you know that you're getting 92 percent or more peanuts. Without a national standard here and elsewhere, consumers would have greater reluctance to purchase.

[11] FDA Act sec. 201(m).

[12] FDA Act sec. 502 (f)(1).

[13] Federal Trade Commission Guides against Deceptive Pricing, Ch. I, tit. 16, pt. 233 (1980).

[14] 16 C.F.R. sec. 233.1 (a)–.1(e) See the recent language in para. 5, p. 3 of the FTC's complaint issue in United States v. Keystone Readers' Service, Inc., 95 F.T.C. 803 (1980). As to significant sales at a stated price, see *In re* Encyclopedia Britannica, Inc., 87 F.T.C. 421, 425 (1977).

[15] N.J. Stat. Ann. Sec. 13:45A-9.2(a) West (1983).

[16] *See* Donovan v. Aclonian Co., 200 N.E. 815 (1936).

[17] *See* FTC Advisory Opinion 120, 71 Op. F.T.C. 120, 1729 (1967), and FTC Advisory Opinion 325, 75 Op. F.T.C. 325, 1113 (1969).

[18] *See, e.g.,* N.J.P.R. 5684, especially sec. 13:45A-9.2(7) and .2(8).

[19] News Release from Congressman Frank Annunzia, "Financial Services Disclosure Act Introduced," April 5, 1979.

[20] FTC Guide Concerning Use of the Word "Free" and Similar Representations, ch. I, tit. 16, pt. 251, sec. 251.1(b)(1).

[21] Spiegel, Inc. v. F.T.C., 494 F.2d 59 (7th Cir. 1975). This case presents an excellent discussion of the free rule.

[22] New York City Dept. of Consumer Affairs, Regulation 201.

[23] 16 C.F.R. sec. 251.1(2)(j).

[24] New York City Dept. of Consumer Affairs, Regulations 13.4, 13.5, and 13.6.

[25] See N.Y. Gen. Bus. Law sec. 581 and New York City Admin. Code sec. B32-206, -209, and -214.

[26] For the best book you'll ever read on Procter & Gamble and maybe the best book you'll read on any corporation, see Oscar Schisgall, *Eyes on Tomorrow: The Evolution of Procter & Gamble,* Doubleday/Ferguson, New York, 1981.

[27] For a good commentary on certain abuses see the editorial viewpoint "If the Shoe Fits," *Advertising Age,* July 5, 1982, p. 12. See also Robert J. Posch, Jr., "Check Revised FTC Guide before Planning Endorsements," *Direct Marketing,* July 1982, pp. 214–217.

[28] Guides Concerning the Use of Endorsements and Testimonials in Advertising, 16 C.F.R. sec. 255.

[29] 16 C.F.R. sec. 255.1.

[30] *See* 16 C.F.R. sec. 255.0: "(a) The Commission intends to treat endorsements and testimonials identically in the context of its enforcement of the Federal Trade Commission Act and for purposes of this part. The term "endorsement' is there-

fore generally used hereinafter to cover both terms and situations." This text likewise uses both terms interchangeably.

[31] 16 C.F.R. sec. 255(b) and example 2.

[32] *Id.*, and examples 1, 4, and 5.

[33] *Id.*, and example 3.

[34] *In re* Mattel and Topper, Inc., [1970–1973 Transfer Binder] Trade Reg. Rep. (CCH) para. 19,735 (Consent Orders 1971).

[35] 3 Trade Reg. Rep. (CCH) para. 21,380 (F.T.C. 1977).

[36] 87 F.T.C. 756 (1976).

[37] 82 F.T.C. 488 (1973), *modified in part*, 442 F.2d 1333 (2d. Cir. 1974), *cert. denied*, 419 U.S. 993 (1974), *order modified*, 85 F.T.C. 404 (1975), *order further modified*, 85 F.T.C. 1052 (1975).

[38] 16 C.F.R. sec. 255.2(a).

[39] 16 C.F.R. sec. 255.1(b).

[40] 16 C.F.R. sec. 255.5.

[41] 16 C.F.R. sec. 255.2(b) and example 3.

[42] 16 C.F.R. sec. 255.2(c).

[43] James P. Forkan, "Maysles Finds 'Great' Copy from Mouths of Real People," *Advertising Age*, November 8, 1982, p. 80. However, to lend a note of caution to this form of testimonial, review Better Business of Metropolitan Houston, Inc. v. Medical Directors, Inc., 681 F.2d 397 (1982).

[44] 16 C.F.R. sec. 255.4.

[45] *Id.*

[46] 16 C.F.R. sec. 255.3, example 1.

[47] 92 F.T.C. 310 (1978). *See also* "Let the Stellar Seller Beware," *Time*, May 22, 1978, p. 66. The effect of this decision hung over the endorsement industry for a long time. For example Marty Ingels of Ingels, Inc. (one of the existing agencies to contact for celebrity endorsers) was quoted in the February 8, 1982, *Advertising Age*, p. 50: "all this, despite the Pat Boone thing still hanging over our heads."

[48] Charles of the Ritz Distribs. Corp. v. F.T.C., 143 F.2d 676 (1944).

[49] Aronberg v. F.T.C., 32 F.2d 165, 167 (7th Cir. 1942).

[50] Liggett & Myers Tobacco Co. v. F.T.C., 55 F.T.C. 354, 370 (1958).

[51] [1967–1970 Transfer Binder] Trade Reg. Rep. (CCH) para. 19,074 (Consent Order 1970).

[52] *In re* Ideal Toy Co., 64 F.T.C. 297 (1964).

[53] *Id.* at 316.

[54] *In re* Sun Oil Co., 84 F.T.C. 247 (1974).

[55] *Id.* at 249; 1974 was a bad year for additive claimants. *See also In re* Standard Oil Co. of Cal., 84 F.T.C. 1401 (1974) (concerning misrepresentation as to its F-310

gasoline additive) and *In re* Crown Central Petroleum Corp., 84 F.T.C. 1493 (1974) (concerning misrepresentation of gasoline additive).

56 Comment, *Illusion or Deception: The Use of "Props" and "Mock-Ups" in Television Advertising,* 72 Yale L. J. 145 (1962).

57 F.T.C. v. Colgate-Palmolive Co., 380 U.S. 374 (1964).

58 *Id.* at 393 (emphasis my own).

59 F.T.C. v. Campbell Soup Co., [1967–1970 Transfer Binder] Trade Reg. Rep. (CCH) para. 18,897 (Consent Order 1970).

60 Robert J. Posch, Jr., "The Technology Is Here—The Laws Aren't Yet," *Direct Marketing,* February 1982, pp. 86–101.

61 ITT Continental Baking Co., v. F.T.C., 532 F.2d 207 (1976).

62 Bob Marich, "Consumerist Earns Grudging Respect," *Advertising Age,* March 16, 1981, p. 12. Another article in this area that is well worth reading is Elrod, *The Federal Trade Commission: Deceptive Advertising and the Colgate-Palmolive Company,* 12 Washburn L. J. 133 (1973).

63 United States v. National Assoc. of Broadcasters, 536 F. Supp. 149 1982).

64 For example, "Wendy's Asks Damages," *Advertising Age,* October 4, 1982, p. 3; Christy Marshall and Richard Kreisman, "Competitors to Fight Burger King Drive," *Advertising Age,* September 20, 1982, p. 2.

65 Richard Kreisman, "Big Mac Ads Hit Back at BK," *Advertising Age,* November 1, 1982, p. 1.

66 On the issue of commercial free speech, see Robert J. Posch, Jr., "Telephone Marketing—It Survived and Prospered," *Direct Marketing,* September 1982, pp. 106–109.

67 15 U.S.C. sec. 45(1982).

68 United States v. J.B. Williams, 492 F.2d 207 (2d Cir. 1974) and ITT Continental Baking Co. v. F.T.C., 532 F.2d 207 (2d Cir. 1976).

69 F.T.C. v. Colgate Palmolive Co., 380 U.S. 374 (1965).

70 *In re* ITT Continental Baking Co., 83 F.T.C. 865 (1973).

71 15 U.S.C.S. sec. 54(a).

72 *See* J.B. Williams Co. v. F.T.C., 381 F.2d 884 (6th Cir. 1967).

73 National Comm. on Egg Nutrition v. F.T.C., 570 F.2d 157 (7th Cir. 1977), *cert. denied,* 439 U.S. 821 (1978).

74 Fisher and Deritis, 49 F.T.C. 77 (1972). *See also* Martin v. J.C. Penny Co., 313 F.2d 689 (1957).

75 *See* Ref. 17.

76 15 U.S.C. secs. 52, 55 (1978).

77 Royal Baking Powder Co. v. F.T.C., 281 F.2d 744 (2d Cir. 1972).

78 *Id.* at 753.

[79] Waltham Watch Co. v. F.T.C., 318 F.2d 28 (7th Cir.), *cert. denied*, 375 U.S. 944 (1963).

[80] *Id.*, 318 F.2d at 32.

[81] United States v. STP Corp., No. 78-559 (S.D.N.Y. 1978).

[82] Campbell Soup [1967–1970 Transfer Binder] Trade Reg. Rep. (CCH) para. 18,897 (1970).

[83] ITT Continental Baking Co., 79 F.T.C. 248 (1971).

[84] Amstar Corp., 83 F.T.C. 659 (1973).

[85] Ocean Spray Cranberries, 80 F.T.C. 975 (1973).

[86] 15 U.S.C. secs. 52, 55 (1978).

[87] *Id.* at 762.

[88] *Id. See also* Robert J. Posch, Jr., "Lingering False Beliefs—The Corrective Advertising Remedy," *Direct Marketing*, December 1982, pp. 88–91.

[89] Gaughan, *Advertisements which Identify "Brand X": A Trialogue on the Law and Policy*, 35 Fordham L. Rev. 445(1966–67), 57 Trade Mark Reporter 309, 310 (1967).

[90] Pitofsky (director of the FTC's Bureau of Consumer Protection), *Network Policy of Preventing Advertisers from Naming Competitors*, Memorandum to the FTC, 1 (March 6, 1977).

[91] FTC News Release, March 30, 1972.

[92] Wilkie and Farris, "Comparison Advertising: Problems and Potential," *Journal of Marketing*, vol. 39, 1975, p. 10.

[93] Rotfeld and Hisrich, *Comparison Advertising: Preliminary Findings on Practitioner's Perspectives*, Working Paper, Marketing Department, Boston College (submitted for presentation to the American Academy of Advertising 1979 National Conference), 13. *See also* Robert J. Posch, Jr., "Commercial Free Speech—The Argument for OUR Side," *Direct Marketing*, February 1983, pp. 92–94.

[94] For our purposes, information is envisioned as any stimulus which is perceived by the consumer as potentially helpful in making a purchase decision or in using a product or service. Technically, a stimulus is not transformed into information until it is actively examined and assigned meaning by the consumer.

[95] 16 C.F.R. sec. 14.15, 44 Fed. Reg. 47378 (August 13, 1979).

[96] Don't forget to refer back to the discussion of comparative pricing in Section 5, Chapter 13.

[97] Lorillard Co. v. F.T.C., 186 F.2d 52, 58 (4th Cir. 1950).

[98] Bakers Franchise Corp. v. F.T.C., 302 F.2d 258 (3d. Cir. 1962).

[99] M & W Gear Co. v. AW Dynamoter, Inc., 424 N.E.2d 356 (1981). *See also* Robert J. Posch, Jr., "Comparative Advertising Yesterday and Today," *Direct Marketing*, May 1982, pp. 106–110.

[100] Resort Car Rental Sys., Inc. v. F.T.C., 518 F.2d 962 (1975).

[101] Standard Oil v. F.T.C., 577 F.2d 653, 658 (1978).

[102] Sears, Roebuck and Co. v. F.T.C., 676 F.2d 385 (1982).

[103] F.T.C. v. Bristol Meyers, Young & Rubicam, Inc. and Pedler & Ryan, Inc. 46 F.T.C. 162, *aff'd,* 185 F.2d 58 (4th Cir.), 47 F.T.C. 1749 (1949).

[104] Carter Prods., Inc. v. F.T.C., 523 F.2d 523, 534 (1963).

[105] F.T.C. v. Merck & Co. 392 F.2d 921, 1929 (6th Cir. 1968).

[106] ITT Continental Baking Co., 83 F.T.C. 865, 1105, 90 F.T.C. 181 (1965).

[107] Sears, Roebuck and Co. v. F.T.C., 676 F.2d 385 (1982). *See also* Robert J. Posch, Jr., "Client/Agency Relationships: Liability of Ad Agency," *Direct Marketing,* April 1983, pp. 119–120. For another article on a related topic, *see* Posch, "Copyrighting Your Advertising Promotions—Both Print and Video," *Direct Marketing,* October 1983, pp. 97–101.

CHAPTER

NINETEEN

PERSONAL PROMOTIONS

Your marketing strategy may include personal selling in which your salespeople (or your current customers, as you will see in a moment) will deal with potential customers on a one-to-one basis. Obviously included in this category are door-to-door sales and telephone sales. Other personal promotions are those in which you reward satisfied customers with a bonus or merchandise when they recruit new customers. Less obvious as a form of personal selling, but an area which rightly belongs in this discussion, is the personal sales pitch which your customers may get when they come into your store to buy an advertised item. Here you must be wary lest your sales pitch revert to bait-and-switch tactics.

Each of these areas entails certain legal issues with which you should be familiar, since your marketing strategy probably does include some form of personal promotions.

DOOR-TO-DOOR SALES AND THE 3-DAY COOLING-OFF PERIOD

For years you've seen the satirized confrontation between Dagwood Bumstead and his nemesis, the door-to-door salesman. The scenario is familiar—the leg in the door, chases from room to room, physical confrontations, and other exhibitions of the "hard sell." The FTC and other consumer groups have argued that a salesperson coming to your door represents an unplanned purchase often after a less dramatic but no less effective hard sell than that to which Dagwood was subjected.

To alleviate the perceived problem of deceptive door openers and high-pressure misrepresentations, the FTC[1] (and many states)[2] promulgated a "cooling-off" rule for door-to-door sales. The major points of the rule are as follows:

1. For purposes of the FTC regulation, a door-to-door sale is one which requires a purchase of $25 or more.
2. The purchase must be made at a place other than the seller's place of business. A door-to-door sale does not include a sale made pursuant to prior negotiation in the course of a visit by the buyer to a retail business establishment with a fixed location and where the goods are available for inspection. The rule does not apply to a sale conducted and consummated entirely by mail.
3. The seller must give oral and written notification of the buyer's right to cancel within 3 days. Any claim misrepresenting this right to cancel or cooling-off period is prohibited. The buyer must receive a copy of the contract or sales receipt before the 3-day period is said to commence.
4. This form must be in the language used in negotiating the contract (e.g., French or Spanish), must be easily detachable, and must contain in *10-point* boldface type the information shown in the form on page 288.

Proof of mailing date and receipt are important, and thus a certified letter is your best protection as a consumer. A firm is not obligated to require certified mail on the form. Finally, no reason is required to cancel.

Within 10 days of receipt of the cancellation form, the seller must:

1. Cancel and return any papers the consumer signed
2. Refund the consumer's money and indicate whether any product left with him or her will be picked up
3. Return any trade-in

Within 20 days, the seller must either pick up the items, or, if the consumer agrees to send back the items, reimburse him or her for mailing expenses. If the 20 days pass without your picking up the goods, your customer can keep them as a gift. No dunning may be instituted.

The FTC exempted sales under $25 or those made totally by mail or phone. The mail exemption is obvious, and the phone's should be too because the high pressure is greatly diminished by the safety valve of a simple hang-up. Further, there is no confrontation presence before you.

Notice of Cancellation
[enter date of transaction]

. . . . .
(Date)
You may cancel this transaction, without any penalty or obligation, within 3 business days from the above date.

If you cancel, any property traded in, any payments made by you under the contract or sale, and any negotiable instrument executed by you will be returned within 10 business days of your cancellation notice, and any security interest arising out of the transaction will be canceled.

If you cancel, you must make available to the seller at your residence in substantially as good condition as when received, any goods delivered to you under this contract or sale: or you may if you wish, comply with the instructions of the seller regarding the return shipment of the goods at the seller's expense and risk.

If you do make the goods available to the seller and the seller does not pick them up within 20 days of the date of your notice of cancellation, you may retain or dispose of the goods without any further obligation. If you fail to make the goods available to the seller, or if you agree to return the goods to the seller and fail to do so, then you remain liable for performance of all obligations under the contract.

To cancel this transaction, mail or deliver a signed and dated copy of this cancellation notice or any other written notice, or send a telegram, to [name of seller], at [address of seller's place of business] not later than midnight of   (date).

I hereby cancel this transaction.
(Date) _____

_____
(Buyer's signature)[3]

However, many states have thought otherwise and have enacted laws which cool off the spontaneity of the telephone sale; telephone marketers should know which states impose various restrictions of this sort.[4]

One final area of note in door-to-door sales is the *Britannica* case.[5] Especially interesting is the up-front notice Encyclopedia Britannica originally was supposed to give the potential customer before beginning a sales presentation. The courts have been whittling down the FTC's penalties, and you should consult with counsel as to the final outcome of the case and its possible implications for your method of promotion.

REFERRAL SALES
AGREEMENTS

When using referral sales agreements, the key to running a successful promotion is to make sure that you are not running any form of direct or indirect chain referral or pyramid-type scheme. The latter invariably boils down to offering a sales device under which purchases are induced on the representation that the cost to buyers will be reduced because they will purchase the right to recruit other participants and receive commissions on the sales of those recruits.

The following is the type of wording included in many, if not most, state unfair trade practice statutes on point (consult your counsel for your state's exact wording):

> It is considered an unlawful act when a person engages in a sale of goods or services, gives or offers to give a rebate or discount, or otherwise pays or offers to pay value to the buyer in consideration of the buyer giving to the seller the names of prospective purchasers, lessers, or borrowers, or otherwise ordering the seller in making a sale, lease, or loan to another person if the earning of the rebate, discount, or other value is *contingent* upon the occurrence of an event subsequent to the time the buyer enters into the transaction.

Most state laws prohibit schemes in which participants invest money to obtain the right to recruit other participants and to receive commissions for such recruiting. The problem with such schemes is that a very large number of potential recruits is necessary for participants to recover their investments and make money.

If you are seeking other forms of relief, you might review with your counsel whether the referral plan involved a lottery. If so, it is illegal.[6] If you are in a commercial setting you should also reference the unconscionability protections in the UCC.[7]

As discussed earlier in this section, your satisfied customer is the *best* recommendation for your product.[8] Many smart firms have established plans which encourage their customers to recruit new customers for them. They know this personal trust relationship among friends and neighbors is an excellent market penetration device. In our society we encourage a fundamental law of nature—that of reward spurring motivation. You wish to reward your customers who get other customers. You also wish to stay within the law. What is to be done?

First the obvious—check your contract. If you are giving away rewards, review with your counsel whether such promotional giveaways are permissible in your state.

Second, review your promotional wording with counsel. As we've stressed throughout, keep in mind the maturity of your target audience. Then make sure that your wording cannot be construed as a false representation for the purpose of inducing consumers to participate in your plan.

You can give away a reward on receipt of a referral, or you might wish to qualify that the reward is contingent upon the referral's buying a food plan or joining a record club, for example. If you do the latter, review the promotional copy with counsel, since all qualifying terms must be *clear* and *conspicuous*—*not* buried in the overall promotion piece. You and your counsel will work out a conspicuous layout (possibly similar to a "rule box" you'll use in your sweepstakes copy). The wording will contain terms such as "*as soon as* your friend pays." You will invite the recruiter to *claim* the gift or reward (not order it) when presenting the referral.

Remember that you are dealing with a *free* offer. As we stated earlier in this section, when you make so-called free or similar offers, all the terms, conditions, and obligations on which receipt and retention of the free item are contingent should be set forth clearly and conspicuously at the outset of your offer. [9] Leave no reasonable probability that the terms of the offer might be misunderstood.[10] Further, remember that terms such as "gift," "given without charge," "bonus," or other words which convey the impression that the article is free are governed by the free rule.[11]

Finally, always have a signature line on your order card for these promotions. The signature requirement discourages forgery by the recruiter and highlights the fact that the applicant is entering a potential business relationship and not merely helping a friend. Finally, if it's a juvenile promotion, you should have parent or guardian sign. This will discourage lark entries by those informed kids who know or may be told by your recruiter that their contractual obligations are generally voidable at *their* initiative.

Despite criticism to the contrary, these promotions work, and, if you do them right, they improve your bottom line while presenting no adverse legal exposure.[12]

BAIT-AND-SWITCH ADVERTISING[13]

You walk into the store prompted by an ad in your newspaper. You request an item on sale. Suddenly you realize that, like a fish on a hook, you have been lured in by "bait" which is not all that rewarding. The procedure is usually as follows: The seller informs you that the bait item is not available, that the original product lacks a guarantee, that parts are hard to replace, and so on. The "switch" item, on the other hand, is available and has none of the failings of the bait item. Of course, it costs "a bit more," too.

The FTC guides against bait advertising should be studied by any manager attempting to trade up, even in good faith.[14] Knowledge of these guides is useful for your own shopping too. The FTC also audits these complaints, so stay abreast of these areas by ordering a copy of the *Digest of Consumer Complaints and Inquiries*.[15]

Since these guides are important to you and your goodwill, we'll review them here.[16] In general, this review applies to retail and/or telephone marketing as well as any other personal contact promotional selling you devise.

WHAT THE FTC SAYS

The FTC defines bait advertising as an "alluring but insincere offer to sell a product or service which the advertiser in truth does not intend or want to sell. Its purpose is to switch consumers from buying the advertised merchandise, in order to sell something else, usually at a higher price or on a basis more advantageous to the advertiser. The primary aim of a bait advertisement is to obtain leads as to persons interested in buying merchandise of the type so advertised."[17]

In short, the offense entails advertising (which is defined as any form of public notice, however disseminated or used) in such an attractive way as to bring customers to your store or have them call, followed by sales staff disparaging the advertised product to get customers to switch to a more expensive product (often with a more lucrative commission for the sales staff obtaining the order).

The initial order which brings your customer to you must be truthful from the start, as we've continually stressed throughout this section. You cannot redeem a deceptive initial offer by presenting the facts to your customer on arrival.[18] In addition to the wording of the ad, the FTC requires that no statement or illustration may be used which creates a false impression to a reasonable person as to the make, value, newness of model, size, color, usability, or origin of the product offered.[19] Many state deceptive-sales statutes specifically state that it is not necessary for a sale to actually take place before a supplier may be liable to a consumer for deceptive acts. A solicitation to sell goods or services intended primarily for personal, family, or household use may be sufficient to give rise to liability, even in the absence of an actual sale, if a deceptive act is committed in connection with the solicitation.

For example, a company circulated advertisements for a piano featured at a specific sale price. The featured piano was from a drawing which was a composite of several more expensive pianos. The composite drawing was used even though a photograph of the piano on sale was available. The court found that this newspaper advertisement, announcing a special sale price on a particular piano model and containing a drawing which was a composite of several more expensive piano models, was a solicitation to supply, which could serve as a basis for a deceptive act for purposes of action under Indiana's Deceptive Consumer Sales Act.[20] The moral of this story is that your entire advertisement can be part of the bait—not merely the price quote or saleperson's in-store conduct.

Assuming that your promotional vehicle is true in all respects, your sales staff cannot discourage a purchase when the customer arrives at your store or phones in the order. Discouragement[21] includes but is not limited to:

1. Failure to show or demonstrate the advertised item
2. Disparagement of the product, its warranty, availability of service, or other aspects of the product by actions or words (including exaggerated exclamations upon inquiry)
3. Failure to make an affirmative offer to sell
4. Failure to have available a sufficient quantity of the advertised product to meet reasonably anticipated needs or to provide a raincheck[22]—unless your advertisement clearly and adequately discloses the *specific quantity* of advertised goods or services available or that your merchandise is available only at designated locations
5. Using any commission or other sales plan which penalizes your sales force from selling the advertised product
6. Subjecting a customer who orders the advertised product to protracted delays in delivery, parts, service, etc. to discourage others from purchasing the product (i.e., general unethical business conduct)[23]

The safest policy is to make clear to your sales force that you intend to sell the advertised item (and stress its benefits in a positive manner) at the advertised price to each and every customer who arrives in your store or calls in the order over the phone.

TRADING UP IS NOT A BAIT-AND-SWITCH TACTIC

When people call or drop in (or you call on them), you already have a buyer of predisposed interest at least in the product about which the potential customer is inquiring. Any additional soft sell will be treated as information. This is a good time to cross-sell. The customer wants a fishing rod—how about a tackle box? A *well-trained* marketer might also attempt to sell up or trade up. Be careful here—you must not get involved in the bait-and-switch areas or even offer the inference of such.

Trading up is not an illegal practice when done in conformity with the guides. What your salespeople actually do and say—not their intentions—determines whether you have a legal violation. If you're within the law, trading up is merely full-line selling, that is, giving your customer the information and opportunity to learn about the various features available in the product line so that each customer can make an informed buying decision by matching his or her *individual* needs and budgetary requirements with the product and features you are offering in your total line. Your customer service relations will be enhanced because your customer will appreciate making a buying decision based on personal attention directed to the customer's own particular need.

Another instance where trading up presents no problems with bait and switch is when customers say no to your advertised offer or are truly undecided. You may then ask prospective buyers if they are interested in obtaining further information. If the answer is affirmative, you may trade up by making the person aware of the top-of-the-line products you are offering.

SWITCH AFTER SALE

Obviously, you may not pursue any practice to "unsell" a product after its purchase with the intent to sell other merchandise in its place. This can occur when you've accepted a deposit and the customer returns to pay the balance or when you fail to make timely or adequate delivery or in any other way discourage the customer from obtaining the goods which you are actively trying to switch away from such customer.[24]

CHECKLIST FOR BAIT-AND-SWITCH COMPLIANCE

The following should be incorporated into any serious in-house program to avoid even the inference of bait-and-switch tactics.

1. Make sure that the issue of bait-and-switch tactics is specifically addressed in all your sales manuals. Include examples of acceptable and unacceptable practices. Make it clear that a violation will result in disciplinary action. Review such manuals (as well as all telephone-marketing sales scripts) with your counsel. If you are involved in telephone marketing and are employing outside service consultants, indicate your policy against bait-and-switch conduct in writing in your contract with each agency and protect yourself against such liability in the indemnification paragraph of your contract.

2. Coordinate your sales advertising campaign with your inventory department. If there are problems, make sure that you have a policy of issuing rain checks to your customers whenever an advertised product becomes out of stock before the advertised termination date (or a reasonable time if no date is specified). If there is any margin for error, specify the quantity of goods available. Review with your counsel how specific your wording must be, e.g., is "16 televisions available" mandated or would "limited quantity available today only" be satisfactory? You need your counsel's input as to the varied state and municipal regulations you're dealing with at each store location.

3. Make sure any photos or illustrations of your item on sale are as accurate as the price.

4. Make your sales staff cognizant of your policy not to disparage or belittle any advertised product you are offering.

5. Make sure your sales staff has corporate goal congruence with you and knows that any comparison of the advertised product with another must be positively oriented. They must stress what each product will do in a positive manner—not what it won't do.

6. No personnel should contradict your promotion piece initiating the call or in-store visit unless there was an objective error (e.g., a typographical misprint). If such an error exists, put the prospective buyer in touch with a customer service professional, *not* another product.

7. If there is any resistance at all to trading up, you must cease. Once a customer reviews your trade-up presentation and elects the original purchase, you must close the sale. The customer should not be requested or in any way encouraged to reconsider.

We are talking smart customer relations here, not just legal compliance. Your customer knows this law from a barrage of consumer education leaflets on point and simple word of mouth and expects compliance and fair treatment. If such expectations are not met, your customer will be someone else's customer in the future. And remember, many customers are no longer just walking away. They're contacting the newspaper, magazine, or other medium that carried your ad. Such media follow-up can turn one customer's bad experience into a cause célèbre at your expense.

REFERENCES

[1] Cooling-off Period for Door-to-Door Sales, 16 C.F.R. sec. 429. If you have problems here a good group to contact (with an excellent newsletter) is the Direct Selling Association, 1730 M St., N.W., Suite 610, Washington, D.C., 20036.

[2] Some of these states include:
a. *California*. Cal. Civ. Code sec. 1689.5–.13 (Deering Supp. 1979): 3-day cooling off; $25 minimum purchase; oral and written notice of right to cancel must be given in the same language used in the sales presentation; seller has 10 days to return down payment and twenty days to pick up canceled goods.
b. *Florida*. Fla. Stat. Ann. sec. 501.021–.035 (West Supp. 1981): 3-day cooling off; $25 minimum purchase; seller may keep part of down payment as cancellation fee.
c. *Georgia*. Ga. Code Ann. sec. 96-902 to -906 (Supp. 1979): 3-day cooling off; credit sales only; seller may assess a cancellation fee and pick up fee for canceled goods even if buyer made no down payment.
d. *Mississippi*. Miss. Code Ann. sec. 75-66-1 to -11 (Supp. 1980): 3-day cooling off; credit sales only; cancellation fee, 40 days to pick up goods; excludes sales on buyer's initiative.
e. *New York*. N.Y. Pers. Prop. Law secs. 425–431 (McKinney Supp. 1980–1981): same provisions as California Civil Code.
Remember that state legislative activity is a constant; monitor it and review your planning with your counsel.

[3] 16 C.F.R. sec. 429.1(b).

[4] The following states have telephone sales incorporated into their home solicitation laws. You should review these with counsel because they vary (e.g., some cover all calls, others cover orders over $25 dollars): Arizona, Arkansas, Indiana, Louisiana, Michigan, North Dakota, Ohio, Oregon, Utah, Virginia (voluntary guides), Wyoming. Certain localities and municipalities also have regulations on point.

[5] Encyclopedia Britannica, Inc. v. F.T.C., 605 F.2d 964 (1979).

[6] Kelly v. Koscot Interplanetary, Inc., 37 Mich. App. 447, 195 N.W.2d 43 (1972) and M. Lippincott Mort. Inv. Co. v. Childress, 204 So. 2d 919 (1968). *See also* discussion of what a "lottery" is in Section 8, Chapter 20.

[7] If you are in a commercial agreement which you believe to be a pyramid scheme, review with your counsel whether you also have relief under U.C.C. sec. 302 (unconscionability provision). *See also* the discussion in Section 4, Chapter 8.

[8] See Section 8, Chapter 18, under "When and How to Use Endorsements and Testimonials."

[9] See Section 8, Chapter 18, under "Copy Headliner Compliance."

[10] 16 C.F.R. sec. 251.1(c).

[11] 16 C.F.R. sec. 251.1(i).

[12] H. R. Ronich, "The Case against Referral Sales," *Case and Comment*, December 1973, p. 20. For other views on this type of promotion, see Comment, *Let the "Seller"*

Beware—Another Approach to Referral Sales Scheme, 22 Miami L. Rev. 861 (1968) and *Pyramid Sales Participants: Victims or Perpetrators?* 47 Temple L. Q. 697 (1974).

[13] Robert J. Posch, Jr., "Is It Trading Up or Bait and Switch?" *Direct Marketing,* January 1983, pp. 92–94.

[14] Guides against Bait Advertising, 16 C.F.R. sec. 238 (1981).

[15] The FTC publishes this every 3 months, and it is available by calling the Public Reference Branch at (202) 523-3598 or by writing to them at the Public Reference Branch, Room 130, Federal Trade Commission, Washington, D.C., 20580.

[16] Don't forget to review with your counsel applicable state and local laws. For example, the following codes are all in the New York City area: N.Y. Gen. Bus. Law sec. 396; New York City Admin. Code sec. 2203.d-2.0(a)(4); Nassau County Admin. Code sec. 21-10.2(5) Westchester County Admin. Code sec. 863.11(7)(c).

[17] 16 C.F.R. sec. 238.0.

[18] 16 C.F.R. sec. 238.2(b).

[19] 16 C.F.R. sec. 238.2(a).

[20] McCormick Piano & Organ Co., Inc. v. Geiger, 412 N.E.2d 842 (1980).

[21] 16 C.F.R. sec. 238.3.

[22] Weaver v. J.C. Penney, Inc., 53 Ohio App. 2d 165, 6 Ohio Op. 3d 270, 372 N.E.2d 663 (1977).

[23] In People by Lefkowitz v. Levinson, 23 Misc. 2d 483, 199 N.Y.S.2d 625 (1960).

[24] 16 C.F.R. sec. 238.4.

CHAPTER
TWENTY
NONPERSONAL
PROMOTIONS

Use of in-store promotions has remained fairly constant the last few years. (For information about coupons and price discounts, reread Chapter 13 in Section 5 as well as applicable topics discussed in this section, e.g., copy headliners and comparative pricing.) As a rule, such promotions are aimed at getting current customers to increase their purchases rather than attracting new customers.

SIMULATED CHECKS

One note about coupon type promotions—don't make them appear as simulated checks, bonds, or other financial instruments, especially if you are mailing them to your target list in a traditional check-bearing envelope. The key is to offer a bona fide check as part of the promotion. Otherwise, you must avoid employing any promotion piece which could be interpreted as a "confusingly simulated item of value." Each of the following could be interpreted as such:

- Check-style paper (because of coloration, use of watermark, and so on)
- Traditional check-style borders
- Wording which might give an air of authenticity to a final document
- A traditional check-size and -style envelope
- Other items normally found on checks, such as any reference to negotiability or lack of same

Obviously, the more of these items actually included, the more you have increased your exposure to marketplace confusion.

You can employ a check promotion using a negotiable document. The promotion may be qualified, provided that the check itself is *not* in the final analysis. *The check must have value apart from its value as a reduction of the cost of membership or service.* A violation in this area can be quite costly. One firm paid a fine of over $1 million.[1]

This is not an issue against which your firm can indemnify itself contractually. Use of simulated checks is against public policy. If an outside creative firm creates your piece, you (as well as possibly they) are responsible for all public FTC decisions (as we discussed in the preceding topic on advertising agency liability). Also, from a tax point of view, a fine is *not* a deductible business expense—it comes right off your bottom line.

A SAFE PROMOTION

A pet favorite of mine in point-of-purchase displays is the matchbook. This can have promotional wording or an 800 number, or it can simply act as a reminder of your business. It has utility value to your customer, so it will be retained. Each time your customer lights a match the matchbook may well be read. This gives you 20 exposures before the book is used, and then there are matchbook collectors. . . . From a legal point of view there are no new copy-wording laws not previously discussed.

A PARTICIPATION PROMOTION— SWEEPSTAKES

For a time you couldn't go to many gas stations and supermarkets without being able to obtain tokens to save toward a prize. A sweepstakes promotion remains very popular for its ability to sell a dream—dreams of a vacation prize or windfall "without paying for it." In general, cash is the preferred prize, followed by travel and then merchandise. However, no matter what your prize, you'll have people happy to enter—especially when they know a purchase *cannot* be required. The market is so competitive that "contesters" have turned to specific literature on point such as *And the Lucky Winner Is—The Complete Guide to Winning Sweepstakes and Contests.*[2]

Because of sweepstakes popularity, we review the rules in detail here and also distinguish a legal sweepstakes promotion from an illegal lottery or chain letter.

CHAIN LETTER OR SWEEPSTAKES?

You've no doubt received chain letters in the mail at some time or another requesting that you send a dollar (or more) to one or more persons whose names appear in the letter and then to send copies of the letter with your name at the top of the list to a certain number of friends. Naturally, the financial remuneration you're promised is tremendous if "the chain is not broken." Fun and games? The government doesn't think so.

First, if you "played," you probably lost your dollar. Secondly, the use of the U.S. Postal Service to send chain letters involving money can result in civil or criminal penalties. Why? This scheme violates the lottery laws, which make illegal any promotion which has *all* the following elements— prize, chance, and consideration.

If you understand the legal concept behind the chain letters, sweepstakes compliance will be fairly easy for you. A sweepstakes or other form of contest is illegal if it contains the "big three"—prize, chance, and consideration. In a legitimate sweepstakes there is no consideration (e.g., payment of time or money) required to enter.

CONTESTS OF SKILL

Contests of skill are also distinguishable from sweepstakes. In a legitimate contest, winners are selected purely on the basis of skill and not *chance* (e.g., the classic country fair animal-raising or pie-baking contest). If any element of chance is present, the contest is illegal, even if some skill is involved.

Sweepstakes are more popular because of the little effort involved. However, sometimes you'll want to run an event requiring writing skill, artwork, or something along this line. You may even require the submission of a proof-of-purchase or an entrance fee to cover the costs of evaluating the contest. Such activity to enter is consideration by your entrant. Do you now have a lottery (chance, consideration, and prize)? No—*there is no chance or luck* because winners are selected purely on the basis of their individual skill, and without all three elements you can't have a lottery.

Note that the contest must be judged by people qualified to do so. This judgment based on merit by qualified people will eliminate any aspect of chance. Otherwise the requirements are similar. To fulfill FTC regulations, you should explain all aspects of the contest in the promotional material. Such aspects include who is an eligible contestant, what are the judging criteria for the contest, what are the prizes and how many are awarded, who are the judges, when is the contest, and when will the winners be announced. Any other information that helps explain the contest and what is expected from contestants should also be included in the promotional material.

To wrap up, in a sweepstakes there can be no element of *consideration*. In a contest of skill, there can be no element of *chance or luck*.

PREPARING FOR A SWEEPSTAKES PROMOTION

You've researched your market and found that the breakdown of the profile of typical sweepstakes entrants is approximately 45 to 55 percent female. In general, they are younger, have larger families, are slightly better educated, and are slightly more upscale in income than the population at large. How to proceed?

A good idea is to enlist the aid of an independent sweepstakes professional firm to advise and assist on all elements of your promotion—not merely as an independent judgment body.[3] The firm will present you with a standard contract outlining its services. With its standard services the firm should, at a minimum:

1. Provide advice on all phases of the offer during the planning of the promotion, including a screen of your copy.
2. File surety bonds in states requiring them.
3. Handle all areas pertaining to the winners, such as generating the winners through a random drawing, notifying them, delivering the prizes, and preparing the formal list of winners to be available to the public.
4. Provide advice on postal and certain legal and regulatory matters, including writing the rules for the promotion. Their advice is advisory only and no substitute for your own counsel.

As in any transaction, the boilerplate agreement you receive should be considered the beginning of negotiations and not the final word. For example, ask yourself whether the contract contains the following minimum points you need for your own protection:

1. Are we being offered vague terms such as "practical knowledge?" Never accept these. Demand that your sweepstakes firm *warrant* all advice they offer. If the firm won't offer you such contractual protection, then your eyes are open and you should consider exactly what, if any, protection you are receiving.
2. Do we retain the right of final approval as to all creative copy, promotional and rules wording as well as layout and mailing dates?
3. Does the sweepstakes firm have the right to assign the contract without our consent? Never accept this, because you could wind up paying for one firm while receiving the services of the later "assigned firm."
4. Is our customer list valuable to us? Direct marketers are well aware of the advantages of the list potential sweepstakes entrants create—even the "no" respondents. More and more retail firms are developing sophisticated data bases. When in doubt have your counsel draft a tight confidentiality clause protecting your lists and any other trade secrets or "know-how" the independent firm may have access to.
5. Have we carefully reviewed the indemnification clause as to all actions *both* private and government? Avoid language which states that you'll only recover on "finally settled" claims. This hurts your cash flow as these matters drag on. Ask your counsel about your exposure to class actions. The recipients of your sweepstakes promotion could be a built-in class, and poor administration of the promotion could expose you to high dollar and goodwill costs.

None of these points is designed to reflect adversely in any way on the independent service you've chosen. They are designed to make you think of self-protection before you sign any form contract they devise. Their contracts are for their protection. This book and your counsel are for your protection.

THE RULES

We'll now examine the aspects of what you might include in your rules in great detail. In fact, the following discussion is probably the broadest review you'll read anywhere.

In addition to the input from your independent consulting firm and your counsel's review and sign-off, you'll have to develop your own philosophy about these promotions. For example, the law doesn't say it has to be easy to enter without a purchase. Provided that it is possible, and provided that a complete reading of the promotional copy and rules make that clear, you are covered legally. However, be aware that ambiguity in the rules will be construed against the sponsor who drafted them and in favor of the participant. Further, remember that customer goodwill is all-important.

If your participants are to feel that they have been dealt with fairly, it is essential that the rules of the sweepstakes and all conditions and terms which will govern the award of its prizes be stated clearly and conspicuously to them. It is not feasible to derive a definite and precise formula for the phrase "clear and conspicuous." In principle, however, terminology should be simple, nontechnical, and unambiguous. Typography in size, style, and location should be such that one can view the promotion piece at a glance, can see that the rules and conditions are there to be read if one chooses to do so, and can read those rules easily.

The following are practical points to consider in drafting the rules. These elements are common to most sweepstakes and should be disclosed, in addition to any others which may be peculiar to a particular promotion.[4] Obviously, the rules of the sweepstakes must be set forth in an area of the copy easily accessible to the reader. The type size must be the same size (or larger) as the type size used in the predominant body copy of the advertisement.

1. Yes or no box. This often appears as a "check box" in the copy or on the envelope. The no and yes boxes must be equally conspicuous. Be clear here. If a purchase is required to win a prize, you are probably running afoul of the lottery laws. Even worse, it means you didn't bounce your rules by your counsel, who would have caught this. Also, being "cute" and offering two different color or size envelopes for the return of yes and no entries is not a legal violation but might encourage a government agency or consumer group to monitor the winners to see if the percentage was skewed in favor of the participants who checked "yes."

2. Facsimile. May a facsimile of the entry blank or promotional piece be used? If a facsimile is made acceptable in lieu of an official entry blank, a potential lottery violation is removed if a purchase is required to obtain the official entry blank. (Remember, the elements of prize, chance, and consideration must *all* be present to be considered a lottery.) The rules should clearly indicate what the facsimile is to state or reproduce. If a facsimile is not acceptable, the rules must specifically say so, e.g., "only official entry blanks will be accepted. No facsimiles permitted." If you do permit facsimiles make sure your systems are set up so that these entries have as much chance of winning as an official entry.

3. "Lucky" or other number. If these are used, they must actually identify the individual and be directly relevant to the award of a prize.

4. Simulated check. Avoid these as entry forms. If you must use them, remember that simulated checks may not be used unless they have value independent of the promotion, they impose no obligation on the recipient, and they may be cashed, redeemed, or exchanged by recipients for U.S. currency.

5. Prizes. The following points should be considered:

a. Listing of prizes. List all prizes by category in detail, including their exact nature and the number to be awarded.

b. Visual depictions. All visual depictions of the prizes must be accurate (e.g., in correct proportion). Especially with sweepstakes promotions, you should be aware that photographs or printed illustrations of U.S. coins may be used for advertising purposes. However, printed illustrations of paper money, checks, and the like are *not* permitted in connection with this form of advertising. (This matter is in flux, and you should consult your counsel as to your current exposure.)

c. Specification of value. No award may be described as a prize unless it has a retail value greater than $1. No prize may be held forth, directly or by implication, to have substantial monetary value if it is of only nominal intrinsic worth. The value test must be substantiated by written records (e.g., prize purchase receipts). Mere opinion is not permissible.

d. Purchase of prizes. All enumerated prizes must have been purchased prior to the commencement of the promotion, and you must be able to verify this with dated receipts. All prizes are then set aside until used for the specific awards.

e. Warranties. Are you prepared to make good on warranty offers? A few years ago a fast-food franchise sought to spur customer traffic with a contest. They offered among their prizes an auto which was supposedly a full-scale replica of the classic 1930 Bentley. The winner found that it was not in the condition promised and sued after numerous attempts to repair. He recovered damages because of the breach of contract.[5] The prizes you offer must be able to do what you hold them out to do or what a reasonable person could infer they'd do.

f. Free-rule requirements. Don't forget that the prizes you are offering are free and are regulated by the free rule. *All* free rule requirements discussed earlier in this section must be complied with. The prize offered must have any qualifications set forth immediately contingent at the outset of the offer. Such qualifications must be set forth clearly and conspicuously to leave no reasonable probability that the offer might be misunderstood. For example, a free prize for two people to anywhere in the United States or to Tahiti, for instance, is wide open, with you footing the bill. Phrases like "first class," "pampered," "travel in style," "all expenses paid," or "luxurious accommodations" will be interpreted literally (i.e., by your winner *against* you).

g. **Personal and/or property injury.** Protect yourself from potential claims of winners by stating that you are not liable for loss of property or personal injury incurred resulting from use of the prize.

h. **Cash substitution.** If you will not substitute cash, say so. Some winners might request this for various reasons, including tax problems. You're not legally required to state "no substitutions" up-front, but it is a good idea from the goodwill angle. Some firms are simply stating "Your Choice—Cash or Travel."

i. **Expiration date.** If the prize is a travel package, it is a good idea (in inflationary periods and a generally unstable geopolitical climate) to state the date by which the trip must be taken.

j. **Prizes by gender (e.g., men's or women's watches)** These are fine provided that there is retail value parity in the prizes *and* that winners may elect either category at their option.

6. Prize procedures. State the total number of prizes to be awarded and the method or manner of selecting the winners (e.g., random drawing from all entries received).

7. Unclaimed prizes. You should state that all prizes will be awarded and describe the procedures for the disposition of unclaimed prizes.

8. Dates. State the *specific* commencement and termination dates for eligibility and whether the termination date refers to date of mailing or of receipt of the entry.

9. Odds of winning. Statements such as "the odds of winning depend on the number of entries received," or "we anticipate the odds to be . . ." may be sufficient for your promotion. (The specific details and procedure of your promotion may require different wording; review same with your counsel.)

10. Age restrictions. Certain age restrictions are patently obvious and necessary (alcoholic beverages, tobacco, and so on). More subtle issues relate to the enjoyment of the prize (e.g., automobiles or vacations). In such situations, you might wish to disqualify minors or restrict delivery to a parent or guardian. Again, all disqualification language must be clear and conspicuous.

11. Restrictions on entries. Is entry restricted to one application per family or address, or may the consumer "enter as often as you wish but only one entry per envelope?" A good idea might be "one person per entry," obviating the need to divide a prize between two or more winners on a single entry. I personally don't like restrictions on entries to one per family or address, but since they're often found in the promotions, let's review them. One entry per person or one person per entry are the only limitations possible. One entry per address would complicate you in various living-together arrangements. The same issue is raised by family. Can you really bar the entry of a 21-year-old son simply because his mother also entered? What about spouses living apart in legal separation? Any limitation other than one entry per person (18 or over) could present legal problems as well as create the potential for the loss of customer goodwill.

12. Exclusions due to employment. Any member of the sponsoring firm and his or her family (plus your independent agency) is routinely disqualified.

13. Voiding clause. As a voiding clause, "void where prohibited by law" is proper; I don't like "void where prohibited *or restricted* by law" because the word "restricted" is too vague. This is a fluid area and the state legislatures must be carefully monitored. Prior to December 1978, sweepstakes were effectively banned in Missouri by action of the state's attorney general. This was altered by a popular vote constitutional amendment ratified November 7, 1978, which redefined consideration (people *like and want* sweepstakes promotions).[6]

14. Endorsements. If you are planning to use the winner's name or picture for future publicity and promotion, notice must be set forth in the rules.

15. Other qualifications. State any geographic limitations (e.g., continental United States). Also, state your disqualification policy for entries which do not substantially conform to the rules of the promotional offer. A record of any disqualifications should be maintained for 30 days after the end of the promotion.

16. Taxes. Contest awards and similar prize winnings are income subject to federal income tax.[7] Your winners will have to report the fair market value of the prizes won. This isn't your headache, but a statement to the effect that income tax liability is the responsibility of the winner is a good idea. However, you do have some tax exposure, and state sales or use taxes should be checked.

17. Applicable law. State that all federal, state, and local laws and regulations apply. When running a sweepstakes promotion in any state, you should obviously comply with the rules of the particular states. For example, the New York General Business Law requires a game of chance bond be obtained and formal registration of the promotion be filed with the secretary of state. Florida currently requires a similar bond with certain qualifications.[8]

18. Customer inquiries. Include in the rules the identity and address of a specific person to whom inquiries concerning the sweepstakes in general and how to obtain a list of winners in particular may be directed. Usually this is the independent judging organization you have retained to assist in the promotion. You can require the customer to send a self-addressed, stamped envelope to obtain the list of winners.

19. Notification of winners. The method by which winners will be notified must be specified (e.g., sign in store or by mail). It is a good idea to obtain a signed affidavit of identity and acceptance, particularly for the larger-dollar-value prizes.

20. Signature line. You can require a signature line. There is no legal requirement for a signature on the entry blank, but it may be legally advantageous for you to obtain the signature of the sweepstakes subscriber. The signature is a specific manifestation of the customer's assent to the terms of the sweepstakes promotion. It helps to remove any ambiguity as to whether all terms and rules were definitely understood and agreed upon—including such issues as sales tax liability and any limitations concerning the recipient (for example, no minors).

Your promotion must be conducted strictly according to its published rules. If an unforeseen development mandates a change, timely notice must be given. This is legally required and important for customer satisfaction.

RECORD KEEPING

You are required to maintain the following data in your records for 3 years after the published termination date for entries for submission on FTC request. (Again, these requirements aren't carved in granite and are changed from time to time; ask your counsel for a current reading on your federal and state requirements.)

1. Approximate number of entries distributed
2. Total number of prizes advertised in each category
3. Approximate number of participants
4. Name and address of each winner of a prize having an approximate retail value in excess of $10, together with a description and the approximate retail value of the prize given to each
5. Method by which winners were determined

Finally, consult your counsel as to the current rules on posting, length of time between games, and other procedural matters which have been subject to change in recent years.

CONCLUSION

If these guidelines are mastered, you will have exhausted the problems apparent in today's state of the art. If you design your sweepstakes promotion in compliance with these guidelines (and a review with your counsel) you can be confident that your successful promotion won't be negated by fines, consent agreements, or an entrant's personal injury or property damage claims. What is just as important is that compliance will enhance your positive image to your entrants, retaining and building customer goodwill.

REFERENCES

[1] United States v. Reader's Digest Ass'n, Inc., 464 F. Supp. 1037 (1979).

[2] Carolyn Tyndall and Roger Tyndall with Ted Tuleja, *And the Lucky Winner Is— The Complete Guide to Winning Sweepstakes and Contests*, St. Martin's, New York, 1982.

[3] Four reputable agencies to investigate for such assistance include: Marden Kane, Inc., 666 Fifth Avenue, New York, N.Y., 10103, (212) 582-6600; Ventura Associates, Inc., 200 Madison Avenue, New York, N.Y., 10016, (212) 689-0011; D. L. Blair Corporation, 185 Great Neck Road, Great Neck, N.Y., 11021, (516) 487-9230; and Weston Group, Inc., 44 Post Road West, Westport, Connecticut, 06880, (203) 226-6933. For further information, write to The Promotion Marketing Association of America, 420 Lexington Avenue, New York, N.Y., 10170.

[4] The body of law to be studied by managers desiring an in-depth knowledge of this area is as follows:

Mail Fraud Law	18 U.S.C. sec. 1341
Fraud by Wire, Radio, TV	18 U.S.C. sec. 1343
Federal Communications Act*	47 U.S.C. sec. 509
Federal Alcohol Administration Act	27 U.S.C. sec. 205c
Federal Food, Drug, and Cosmetic Act	21 U.S.C. sec. 342
Fair Package and Labeling Act	15 U.S.C. sec. 1451
FTC Guide on Use of Word "Free"†	16 C.F.R. sec. 251
Robinson-Patman Act	15 U.S.C. sec. 13
FTC Guides on Advertising Allowances	16 C.F.R. sec. 240

*This act enforces a federal law that bars broadcast of lottery information or advertising except for state government–conducted lotteries.

† Generally applicable to all promotions. The others will vary by reason of the nature of the product being promoted or the article being awarded as a prize.

THE LAW AFFECTING YOUR PROMOTIONAL POLICY

FTC Guide—Deceptive Pricing*	16 C.F.R. sec. 233
Hazardous Substances Act	15 U.S.C. sec. 1261
Consumer Product Safety Act	15 U.S.C. sec. 2051
Federal Bank Regulations	12 C.F.R. sec. 526

As demonstrated, the laws affecting this area are quite comprehensive. Do not think that the FTC rules will *only* apply to "Games of Chance in the Food Retailing and Gasoline Industries." Voluntarily comply, because the FTC has indicated that it expects other firms running similar promotions to take these guidelines under advisement. For example, between January 1970 and March 1977 the FTC was involved with nine cases involving sweepstakes:

D'Arcy Advertising Co., 78 F.T.C. 616 (1971)

McDonald's Corp., 78 F.T.C. 606 (1971)

Reuben H. Donnelley Corp., 79 F.T.C. 599 (1971)

Procter & Gamble Co., 79 F.T.C. 589 (1971)

Reader's Digest Ass'n, Inc., 79 F.T.C. 696 (1971)

Longines-Wittnauer, Inc., 79 F.T.C. 964 (1971)

Revere Chem. Corp., 80 F.T.C. 85 (1972)

Lee Rogers d/b/a American Holiday Ass'n, 81 F.T.C. 738 (1972)

Coca-Cola Co., 88 F.T.C. 656 (1976)

If you follow the FTC guidelines, you'll avoid complaints from entrants and be within almost all provisions of state law. Compliance follows the old axiom of "do thy patient no harm."

[5] Rutherford v. Whataburger, Inc., 601 S.W. 441 (1980).

[6] Formerly Missouri did not recognize federal preemption of control over mailed offers (Missouri v. Readers Digest Ass'n, Inc., 527 S.W.2d 355, 1975). Subsequently the people of the state endorsed sweepstakes promotions by popular referendum (1978). This was a demonstrative endorsement that people *want* these promotions and don't regard them as junk mail. Self-appointed consumer representatives should take note.

[7] 96 L. Ed. 1242 (1952).

[8] The Games Registration Law, Sec. 849.094(4)(a) requires a 30-day advance registration of a sweepstakes promotion with the attorney general. Effective July 1, 1981, this was amended to permit the Department of Legal Affairs to waive the bond or trust account requirement for operators who have conducted game promotions in the state of Florida for not less than 5 *consecutive* years and who have

*Generally applicable to all promotions. The others will vary by reason of the nature of the product being promoted or the article being awarded as a prize.

stayed within the law during this period. Prior to 1967, Florida banned sweep-stakes altogether.

Rhode Island requires registration if retail stores participate in the promotion. For a good overall marketing analysis of this promotional device see F. Peterson and J. Turkel, "Catching Customers with Sweepstakes," *Fortune*, February 8, 1982, p. 84.

SECTION
NINE
CONCLUSION_____

I hope you have resolved to stay abreast in legal areas of concern to you and your firm. One way to do this is to follow trade association newsletters, and most business magazines allude to legal areas. Three periodicals that will keep you abreast of current marketing law are *Advertising Age, Journal of Marketing's* "Legal Briefs" (each issue), and *Direct Marketing* (my own column, "Legal Outlook").

Finally, take your lawyer to lunch, even when nothing in particular is on the horizon. Your counsel can discuss with you the topical areas you've read as well as marketing ideas you're thinking of. This type of personal contact builds mutual trust and friendship for when you need each other in more serious matters.

Before we depart, I'd appreciate any comments and opinions you have as to any topic contained herein (a word of legalese has surfaced). Write to me at 242 Elsie Avenue, Merrick, N.Y., 11566, or call me at (516) 868-9849. All correspondence and calls will be answered. I look forward to hearing from you.

GLOSSARY

As stressed throughout, these terms are defined to facilitate general reading of the text. They should not under any circumstances be considered a substitute for legal advice in a specific situation. Please consult your counsel in such circumstances.

Advertising Medium The vehicle (e.g., newspaper or direct mail) used to carry the advertising message from the sender to the intended receiver.

Allowances Compensation (e.g., space or price discounts) by a wholesaler or manufacturer for services such as advertising or in-store point-of-purchase displays provided by a retailer or wholesaler. Such allowances must be generally available to all qualified customers on a proportionately equal basis.

Antitrust Law General body of law which regulates or prohibits combinations, conspiracies, agreements, monopolies, and certain distribution practices which restrain free trade.

Bailment The transfer of the possession of personal property without the transfer of title in which it is understood that the personal property is to be returned to the owner after some period of time has elapsed or some particular purpose has been accomplished.

Bait and Switch A bait offer is an alluring but insincere offer to sell a product or service which the seller does not intend to sell. Its primary purpose is to switch consumers from the advertised bait product or service to sell something else, usually at a higher price or on a basis more advantageous to the seller. Its secondary purpose is to increase store traffic (see Trading Up).

Bona Fide Prices Prices which under the Federal Trade Commission Act must represent the prices of actual purchases for a reasonable period of time in the same geographic area before they can be referred to in a sale that advertises price comparisons.

Boycott An agreement or conspiracy to restrain or prevent the carrying on of a business by preventing or excluding potential competitors, suppliers, customers, or others from freely engaging in business or desired transactions with other businesses.

Brand The name or symbol used to identify and differentiate a product or service from competing products or services.

312

Cable Television Television service with large antennae positioned to receive television broadcasts, amplify the signals, and deliver them, via coaxial cable, to subscribers; originally designed to be a service to those unable to obtain adequate television reception. Increasingly cable systems are being used to deliver a wide selection of stations, features, and services (also referred to as CATV–Community Antenna Television).

Cash Discount A reduction in price granted to buyers who pay cash.

Collusion A secret cooperation, usually in fraud or in illegal activities between two or more persons, to accomplish a common result, usually to injure a third party.

Common Carrier A firm obligated by the terms of a government license to transport goods under stated conditions for all who wish to employ their services (see Contract Carrier).

Consignment Merchandise delivered or made available to an agent, with title or ownership to the goods remaining with the supplier.

Conspiracy A criminal partnership in which two or more people combine formally or informally to accomplish an unlawful act. In a price-fixing situation, there must be express or circumstantial proof that a combination was formed for the purpose of fixing prices and that it caused them to be fixed or contributed to that result.

Contest A sales promotion device that offers prizes as a reward for some form of specific creativity or skill.

Contract Carrier A transportation company that provides its services to one or more shippers on an individual contract basis, usually does not operate on a regular schedule, and has rates more easily adapted to specific situations than those of common carriers (see Common Carrier).

Cooling-Off Period The period (a certain number of business days) in which the buyer has the right to cancel after a sale. The buyer must receive written notification of this right and often must receive a copy of the contract or sales receipt.

Cooperative Advertising Advertising in which the supplier reimburses an agreed upon portion of buyer's advertising expenses for a certain product or service.

Coupon A sales promotion certificate that entitles the holder to either a specified saving on a product or service or a cash refund.

Credit Deferred time to pay debt. May involve finance charges and/or installment payments.

Credit Bureau An organization that collects credit information for dissemination to members or subscribers upon request. Credit bureaus are sometimes cooperatives, owned by the users of the service.

Demographic Segmentation Selecting target markets on the basis of statistical information such as age, sex, income, or a geographical unit such as a zip code.

Direct Mail Mailing of advertising solicitations directly to consumers using the U.S. Postal Service or private direct-delivery service. The term may refer to a mail-order firm selling only by mail with no retail outlets and a retail store that sells by mail.

Direct-Response List List of persons who answered a direct-response offer of another firm. Purchased from the firm or through a broker for a one-time promotion.

Distribution Channel Route taken by a product as it passes from the original owner or maker to the ultimate consumer.

Dual Distribution Use of two channels to market a product.

Endorsement A product recommendation, usually paid for, given by a prominent celebrity.

Escheat The statutory reversion of property to the state after a specified period of time if the property holder or claimant cannot be located or if the property is abandoned.

FOB Free on board. A provision of the contract specifying at which point shipping costs are to be paid by the buyer.

Franchise In marketing, a contract right or license granted by a franchisor for compensation, usually to multiple franchisees, to do business under a certain name legally controlled by the franchisor and usually involving specific territorial, field-of-use, and product-quality traits.

Free A product or service that is an unconditional gift or, when a purchase is required, all the conditions to the receipt and retention of the product or service offered are clearly and conspicuously set forth in immediate conjunction with the first use of the word "free," leaving no reasonable probability that the terms of the offer will be misunderstood.

Freight Goods which one party entrusts to another for transportation.

FTC Rules and Guidelines Refers to rules and guidelines adopted by the FTC. The terms are not synonymous. Trade regulation rules define with specificity acts or practices which are unfair or deceptive. Industry guides do not have the force of substantive law. However, the guides do advise the industry how the FTC will interpret the law. A violation of a guide may lead the FTC to issue a complaint.

Functional Discounts The means by which your intermediaries are compensated for reselling to subsequent distributors in the distribution channel.

Fungible Goods Goods composed of units that are considered commercially alike, e.g., a particular grade of wheat.

Game In marketing use, a sales promotion device that requires no skill on the part of the participants, since pure chance determines the winner (see Contest).

Horizontal Agreements Agreements between competitors at the same level of market structure (for example, between two producers or retail chains).

Horizontal Territorial Division of Markets An agreement by which competitors on the same production or distribution level restrict their competitive activity to an agreed upon area.

Informercial A 5- to 15- minute hybrid cable program having an informational and entertainment component similar to a typical television program but designed as an extended advertisement for a particular product.

Installment Buyer One who orders goods or services and pays for them in two or more periodic payments after delivery of the products or services.

Interactive A two-way information system whereby the information receiver can communicate directly with the information supplier.

Interbrand Competition Competition among the manufacturers of the same generic product. This area, under certain federal court decisions, can be important in evaluating vertical territorial marketing plans.

Internal Data Operational data on such items as sales, credit, and lists generated within the firm.

Interstate Operations crossing state lines or involving more than a single state. An important factor in many areas of law; whether you are selling interstate may determine whether you have antitrust exposure. For trademark registration, you must place your product in interstate commerce. Telephone services interstate come under the jurisdiction of the Federal Communication Commission.

Intrabrand Competition Competition between or among the distributors, wholesalers, or retailers of the product of a particular manufacturer in that product.

Intrastate Operations that remain within the boundaries of a specific state. Telephone services remaining intrastate are under the jurisdiction of the respective state's public service commission or board of public utilities.

Label Written, printed, or graphic matter attached to a product or inscribed on its package and used to give certain information about the producer, ingredients, weight, or how it should be used (see Warranty).

Liquidated Damages A sum of money which the parties to a contract agree in advance will be paid to either as damages if the other is guilty of a breach of the contract.

List Price Comparison May be advertised as comparable to the advertised sales price of another only to the extent that it is the actual selling price currently charged in the market area where the claim is made and the comparable products are of at least like grade and quality, demonstrable by objective evidence.

List Rental An arrangement in which a list owner furnishes names and/or addresses on a list to a mailer, together with the privilege of using the list (unless specified) one time only. A list can be selected from a mass-compiled list on geographic, demographic, or psychographic bases, or it can be rented from a firm whose clientele closely resembles that desired (subject to the practice of many mailers and the **Direct Marketing Association** to permit consumers to remove their names from unwanted lists). The list owner is paid a royalty by the mailer, usually a specific fee per name. The list owner will establish a specific date on which the user has the obligation to mail to a specific list.

Location Clause A clause that limits the area in which the distributor may establish a sales outlet but does not limit the distributor to servicing customers who live within that area.

Lottery An offering to the public, illegal under most state and federal statutes (often ignored in the case of charitable or other nonprofit institutions), containing elements of chance, consideration, and prize.

Market Power Ability of producers to expand their share of a prevailing competitive market. Factors to consider include current market share of firm, degree of concentration in the industry, the extent of product differentiation, and actual or potential government regulation.

Material Statement Any statement in a promotion which is capable of affecting the decision to purchase.

Member Get a Member A phrase indicating a broad range of referral promotions by various firms whereby a current customer is offered free merchandise for soliciting other customers.

Monopoly Individual action, joint acquisition, or maintenance by members of a conspiracy formed for that purpose of the power to control and dominate interstate trade and commerce in a commodity or service to such an extent that actual or potential competitors are excluded from the field *accompanied with* the intention and purpose to exercise such power.

Negative Option A buying plan in which a customer or club member agrees to accept and pay for merchandise announced in advance at regular intervals unless the individual formally notifies the company not to send the merchandise within the time period specified with the announcement.

Oligopoly Market in which a few sellers control the supply of a product or service and hence its price or other terms of sale.

Out of Stock Merchandise that is not presently available but will be at some future date.

Per Se In itself, or by itself.

Place Utility Value added to a product by making it available to consumers at a convenient location, i.e., their homes.

Point-of-Purchase Advertising A nonpersonal sales promotion implemented through window displays or counter set-ups in stores.

Premium A product offered free or at less than its usual price to encourage the consumer to buy another product or make a commitment to a membership.

Price Discrimination Generally, charging different prices to different customers. This area is quite complex; read Section 5, Chapter 12 under "Price Discrimination and the Robinson-Patman Act."

Puffery An expression of opinion (often exaggerated) by a seller not made as a representation of fact.

Resale Price Maintenance Program A situation in which a seller of goods, such as a manufacturer, regulates the price at which the goods may be resold by the retailer. Presently illegal under the antitrust laws in most cases.

Sale A significant temporary reduction from the usual and customary price of the product or service offered.

Shipping and Handling Cost to seller of fulfilling and delivering orders. If an extra charge is required to make delivery of an advertised product, that fact must be clearly and conspicuously stated in the offer under FTC rules.

Sweepstakes A sales promotion device that offers prizes to participants but, unlike contests, requires no skill or analytical thinking. Consumers need only enter their names, numbers, or other identification symbol to qualify for random drawing. No purchase is necessary.

Target Market The most likely purchasers of your product.

Tie-In Express or implied contract arrangement whereby a party with significant economic power requires a purchaser, lessee, or licenser to purchase or acquire one or more additional products to be able to carry or deal in the desired product.

Trading Up Attempting to interest your customers in better, and usually more expensive goods than they expected to buy.

Unique Selling Proposition Advertising claim concerning a product which is thought to be strong enough to cause customers to buy the product about which the claim is made rather than a rival product. To be unique, the proposition must be one that the competition either cannot or does not offer.

Vertical Agreements Agreements between people at different levels of the market structure (e.g., manufacturers and distributors).

Vertical Territorial Restraint Specified territorial area imposed by a manufacturer or supplier as a condition of doing business with a customer such as a distributor or retailer.

Void Null; of no legal effect.

WATS Wide Area Telephone Service, a long-distance service offered to business customers enabling them to use large amounts of long-distance service for high volume and short duration of conversation at a discount rate. Excellent service for any telephone-marketing program.

Waiver The act of relinquishing or giving up some legal right.

Warehouse A storage facility whose operators (if not the owner) do not take title to the goods they handle and whose receipts, if any, are often used as collateral for loans.

Warranty A subsidiary promise or collateral agreement, the breach of which entitles the buyer to make certain claims for damages, replacement, or repair against the warrantor. The warranty may be full or limited (depending on the express agreement) or implied in law.

Index

ABOUT THE AUTHOR

Robert J. Posch, Jr., brings a unique perspective to the specialized area of marketing and the law. He is an attorney with an MBA from Hofstra, and he is an elected member of the National Honor Societies of Business and Marketing. For the past nine years, Mr. Posch has worked in the legal department of Doubleday & Company, Inc., where he monitors legal compliance with government regulation. He publishes frequently in marketing journals, such as *The Journal of Marketing* and *The Market Place*, and is the author of the book *The Direct Marketer's Legal Adviser* and the monthly column "Legal Outlook," appearing in *Direct Marketing* magazine.